FIRST LOGIC

Second Edition

Michael F. Goodman

University Press of America, Inc.
Lanham • New York • London

Copyright © 1997 by
University Press of America,® Inc.
4501 Forbes Boulevard, Suite 200
Lanham, Maryland 20706

12 Hid's Copse Rd.
Cummor Hill, Oxford OX2 9JJ

Library of Congress Cataloging-in-Publication Data

Goodman, Michael F.
First logic / Michael F. Goodman--2nd ed.
p.   cm.
l. Logic. I. Title.
BC71.G66   1996   160--dc20   96-33419 CIP

ISBN 0-7618-0501-X (pbk: alk. ppr.)

Preface to the Second Edition

The usual reasons for a second edition of a textbook being issued are, one, to correct significant errors, and two, to incorporate new and/or revised materials. These reasons apply here. The exercises in most chapters have been both revised and expanded, sometimes largely. A number of significant changes (read "improvements") have taken place in chapters 1, 5, 6, and 7, not the least of which has had to do with the presentation of the matters treated therein. I remain convinced that presentation is *the* crucial element in teaching and learning and am continually on the hunt for the better way of tendering the discipline of logic. The probability is high that some errors still exist within, both in the simple aspect of the typography as well as in the substantive areas of logic itself. Whatever errors there may be are my responsibility alone.

I wish to thank the following people for, one way or another, helping to make clearer to me ideas surrounding the concepts and techniques of logic: Dick Anderson, Jim Derden, Ken Faber, Alan Fletcher, Joe Hanna, Herb Hendry, Stan Mortel, Arthur Morton, John Powell, Benjamin Shaeffer, Bob Snyder, William Wheeler, Stan Weissman. Also, thanks are due to the many students in both my lower and upper division logic classes over the years for helping this sometimes backward teacher.

To Hollie, Matthew, Anna, Jay and Moira, for their understanding of my spending so much time away from home to pursue this project, goes my deepest gratitude and respect.

MFG
Arcata, CA

This book is dedicated to

Dave Whitlow and Steve Castaneda

The true logicians of my youth;
Friends and companions;
"Let's go down to George's and play some pool."

Table of Contents

1. Core Concepts of Logic

1.1 Preliminaries

It is impossible to define the term "logic" in one sentence, unless one is willing to overlook detail. It is the study of the nature of argument-ation, good and bad reasoning, language, statements and assertions, inference, induction and deduction, soundness, consistency and much, much more. Essentially, the logician (one who studies logic) begins with the search for the distinguishing features of correct and incorrect argu-ments. And since some of the features of arguments in general are soundness and validity, it follows that the logician will also be interested in these concepts.

The study of logic has a practical as well as a theoretical side; it is simple and complex, even in a first course. On the practical side we might ask, "How is the study of logic to be of help in my everyday activities?" Part of the answer to this question is that since we already know how to reason pretty well already, without studying logic formally, and since we use this knowledge everyday, and since studying logic can only heighten this ability, it follows that studying logic will help us to reason better in the everyday, ordinary world.

For instance, let's say you have a friend who feels quite strongly about which Senatorial candidate should be elected. Your friend says, "My candidate is for strong but fair measures in timber harvesting, while the other candidate has expressed no interest in environmental concerns whatsoever." You're friend has just given a reason for voting a certain way. Behind that reason is an argument. And, though it is unstated, you understand the argument well enough not to ask your friend to make it explicit. The argument might be:

> Whichever candidate expresses environmental concern should be voted for. My candidate expresses environmental concern; the other candidate doesn't. You are concerned with the environment. Hence, you should vote for my candidate.

But there are arguments that are not so straightforward, ones we can't be quite so confident about accepting. Consider:

> The Christian God commands people to love one another.
> This God would never command people to do something
> which is impossible for them to do. It is impossible for
> people to control their emotions. Hence. love is not an
> emotion.

Analyzing these arguments from a logical point of view is but one way we have of determining whether or not they are acceptable. We will be outlining various techniques used by logicians in following chapters.

There is a way of testing the acceptability of an argument which is not within the purview of the logician as logician. Quite simply, if one or more of the premises (sentences supporting the conclusion) in an argument is false, the argument is unacceptable. And of course you don't have to be a logician to tell when some sentence is true or false. Consider the following two arguments:

(A)	(B)
All beds are lamps.	All dolphins are mammals
All lamps are tables.	All mammals are warm-blooded.
So, all beds are tables.	So, all dolphins are warm-blooded.

Both (A) and (B) are acceptable from the logician's perspective. This is to say that *if* each of the first two sentences of each argument is true, then the last sentence of each argument will also be true. The operative word here is "if". We note however that each of the sentences in (A) is false. Hence, we would never find ourselves being convinced by this argument. That is, we would never come to believe that beds are tables. Argument (B), on the other hand, is a different matter. It has the same form or structure as (A), but the sentences are different. If you believe that the first two sentences in (B) are true, then presumably you also believe the last is true. But what if you aren't sure about the truth of, say, the second sentence in (B)? If you want to find out whether it *is* true, you might find a marine biologist and ask. It wouldn't be a good idea to ask a logician because matters of marine biology are not the kinds of things logicians are formally trained to know about. In fact, the study of logic itself is not designed to give a person increased knowledge about what is and what is not true about the world, as far as factual information is concerned. One must go outside one's study of logic to obtain this sort of knowledge.

An important fact to remember about logic is that it is a tool. Aristotle, who wrote the first treatise on logic, called it "Organon" (organ or instrument). Some people find the study of logic fun, simply learning about it. Nonetheless, we *use* logic, everyday. We are constantly bombarded with arguments attempting to persuade us to buy this product, vote for that person, accept this proposal, arrive on time for that meeting, and so on. One of the most effective methods that has been devised for deciding whether to accept or reject any given argument is logical analysis of arguments themselves. And this logical analysis is what much of this book explores; its concepts, content, and techniques.

1.2 Basic Terms and Concepts

An **argument** consists in a series of assertions (two or more) about the world, one of which is intended to follow from the other(s). Example:

(1) If infanticide is morally permissible, killing is not wrong.
(2) If killing is not wrong, then suicide is not wrong.
(3) So, if infanticide is morally permissible, so is suicide.

Sentences (1) and (2) above are called the **premises**. They are supposed to provide a certain amount of support for the **conclusion** (3). When the premises provide conclusive support, the conclusion is said to follow from the premises with logical necessity. This is to say that, necessarily, if the premises are true, the conclusion is true, or, if one accepts the premises (as true), then one is bound to, or *must*, accept the conclusion (as true). When premises provide less than conclusive support for a conclusion, but do provide *some* support, the conclusion is said to follow from the premises with some degree of probability. For example,

(1) When Jim goes camping, he takes a lantern.
(2) Jim has his lantern with him now.
(3) It follows that Jim is going camping now.

In the above argument, the conclusion does not follow with necessity from the premises. Even if the premises are true, Jim may not be going camping at all, but perhaps taking the lantern to the shop to get it fixed. Jim might be intending to do many other things by having the lantern with him, none of which involve going camping at that moment. However, we say it is *probable* that Jim is going camping, because *usually* when someone is carrying a lantern around, that person is indeed going camping.

An argument is said to be **valid** if it is impossible for the premises to be true while the conclusion is false. Any argument that is not valid is termed **invalid**. The following arguments are valid and invalid, respectively.

(A)

Some nurses are trained in surgical techniques.
All those trained as such can perform surgery.
Hence, some nurses can perform surgery.

(B)

All pigs are good truffle hunters.
Some good truffle hunters are not four-legged.
We can conclude that some pigs are not four-legged.

It can be seen that if the premises in (A) are true, then the conclusion cannot be false, while in (B) it is quite possible that even if the premises were true, the conclusion could be false.

As will become increasingly apparent, the concept of truth is extremely important for much of the logician's work. Recall, however, the earlier remark that it is not the logician's job to determine which sentences in arguments are in fact true and which are false. The basic question that concerns the logician at this level is about the validity or invalidity of arguments. But on our definition of validity, we appeal to the notion of truth. The closest the logician comes to talking about the actual truth of sentences is when a certain kind of argument is referred to, namely, a **sound argument**. *A sound argument is an argument that is valid and has true premises.* For example, consider the following two arguments:

Christian Huygens was either a scientist or a poet.
He lived between 1629 and 1693 and wasn't a poet.
It is shown, hence, that Christian Huygens was a scientist.

Christian Huygens was either a scientist or a poet.
He lived between 1630 and 1692 and wasn't a scientist.
Hence, Christian Huygens was a poet.

The first is sound while the second is unsound, because Huygens lived between 1629 and 1693 and not between 1630 and 1692, which fact renders the second premise of the second argument false. The second argument *is* valid, however. This is so since *if* the premises of the second argument *were* true, the conclusion would also be true. The primary way valid unsound arguments differ from sound arguments is that the former have one or more false premises.

1.3 Validity and Acceptability

Perhaps it will sound strange that a valid argument may be unacceptable and that an invalid argument may be acceptable. But on the definition of validity we have adopted both of these oddities are quite possible. Consider the following argument.

If Yuma is 20 miles east of San Diego, then Yuma is in California.
Yuma is 20 miles east of San Diego.
Therefore, Yuma is in California.

This is a valid argument because if the premises were true, it would be impossible for the conclusion to be false. However, since the second premise *is* false, and would be rejected by anyone who knows this fact, the argument itself is also to be rejected. In other words, where one or more of the premises in any argument is/are unacceptable, the entire argument is unacceptable. If this argument were presented to a person who knows that Yuma is not 20 miles from San Diego, but does not know whether Yuma is in California, this person would not come to believe that Yuma is in California on the basis of the premises alone. This is not meant to imply that the person would come to believe that Yuma is not in California simply because the second premise is false, however. Consider the following argument:

Earp is the easternmost town in California.
Reno is west of Earp.
Therefore, Reno is in California.

Each of the premises of the argument above is true. But the con-clusion is not true. These facts show that the argument is invalid. Owing to the particular geographical shape of California, some towns outside of

California are west of the easternmost town in California. A person could, however, come to believe that Reno is in California on the basis of the premises above. But this could only be so if the person failed to consider, or was perhaps incorrect about, the shape of California. A crucial point here is that since the conclusion is false, the argument is unacceptable, which point should make it clear that any argument containing one or more false sentences (whether as a premise or as a conclusion) is unacceptable.

As can be seen from the examples above, arguments can have premises with varied truth values and still be valid. That is, a valid argument can have all true premises and a true conclusion, or all false premises and a false conclusion, or all false premises and a true conclusion, or one or more false premises and a true conclusion, or one or more (but not all) true premises and a false conclusion. What a *valid* argument cannot have is all true premises and a false conclusion. Each of the following four arguments is valid.

John F. Kennedy was the 35th U.S. President.	True
Kennedy was born in Massachusetts.	True
So, the 35th President was born in Massachusetts.	True
Cantinflas starred in the movie "Key Witness".	False
"Key Witness" was a biography of Einstein.	False
So, Cantinflas starred in a biography of Einstein.	False
London is the capital of England.	True
If London is the capital of England, Charles is King.	False
Hence, Charles is King.	False
Hillary reached the summit of Mt. Everest in 1954.	False
Campanella hit 40 home runs in 1954.	False
Hence, Hillary reached the summit in the same year that Campanella hit 40 home runs.	True

Each of these arguments is valid because if the premises were all true, it would be impossible for the conclusions to be false. The last of the arguments is the most interesting I think, as it is hard to believe that false premises could lead to a true conclusion. What is important is not that the premises are in fact false, but that *if* they were true, the conclusion would also have to be true. It turns out that Edmund Hillary reached the summit of Mt. Everest on 29 May 1953, and Roy

Campanella hit 40 home runs in 1953. It really is true, then, that Hillary reached the summit in the same year that Campanella's hit 40 home runs.

What makes an argument valid or invalid has nothing to do with the content of the argument. Validity and invalidity are products of the form of arguments. *It is form that matters, not content.* For example, we can use the same form as in the third argument above, borrow some nonsense from Lewis Carroll and Dr. Seuss, and still get a valid argument:

Snarks are sneeches.
If snarks were sneeches, then oceans would be beaches.
Hence, oceans are beaches.

The important question regarding the validity of any argument is always, *Could the conclusion be false while the premises are true?* When one applies this question to any argument, if the answer is *yes*, then the argument is invalid. If the answer is *no*, the argument is valid.

Consider another example where form clearly determines validity.

All seagulls have four chambered hearts.
All sparrows have two chambered hearts.
Therefore, all sparrows are sparrows.

The first thing to notice here is that the conclusion is logically true, which is to say that there is no case in which the conclusion is false. On this consideration alone, we see that it would be impossible for the premises to be true while the conclusion is false because the conclusion cannot be false. So, the argument is valid. It is valid based strictly by virtue of the definition of *valid argument* we have adopted. Even if the conclusion had nothing to do with the premises, say, All mice are mice, the argument would still be valid. **It's all form.**

Back to acceptability. To repeat, each of the arguments above is valid. However, with the exception of the first, each argument is to be rejected solely on the basis of there being at least one premise that is false. The important point to remember is that validity and acceptability are neither mutually inclusive nor mutually exclusive. The same point can also be made with respect to invalidity and unacceptability. From the strictly logical point of view, all invalid arguments are unacceptable because the premises do not establish the conclusion in an invalid argument. However, in the lived world, i.e., the world of our everyday experience, we rarely, if ever, take the strictly logical point of view. There are always other factors to consider. This leads us to affirm that some invalid arguments are not to be rejected lightly. Consider the argument below:

> The Southern Pacific Railroad has passed Ned's house at 2am for the last 15 years.
> The time is now 1:51am.
> Hence, the Southern Pacific will pass Ned's house in 9 minutes.

The extreme regularity of the Southern Pacific, as evidenced by the first premise above, would lead us to believe that it is quite probable that the train will again come by at 2am. "Probable" is the key term here, for we realize that it is possible for a train to be early or late on any given day for any given destination. Strictly speaking, it is possible for the premises to be true and the conclusion false in the above argument, that is, that the Southern Pacific will pass Ned's house in more or less than 9 minutes. But since the conclusion follows from the premises with (in this case) a high degree of probability, we would accept the argument.

In accepting the argument, we would by no means be affirming that the conclusion follows with any sort of logical necessity. We would simply be saying that, based on past evidence, it is highly likely that the train will pass in 9 minutes.

A more difficult argument to assess is the following:

> On 43% of the days with weather patterns of kind R, it has rained.
> Today's weather pattern is of kind R.
> Hence, it will probably rain today.

Weather forecasting is notoriously difficult, and it comes as no surprise if we find ourselves undecided about accepting or rejecting the above argument, because 43% is not such a high percentage that we can be very confident that it will rain. Our first inclination might be to point out that even a 75-90% chance of rain only yields that much probability; and probability it remains. However, that we are dealing in percentages here no one denies. What is important is the fact that as the probability that it will rain increases, it seems natural to say that the acceptability of the argument increases in due proportion.

This being so, we say there are degrees of acceptability of arguments.

The imprecision we note of arguments with only probable conclusions bespeaks the difficulty students of logic typically recognize in assessing them. No attempt will be made here to treat these sorts of arguments in detail. The point in devoting space to them at all is that arguments of this kind frequently occur and it is well to be able to distinguish arguments whose conclusions follow with some degree of probability from those whose conclusions do not, and also to recognize that just because these arguments are formally invalid, that in itself is not a reason to dismiss them out of hand.

One important conclusion of this section is that some valid arguments are not arguments we would accept, while some invalid arguments are arguments that we *would* accept.

This writer believes that an argument's acceptability is conditioned by the unique beliefs held by the judge of the argument. An argument will be acceptable to a person if the person has good reason to believe that the premises are true and if the conclusion follows with a somewhat high degree of probability (there is no clear answer as to what level of probability is itself acceptable). Consider, for example, the following argument:

Stretch-a-Neck has been out of the money in each of the last 5 races on turf.

Stretch-a-Neck has been in the money in only 3 of the last turf races.

Stretch-a-Neck's best time at 8 1/2 furlongs on turf is 2:57.

Yet Stay has been in the money in the last 8 races on turf.

Yet Stay's best time at 8 1/2 furlongs on turf is 2:54.

Today's race is a turf race.

Stretch-a-Neck and Yet Stay are in the race today.

No other horse in the race has as good a time on turf as these two horses.

Hence, the best bet in this race is Yet Stay.

On the basis of this eight-premise argument alone, we might affirm that it would indeed be most prudent to bet on Yet Stay. But, what if you saw Stretch-a-Neck's workout on the morning of the race, were impressed, and came to believe that Stretch-a-Neck was "due for a win"? You might also note that the difference in turf times for Stretch-a-Neck and Yet Stay is only 3 seconds. "That's not much", you think. Now a friend points out that these two horses have been in seven races together, and that Stretch-a-Neck has never come in ahead of Yet Stay. But you reply that Yet Stay has just gotten over a cold and must be a bit weak from the illness. Your friend notes that Yet Stay is carrying two pounds less weight, including jockey and gear, than Stretch-a-Neck. You reply that this is the first time this jockey has ever ridden Yet Stay but that the jockey on Stretch-a-Neck has ridden Stretch-a-Neck six times previously, with two wins, one place, and one show.

And so it goes, with seemingly good reasons for betting on either horse. It seems especially difficult to determine just what is to count as an overriding reason for choosing to bet on one horse rather than the other. The set of beliefs held by the person betting will surely lead that person to bet one way or the other. Hence, one set of premises will "move" the person betting in a way which the other set won't. Perhaps, for example, the person thinks it's much more important that Yet Stay had a cold than that Big John A is carrying two pounds less than Stretch-a-Neck. Since the logic of psychology is not within the scope of this book, this is a good place to stop, the point having been made that some arguments are more difficult to analyze for acceptability than others.

As a general principle, we will say an argument is **acceptable** if there is sufficient reason to believe the premises to be true and if the conclusion follows from the premises with at least a high degree of probability.

The usual name applied to any argument in which the conclusion follows with some degree of probability (but does not follow conclusively) is **inductive argument**. For example,

> Pavlov's dogs have been trained to salivate at the sound of a certain bell. Don recently acquired one of Pavlov's dogs. So, Don's dog will salivate at the sound of a certain bell.

Now, unless Don's dog was somehow "deprogrammed", we can be confident that it will salivate when it hears a certain kind of bell ring. Confidence, however, is not identical with knowledge. Many things may happen/have happened which might prevent Don's dog from salivating when it hears the bell, e.g., it may not have been trained as well as some of the other dogs, or it might, unknown to us, actually have been retrained. The point is that though it is *logically possible* that the conclusion is false while the premises are true, we have good reason to believe that the dog will indeed salivate on command, i.e., reason to believe that the conclusion is *not* false. Hence, since it is possible that the premises are true and the conclusion is false, we admit that the argument is formally invalid, but, for all that, that the argument is more or less acceptable. Now consider the following argument:

> No Republicans are Democrats.
> Some college administrators are not Republicans.
> Therefore, some Democrats are college administrators.

This argument contains no statement of probability, either in the premises or in the conclusion. In fact, it looks as though anyone who presented this argument might presume that the conclusion followed, not with mere probability, but with certainty, or, that the premises provided conclusive support for the conclusion. We know that this is not so, however, since the argument can be shown to be invalid, i.e., that it is possible that the premises are true while the conclusion is false. Given that it would not be appropriate to call this argument *inductive*, since the conclusion doesn't seem to follow with any degree of probability whatsoever from the set of premises, another name is applied to arguments of this sort; we call them **deductive arguments**. The following two arguments are inductive and deductive, respectively.

> When Jill goes fishing, she takes her fishing rod along.
> She has her fishing rod with her now.
> Therefore, Jill is going fishing.

> When Jill goes fishing, she takes her fishing rod along.
> Jill is going fishing now.
> Therefore, Jill has her fishing rod with her now.

But notice that the first argument above doesn't say that there is a probability that Jill is going fishing. It says nothing about probabilities at all. The point is that even though the argument doesn't state as much, it is indeed probable (given the premises) that Jill is going fishing. The probability may be high or low, depending on whether the evidence is strong or weak. That is, perhaps Jill's having her rod with her really isn't very good evidence that she's going fishing. The first argument, then, would be counted by us as less acceptable than the following argument:

When Jill goes fishing, she takes her fishing rod along.
She also takes her waders and her tackle box.
Jill has her rod, her waders, and her tackle box with her now.
Therefore, Jill is going fishing.

The more evidence we mount for the conclusion, the more acceptable the argument becomes, because an increase in evidence increases probability. However, the argument is still invalid just because the premises may all be true and, still, Jill may not be going fishing but rather, say, to a costume party. Note that the second argument above is purely valid. Necessarily, if the premises are true, then Jill does indeed have her rod with her.

The dual concepts of induction and deduction will not be stressed in further chapters. While the above discussion is important for understanding two forms in which arguments are presented, it is still the validity of arguments that the logician has as a major object of concern. The concept of validity will be a crucial part of much that follows.

1.4 Recognizing Arguments

As mentioned previously, the two major constituents of an argument are the premise(s) and the conclusion. When one is being careful in constructing an argument, one usually makes it explicit just what conclusion one has in mind. When we want to call anyone's attention to the conclusion of an argument, we mark off the conclusion from the premises by including a word or phrase intended to draw attention to the fact that the sentence coming up is the conclusion. We call such words and phrases **conclusion indicators**. Some conclusion indicators are:

Therefore	So	Hence
Thus	In conclusion	It follows that...
Consequently	We may conclude that...	We may infer that...
This proves that..	This entails that...	This shows that...

Similarly, to note that some sentence in an argument is a premise, rather than the conclusion, we use a **premise indicator**. Some premise indicators are found on the following page.

Since	For	Inasmuch as
As	Because	For the reason that
Follows from	As indicated by	May be inferred from

In the examples that follow, it will be shown that the structures of arguments are as diverse as the subject matters themselves with which they deal. Consider the following argument, in which the conclusion is stated at the beginning.

A great uncertainty surrounds the concept of the nature of mind, inasmuch as science explains it in physical terms whereas religion explains in spiritual terms.

There are a number of points to be made here. First, up until now I have presented most arguments in a quite linear fashion, stating premises first and conclusion last. But second, note that the argument above is presented as one sentence. This should cause no concern because we can pick out at least three separate ideas being put forward. Each of these ideas can be seen as assertions about the world and can be translated into premises and conclusion. The premise indicator "inasmuch as" appears directly after the first complete thought in the argument. We analyze what follows the indicator phrase and come up with the following two sentences:

Science explains the mind in physical terms.
Religion explains mind in spiritual terms.

Since these two sentences follow the premise indicator, these two sentences are the premises. The next argument is different.

As mind can be explained in physical terms, it follows that mind is a physical entity, since it would be impossible for mind and body to interact if mind were spiritual.

Here, the conclusion appears as the middle sentence, bounded by sentences each of which contains a premise indicator. In general, an indicator word or phrase comes directly prior to the sentence it indicates as premise or conclusion. The next argument is again different.

For the reasons that John Locke and Baruch Spinoza were born in the same year, and that the year was 1632, and that they were both interested in the study of philosophy, we can conclude that Locke and Spinoza were contemporary philosophers of the 17th century.

The above is a three-premise argument, with the (plural) premise indicator 'for the reasons that' appearing at the beginning of the sentence itself and the conclusion indicator 'we can conclude that' appearing directly before the conclusion. Another way of representing the same argument would be:

> Since Locke and Spinoza were born in the same year, and
> since they were born in 1632, and since they were interested
> in philosophy, it follows that they were contemporary 17th
> century philosophers.

This shows that it is not so much how one expresses an argument that matters as long as the meaning of the sentences is uniform throughout. Premise and conclusion indicators are interchangeable whenever they occur. That is, 'as', for example, is no less an indicator of a premise than 'since' or 'because' or 'inasmuch as'.

The occurrence of premise and conclusion indicators greatly increases one's chances of recognizing not only the premise(s) and conclusion in some argument but also that some set of sentences comprises an argument at all. The following two sentences are not arguments, even though they contain what look like premise and conclusion indicators.

> As you can see, WWII was preceded by economic uncertainty.
> With the decline in social status of the poor, so too an increase in
>   crime follows.

A crucial point to remember when attempting to pick out an argument is that an argument is intended to show (explicitly or implicitly) that one of the sentences follows from another, or some   others. Consider the following argument, without indicators:

> In Missouri and Alabama you can get yourself imprisoned
> for having one marijuana cigarette in your possession, while
> in Oregon you get a slap on the hand and in California you
> can make a few bucks. The Law sure is strange.

If you're not sure what to make of this argument, at least you're not alone, as it isn't very clear exactly what conclusion the arguer is putting forth. It could be that the arguer is just misinformed about the fact that various states have various laws regarding drug possession. Or, it could be that the arguer is making some claim about the concept of law itself. The conclusion is ambiguous and would need to be made explicit for purposes of analysis. For all that, there really does seem to be an argument here.

1.5 Counterexamples

Thus far, the discussion has worked mainly around the concepts of validity and invalidity of arguments, but without indicating how one can determine whether any given argument is or is not valid. In this section, a method for showing invalid arguments to be invalid is presented. It is typically known as the **counterexample method** or as **refutation by analogy**. It is important to keep in mind that this method is designed to show invalid arguments to be invalid; it is not designed to show valid arguments to be valid.

Let's say someone presents the following argument,

Since no IQ tests are reliable intelligence indicators, it follows that some reliable intelligence indicators are culturally neutral, because some culturally neutral exams are not IQ tests.

It will help in analyzing the argument by putting it into a more simple form, clearly indicating the premises and the conclusion, like so,

Some culturally neutral exams are not IQ tests.
No IQ tests are reliable intelligence indicators.
So, some reliable intelligence indicators are culturally neutral.

In terms of the acceptability of the argument, one might first try to show one or both of the premises to be false. The second premise might look especially vulnerable, since some people would say that IQ tests are definitely not reliable for measuring intelligence. But this sort of consideration, i.e., whether or not the argument is acceptable, doesn't tell us much about the actual validity of the argument. For that, we need some way of determining whether it is possible for the premises to be true and the conclusion false.

To show that the above argument is invalid, it suffices to show that there exists a second argument, *which has exactly the same form as the first*, in which the premises definitely are true and the conclusion definitely is false. Such an argument is the following:

Some racquetball players are not teenagers.
No teenagers are penguins.
So, some penguins are racquetball players.

That this argument has the same *form* as the first is shown by noting that the only changes made are the replacements of 'culturally neutral exams' with 'racquetball players', 'IQ tests' with 'teenagers', and 'reliable intelligence indicators' with 'penguins'. The second argument is clearly invalid, since each of the premises is obviously true and the conclusion is obviously false. The second argument shows that any argument with the same form as the original is invalid. This is true no matter what the content of the counterexample argument may be, i.e., no matter what the counterexample argument is about in terms of subject matter. What the counterexample method shows is that the original argument has an analogous argument in which the conclusion is false while the premises are true, or, that the conclusion does not follow from the premises. Since it is the form of arguments that matter, in terms of their validity, rather than their content, if one can show that the form of some argument disallows the conclusion following from the premises, one will have refuted all arguments of the same form, regardless of content.

Consider now the following argument:

All people who appreciate a good pass like to win.
All hockey fans like to win.
So, all hockey fans appreciate a good pass.

It is vitally important to recognize that just because the conclusion in an argument is true, that does not mean that the conclusion follows from the given premises. In the above example, it is likely that, taken in a certain way, the conclusion is indeed true. If we say that a hockey fan is a person who knows much about the game, has watched the game played more than just a few times, understands many of the nuances of the game, including offensive and defensive maneuvers, likes the game, etc., then it would seem that, given that passing is a special kind of maneuver of hockey, the fan would appreciate a pass that is well executed. A counterexample to the above argument is,

All bees are social creatures.
All chimpanzees are social creatures.
So, all bees are chimpanzees.

with the same form as the one presented, but which has true premises and a false conclusion. It is important that the counterexample argument contain sentences that are clearly true and false, i.e., try to make the premises trivially true, as in "All bees are social creatures", and the conclusion trivially false, as in "All bees are chimpanzees". Most people find that beginning with a trivially false conclusion is the easiest. Then, simply match the counterexample premises with the premises of the original argument. An example:

> No retired corporate lawyers are people who have contributed to the literature on Freudian psychology.
> All people who have contributed to the literature on Freudian psychology are famous Freudian psychiatrists.
> So, no retired corporate lawyers are famous Freudian psychiatrists.

The form of this argument is:

> No xxx are yyy.
> All yyy are zzz.
> So, no xxx are zzz.

Now we must choose the subject matter of the refuting argument. We can use the following classes: {lions} {tigers} {animals}. The first step is to create a trivially false conclusion, such as,

> No lions are animals.

Filling in the blanks, the form of the refuting argument now is,

> No lions are yyy.
> All yyy are animals.
> So, no lions are animals.

What remains is to "plug in" the remaining category to replace 'yyy', the result being the following argument, which, being a counterexample, refutes the original argument:

> No lions are tigers.
> All tigers are animals.
> So, no lions are animals.

Until now, we have been considering arguments with quite simple forms. The counterexample method of proving invalidity can be used, in principle, on any invalid argument. The following is an example of a different kind:

> If the U.S. Space Program would have landed a person on the moon in 1961, the conspirators in the Kennedy assassination would have had second thoughts about their intentions. Since the first person to land on the moon landed in 1969, we can conclude that the conspirators had no second thoughts about the assassination.

Setting out the argument with its premises and conclusion shown explicitly, we can rephrase it as follows:

> If the U.S. Space Program would have landed a person on the moon in 1961, the conspirators in the Kennedy assassination would have had second thoughts about their intentions.
>
> The first person to land on the moon landed in 1969.
>
> Hence, the conspirators had no second thoughts about the assassination.

To begin our counterexample, we put the argument in a simple form, as it were, deleting subject matter.

> If xxx, then yyy
> It is not the case that xxx.
> Hence, it is not the case that yyy.

Next, we can choose classes to use: {Abraham Lincoln}, {Libertarians}, {People who value freedom}. We create a false conclusion and the result is the following counterexample:

> If Lincoln was a libertarian, then he valued freedom.
> Lincoln was not a libertarian.
> Hence, Lincoln didn't value freedom.

It will be noticed that the counterexample method is not a purely mechanical method for proving the invalidity of arguments. One has to be creative, to pick an appropriate subject matter for showing true premises and false conclusion. Take the "Freud" example above; the following classes would not have worked in a counterexample to that argument: {triangles}, {cubes}, {three-sided figures}, because the attempted counterexample argument would have been,

> No three-sided figures are cubes.
> All cubes are triangles.
> Hence, no three-sided figures are triangles.

which does not have all true premises (#2 is false) and a false conclusion, which is the precise point of the counterexample method. This leads to the important point that just because one is, at the moment, unable to come up with a counterexample for some argument that one suspects to be invalid, that does not show that it is impossible to come up with such an argument. It may be a simple matter of using different classes.

To create premises and conclusion that are clearly true and false, it is best to choose one's subject matter carefully. For example, many people who would be interested in a counterexample to some argument would know that all dogs are mammals, that all brothers are siblings, that no cubes are triangles, that libertarians value freedom, and so on. Probably fewer people know that the seat of origin for the emotions resides in a part of the brain called the amygdala, or that Phil Edwards was the first person to surf a place called Pipeline, or that Michigan State University was founded in 1855. Hence, these facts are not very good candidates for inclusion in counterexamples, albeit, strictly speaking, they *could* be used as premises in a counterexample because they are indeed true. It might be guessed that the nature of one's audience can be of importance here, for a biologist is more likely to know about the amygdala than, say, a band leader, and a person interested in water sports is more likely to know about surf spots than a person who isn't. Notwithstanding all of the above, it is just plain easier to create counterexamples when one chooses very common objects of reference.

Exercises 1

Notes: Solutions to starred exercises are to be found in the back of the book. The words "sentence", "statement", "assertion", and "proposition" will be used interchangeably throughout the exercises.

A. Which of the following sentences are true and which are false?

1 No valid argument is an unacceptable argument.
2 "Aristotle was a philosopher" is a valid statement.
3 No argument with a true conclusion is invalid.
4 No valid argument can have one or more false premises.
5* All sound arguments are true arguments.
6 No argument with a true conclusion is unsound.
7 All arguments with true premises are acceptable.
8 "Since" and "hence" are both conclusion indicators.
9 All arguments with false premises are invalid.
10* No valid argument can have any false premises.
11 The conclusion of one argument may appear as a premise in another.
12 All arguments have either premise or conclusion indicators.
13 Validity has to do with form, not content.
14 Soundness has to do with form, not content.
15* Acceptability has to do with content, not form.

B. Which of the following contain arguments and which do not? Specify the premise(s) and the conclusion of each argument.

1. The more different manifestations you observe of one phenomenon, the more deeply you understand the phenomenon, and therefore the more clearly you can see the vein of sameness running through all those different things. [Douglas Hofstadter, *Metamagical Themas*]

2. Philosophers push or iterate a question, usually about justification, so far that they cannot find any acceptable deeper answer. [Robert Nozick, *Philosophical Explanations*]

3. Fresnel's view of the dependency involved here (the intensity is dependent on the propagations along all possible paths of the wavefront) is endorsed in contemporary physics, his mathematics for articulating the dependency is enshrined in elementary texts and is embedded in a richer mathematical framework in advanced discussions. So, by contemporary lights, it is hardly surprising that his discussions of interference and diffraction were so strikingly successful. [Philip Kitcher, *The Advancement of Science*]

4. There is a long philosophical tradition of distinguishing between *necessary* and *contingent* truths. The distinction is often explained along the following lines: a necessary truth is one which could not be otherwise, a contingent truth one which could; or, the negation of a necessary truth is impossible or contradictory, the negation of a

contingent truth possible or consistent; or, a necessary truth is true in all possible worlds, a contingent truth is true in the actual but not in all possible worlds. Evidently, such accounts aren't fully explanatory, in view of their 'could (not) be otherwise', '(im)possible', 'possible world'. So the distinction is sometimes introduced, rather, by means of examples: in a recent book '7 + 5 = 12', 'If all men are mortal and Socrates is a man, then Socrates is mortal' and 'If a thing is red, it is coloured' are offered as examples of necessary truths, and 'The average rainfall in Los Angeles is about 12 inches' as an example of a contingent truth. [Susan Haack, *Philosophy of Logics*]

5* A complementary objection would be that I have exaggerated the degree to which a fine-grained naturalistic view can accommodate traditional ideas about the authority of morality. It might be said, in this spirit, that I have not given any reason to think that the considerations that are authoritative for an individual will always be moral considerations, in any plausible sense of that term. For I have not said anything that would rule out the possibility of someone's treating considerations as authoritative that would ordinarily be regarded as amoral, or morally eccentric, or even immoral. [Samuel Scheffler, *Human Morality*]

6. There is no hope whatever that man's biological nature can be changed enough to enable him to survive without the earth's atmosphere; in fact, the very statement of this possibility is meaningless. *Homo sapiens* achieved his characteristics as a biological species more than 100,000 years ago, and his fundamental biological characteristics could not be drastically altered without destroying his very being. He developed his human attributes in the very act of responding to the environment in which he evolved. The earth has been his cradle and will remain his home. [Rene Dubos, *So Human An Animal*]

7. Not for a single instant can I believe that David's schoolfellows did not recognize his superior mentality and, to some degree, acknowledge it. Who does not recall that the big and awkward Samuel Johnson, who also was to remain ungainly all his life, was occasionally carried to school on the shoulders of the pupils in honourable tribute to his intellectual attainments? [E.C. Mossner, *The Life of David Hume*]

8. We have not seized any foreign land: what we took is not the property of others, but our ancestral heritage which for a time had been unjustly held by our enemies. Now that we have the opportunity, we are holding on to the heritage of our ancestors. [Maccabees: 1,15,33]

9. Sometimes I feel like I will *never* stop
   Just go on forever
   Till one fine mornin'
   I'm gonna reach up and grab me a handfulla
       stars
   Throw out my long lean leg
   And whip three hot strikes burnin' down the
       heavens
   And look over at God and say
   How about that!   [Samuel Allen, "To Satch"]

10* When we compare the individuals of the same variety or sub-variety of our older cultivated plants and animals, one of the first points which strikes us is, that they generally differ more from each other than do the individuals of any species or variety in a state of nature. And if we reflect on the vast diversity of the plants and animals which have been cultivated, and which have varied during all ages under the most different climates and treatment, we are driven to conclude that this great variability is due to our domestic productions having been raised under conditions of life not so uniform as, and somewhat different from, those which the parent species had been exposed under nature.   [Charles Darwin, *The Origin of Species*]

C. State the premises and the conclusions in the arguments in the passages below. Some passages contain more than one argument. Some passages may not contain any argument at all.

1. We know that there is a level of naive, commonsense, grandmother psychology and also a level of neurophysiology -- the level of neurons and neuron modules and synapses and neuro-transmitters and boutons and all the rest of it. So, why would anyone suppose that between these two levels there is also a level of mental processes which are computational processes? And indeed why would anyone suppose that it's at that level that the brain performs those functions that we regard as essential to the survival of the organism -- namely the functions of information processing? [John Searle, *Minds, Brains and Science*]

2. When in broad daylight I open my eyes, it is not in my power to choose whether I shall see or not, or to determine what particular objects shall present themselves to my view; and so likewise as to the hearing and other senses, the ideas imprinted on them are not creatures of my will. There is therefore some other will or spirit that produces them. [George Berkeley, *Principles of Human Knowledge*]

3. He spoke, and many were willing to go with Diomedes.
    The two Aiantes were willing, henchman of Ares, and
       likewise
    Meriones, and Nestor's son altogether willing,
    and Atreus' son was willing, Menelaos the spear-famed,
    and patient Odysseus to was willing to enter the multitude
    of Trojans, since forever the heart in his breast was daring.

                                            [*The Iliad of Homer*]

4. Fires were burning in the town, tall, fierce flames leaping high
into the air. It was pointless to order the troops to put them out. Here
and there, smoke was rising from the fires which they had lit in ovens
and out of doors. Having collected their loot, soldiers were sprawled
around their camp-fires like gypsies. How the Narva regiment had
changed in two hours. [Alexander Solzhenitsyn, *August 1914*]

5* Alice was beginning to get very tired of sitting by her sister on
the bank, and of having nothing to do; once or twice she had peeped into
the book her sister was reading, but it had no pictures or conversations
in it, "and what is the use of a book", thought Alice, "without pictures or
conversations?"

So she was considering in her own mind (as well as she could, for
the hot day made her feel sleepy and stupid), whether the pleasure of
making a daisy-chain would be worth the trouble of getting up and
picking the daisies, when suddenly a white rabbit with pink eyes ran
close by her. [Lewis Carroll, *Alice's Adventures in Wonderland*]

6. The regulation of aggregate demand, it will be evident, is an
organic requirement of the industrial system. In its absence there would
be unpredictable and almost certainly large fluctuations in demand and
therewith in sales and production. Planning would be gravely impaired;
capital and technology would have to be used much more cautiously and
far less effectively than now. And the position of the technostructure,
since it is endangered by the failure of earnings, would be far less secure.
The need for regulation of aggregate demand is now fully accepted. [John
Kenneth Galbraith, *The New Industrial State*]

7. Since 'conscious that' is at least unusual if not outright one of
those things we 'do not say', and since 'conscious of' and 'aware of' are
as close to being synonymous -- to my ear -- as any terms we are apt to
find in ordinary language, a step in the direction of clarity and order can
be taken by abandoning 'conscious that' and rendering 'conscious of'
always as 'aware of', thus forming all the Intentional idioms with 'aware'.
[D.C. Dennett, *Content and Consciousness*]

8.   When we run over libraries, persuaded of these principles, what havoc must we make? If we take in our hand any volume; of divinity or school metaphysics, for instance; let us ask, Does it contain any abstract reasoning concerning quantity or number?   No.   Does it contain any experimental reasoning concerning matter of fact and existence?   No. Commit it then to the flames: for it can contain nothing but sophistry and illusion.   [David Hume, *Enquiry Concerning Human Understanding*]

9.   There is no doubt that the formalism of theories *can* be interpreted in terms of iconic models and that doing so is heuristically fruitful in suggesting hypotheses, developing theories, and so on.   Nagel's and Hesse's position, however, is not merely that such models *can* be given and are useful in such a way, but that they are *essential* and *integral* components of theories.   [Frederick Suppe, *The Structure of Scientific Theories*]

10* The self presents itself, then, as an organized whole, an integrated structure, and experiences are related to one another not through but within the whole.   For that reason, when the structure is modified the nature of the experiences and relationships between them are also modified.   The interdependence of different experiential groups shows that the self is a structure which is organized and "makes sense" and that each member occupies its proper place within the structure. [Risieri Frondizi, *Nature of Self*]

11 Whatever features an individual male person has which tend to his social and economic disadvantage (his age, class, height, etc.), one feature which never tends to his disadvantage in the society at large is his maleness.   The case for females is the mirror image of this.   Whatever features an individual female person has which tend to her social and economic advantage (her age, race, etc.), one feature which always tends to her disadvantage is her femaleness.   Therefore, when a male's sex-category is the thing about him that gets first and most repeated notice, the thing about him that is being framed and emphasized and given primacy is a feature which in general is an asset to him.   When a female's sex-category is the thing about her that gets first and most repeated notice, the thing about her that is being framed and emphasized and given primacy is a feature which in general is a liability to her.

---Marilyn Frye, "Sexism"

12 At that time, which we call the big bang, the density of the universe and the curvature of space-time would have been infinite. Because mathematics cannot really handle infinite numbers, this means that the general theory of relativity (on which Friedmann's solutions are

based) predicts that there is a point in the universe where the theory itself breaks down. Such a point is an example of what mathematicians call a singularity. In fact, all our theories of science are formulated on the assumption that space-time is smooth and nearly flat, so they break down at the big bang singularity, where the curvature of space-time is infinite. This means that even if there were events before the big bang, one could not use them to determine what would happen afterward, because predictability would break down at the big bang. Correspondingly, if, as is the case, we know only what has happened since the big bang, we could not determine what happened beforehand. As far as we are concerned, events before the big bang can have no conse-quences, so they should not even form part of a scientific model of the universe. We should therefore cut them out of the model and say that time had a beginning at the big bang. ---Stephen W. Hawking, *A Brief History of Time*

13 At the present time, the philosophical world is curiously divided. If positivism be taken in its widest sense, the sense in which it embraces all shades of analytical, linguistic, or radically empirical philosophy, it is dominant in England and in Scandinavia, and commands considerable allegiance in Holland and Belgium, in Australia and the United States. Elsewhere, it makes hardly any showing at all. [A.J. Ayer, *Logical Positivism*]

14 The word "snob" has had many meanings since it surfaced in the late Middle Ages, none of them good. It began as an all-purpose insult, used to express contempt. By now it has certainly earned its evil reputation. For us snobbery means the habit of making inequality hurt. The snob fawns on his superiors and rejects his inferiors. And while he annoys and insults those who have to live with him, he injures himself as well, because he has lost the very possibility of self-respect. To be afraid of the taint of associations from below is to court ignorance of the world. And to yearn for those above one is to be always ashamed not only of one's actual situation, but of one's family, one's available friends, and oneself. Snobbery is simply a very destructive vice. [Judith Shklar, *Ordinary Vices*]

15 Relations of power are not in a position of exteriority with respect to other types of relationships (economic processes, knowledge relationships, sexual relations), but are immanent in the latter; they are the immediate effects of the divisions, inequalities, and disequilibriums which occur in the latter, and conversely they are the internal conditions of these differentiations; relations of power are not in superstructural positions, with merely a role of prohibition or accompaniment; they have

a directly productive role, wherever they come into play. [Michel Foucault, *The History of Sexuality*]

D. Refute the following arguments via the counterexample method.

1. Some puzzles have solutions and some puzzles do not have solutions. So, some things with solutions are not puzzles.

2. Franklin Delano Roosevelt was either a democrat or a New Englander. He was certainly a democrat, from which it follows that he was not a New Englander.

3. All writers are literate and all poets are writers. We may conclude that some poets are literate.

4. The last seven times Gary has added STP to his fuel supply, the pinging noise in his engine has disappeared. Since he just added another quart of STP, when he starts the car, the pinging noise will be gone.

5* Oliver North either lied to Congress or had been brain-washed by some sinister Marxist group planning a takeover of the United States. North *did* lie to Congress. Hence, he wasn't brainwashed by the Marxist group.

6. If Robert E. Lee had been born in Baton Rouge, then he would have fought for the South. But he did fight for the South. Hence, Lee was born in Baton Rouge.

7. Buckingham Palace is not the most regal mansion in all England; but if it was the most regal mansion, every British girl would want to go to a slumber party there. It follows that it is false that every British girl wants to go to a slumber party at Buckingham Palace.

8. If Darwin's Theory of Evolution is correct, then both the snake and the rabbit are descendants of a single-celled organism. Hence, the snake is a descendent of a single-celled organism.

9. Some soldiers are pacifists. So, some soldiers are not pacifists.

10* No Pit Bulls are cuddly. No Vampire Bats are cuddly. Thus, no Pit Bulls are Vampire Bats.

2. Aristotelian Logic A

2.1 Preliminaries

The following two chapters are devoted to outlining what is traditionally known as Aristotelian Logic. Sometimes it is called syllogistic logic. This logic is, at its core, the result of the work of Aristotle, the exalted Greek philosopher (father of logic, scientific method, biology) as presented in his treatise *Organon*. Even though modern logicians are far less concerned with this sort of logic than in previous times, it is well worth the time and effort to acquaint ourselves with what has gone before us. To study this system of logic is to study what every student prior to Russell and Whitehead's writing of *Principia Mathematica* had to master to be considered "educated".

This historical basis in itself is not the only reason to work through Aristotelian logic, however. Here we have a system that allows one easy access to the applicability of the many concepts presented in Chapter 1. The sentences and arguments treated by Aristotelian logic are straightforward, without the highly complex structure of sentences and arguments encountered further along. Hence, their analysis is much simpler than in other areas of logic. In short, this is a good place to start one's study of logic.

As mentioned, the heart of what we will study here was first presented formally by Aristotle. There have been many additions by various logicians in the 2300 years since, however, refinements and articulations that have gone to make the system what it is today. A classic example of this is the work of the 19th century mathematician/logician John Venn, who constructed a method for determining the validity of arguments via diagrams. We will study Venn Diagrams in detail further along as well as in the next chapter.

In Aristotle's *Organon*, the first section is called "Categories", and has to do with predicates. For example, to say

My shirt is blue.

is to predicate blueness of my shirt. The phrase "is blue", then, is taken to be a predicate, as, for example, are 'is next to', 'is running', and 'is late'. Aristotle presented ten types, or categories, of predicate. These follow, each with an example.

> Substance: David Whitlow is a *man*.
> Quantity: Some manuscripts have over *1250 pages*.
> Quality: Oxygenated blood is *red*.
> Relation: Nine is *greater than* three.
> Place: No Senators have a booth *in the market place*.
> Time: The Cubs didn't win the World Series *last year*.
> Position: Courtney is *sitting* on the desk.
> State: The debaters were *armed* with clever arguments.
> Action: Guidry is *throwing* nothing but fast balls today.
> Affection: The Redwoods need to be *protected*.

The sentences we will study are typically known as **categorical sentences**. The structure of **normal form categorical sentences** is uniform in that each has a **quantifier, a subject term**, a **copula**, and a **predicate term**. The following are instances of normal form categorical sentences:

(1) All even numbers are divisible by the number 2.
(2) No odd numbers are divisible by the number 2.
(3) Some prime numbers are divisible by the number 2.
(4) Some prime numbers are not divisible by the number 2.

The words "all", "no", and "some" are called the quantifiers in these sentences. They have to do with quantity, and indicate how much of the subject class is included in the predicate class. In normal form categorical sentences, these are the only quantifiers used. However, corresponding to (1) above is the following sentence:

(5) Every even number is divisible by the number 2.

This sentence has the same meaning as (1), but is not in normal form because the word "every" appears as the quantifier rather than 'all'. Our concentration will be primarily on normal form categorical sentences here. At this point, we can drop the phrase "normal form" and simply refer to the sentences as categorical sentences.

The subject and predicate terms of categorical sentences are known also as **class terms**, because they specify classes of objects. For example, the subject term in (1) is "even numbers". It is the class of even numbers that is being referred to here and what is being said is that the whole of the one class is included in the other class, i.e., in the predicate class, or in the class referred to by the predicate term "divisible by the number 2".

Note again our previous mention of Aristotle's categories (predicates). In each of the above sentences, the predicate term is the same, i.e. divisible by the number 2. Sentence (1) predicates divisibility by the number 2 of each member of the class of even numbers; sentence (2) denies divisibility by the number 2 of each member of the class of odd numbers; sentence (3) predicates divisibility of some member(s) of the class of prime numbers; and sentence (4) denies divisibility of some member(s) of the class of prime numbers.

The copula is the word, which is always some form of the verb "to be", that connects the subject term with the predicate term. Hence, we can have the following sorts of categorical sentences:

(6) All students *have been* tested for measles.
(7) No matches *were* found at the scene of the crime.
(8) Some comedy *will be* presented in the form of poems.
(9) Some jobs *have not been* offered to women.

Again, as can be seen, the structure of these sentences is similar. Each sentence has a quantifier, a subject term, a copula, and a predicate term. The order of the components of categorical sentences **never** changes, and is shown on the following page.

Quantifier	Subject Term	Copula	Predicate Term
(10) All	lemons	are	sour.
(11) No	Rabbis	are	Catholic.
(12) Some	peaches	are	sweet.
(13) Some	Priests	are not	theologians.

It will be noticed that the copula in (13) includes the negative, as does the copula in (9), viz., "might not be". This is the proper way of characterizing the copula in these sorts of sentences, i.e., negatives do not belong in either the subject or predicate terms.

There are many ways of presenting categorical sentences in **nonnormal form**. For example:

Jody was late for the dance.

could be put in normal form by specifying exactly what the subject and predicate terms are. Although it might, at first, seem that "Jody" is the subject term, actually the subject term is "people identical to Jody". The copula becomes "are" and the predicate term is "people who were late for the dance". In effect, we derive an **A** sentence, as follows:

All people identical to Jody are people who were late for the dance.

The key to putting any nonnormal form categorical proposition into normal form is understanding what the sentence is saying. This means that one must be sensitive to the number of items being referred to, the classes (designated by the subject and predicate terms), the copula and its placement, and whether or not there appears the words "no" or "not" in the sentence (or some variant). Following are a number of pairs of sentences. The first in each pair is in nonnormal form. The second in each pair is a normal form categorical sentence.

Every hump-backed whale has a humped back.
All hump-backed whales are whales with humped backs.

Cheerleaders are at the game.
Some cheerleaders are people who are at the game.

Dolphins may be persons.
All dolphins are beings that may be persons.

Not all politicians have unanimous support.
Some politicians are not people with unanimous support.

If any fish is caught, it's let go.
All fish caught are fish that are let go.

Computers are tools.
All computers are tools.

Teddy doesn't ever wear his high school ring.
No times are times when Teddy wears his high school ring.

Exercises 2.1

A.   Identify the subject and predicate terms of the following sentences.

1   All poems written by T.S. Elliot are beautiful.
2   Some San Francisco nightclubs are not places one would want to take the Queen of England.
3   No books in the philosophy of science are written for popular consumption.
4   Some photographs of "muscle men" are touched-up so as to make the person photographed appear more "human".
5*   All toreadors who have bloodied the suit of lights are fearless in the ring.
6   Some guitars are prized for their design innovation.
7   All Marian churches are devoted to the mother of Jesus.
8   No telephone operators are glad to have a job.
9   No Care Bears are named "Bummed-out Bear".
10* Some physicians are not confident in placebos.

B.   Rewrite the following sentences into normal form.

1   Socrates is mortal.
2   Recent findings in medicine have affected research in psychology.
3   A few of the paintings in the gallery were painted by Goya.
4   Not all Porsches can go 144 mph all day long.
5*   "Coke is it".
6   "MJB is good to the last drop".
7   All solipsists deny the existence of other people.
8   *Taltos* was written by Anne Rice.
9   Santa Claus is coming to town.
10* At least one U.S. President was guilty of treason.

C. Specify full subject and predicate terms in the following sentences.

1. Some categorical sentences are in nonnormal form.
2. All typical U.S. children are slightly overweight.
3. No jockies over 5' 7" are successful.
4. Some apartments in Los Angeles are rat-infested dumps.
5* All articles by psychologists who graduated between 1934 and 1964 from Harvard University are read by Harvard's Society of Fellows.
6. All those who say and do things hated by patriarchs are revolutionaries.
7. Some panthers are invisible at night.
8. Some stamp collectors are ruthless when certain stamps are marketed.
9. All conscious beings are unable to feel pain.
10* No conservatives are socialists.

2.2 Quantity and Quality

Every categorical sentence is classified in a number of ways, depending upon its form. Each refers to a more or less specific number of individual class members as being included or excluded in the membership of a second class. For example, in the sentence

(14) All tigers are mammals

the claim is that every member of the class of tigers is also a member of the class of things that are mammals. By referring to every member of the class of tigers, the sentence marks itself as **Universal** in quantity. The same is true of the sentence

(15) No tigers are herbivores.

since the claim here is that every member of the class designated by the term "tigers" is *ex*cluded from the class of things designated by the term "herbivores". 'All' and 'no' are called **Universal Quantifiers**, and any categorical sentence containing one of these quantifiers is itself said to be a Universal Sentence.

Since the quantity of a categorical sentence is defined by the sort of quantifier found in the sentence, and since 'some' is not universal in quantity, it follows that the following two sentences will have a different quantity from (14) and (15).

(16) Some tigers are reddish in color.
(17) Some tigers are not found in Siberia.

The quantifier "some" has a specific meaning in the world of logic. 'Some' is taken to mean "there exists at least one", and hence, (16) claims that there is at least one tiger that is a member of the class of things that are reddish in color. We know that there are many tigers that have a reddish hue, and also that there are many that do not, but (16) is referring to a particular instance of a tiger having a reddish hue and not to the fact that many more than just one have this hue. (16) is said to have **Particular Quantity**, and "some" is called an **Existential Quantifier** since the sentence claims that at least one red plum exists.

What is said about (16) is equally true of (17). Since its quantifier is 'some', it has Particular Quantity. Hence, it also makes an existential claim, viz., in this case, that there exists at least one tiger that is excluded from the class of things found in Siberia.

The **quality** of a categorical sentence is either Affirmative or Negative, depending on whether the sentence contains a negative term such as "not" or "no". The following two sentences are Affirmative:

(18) All scientists are students of mathematics.
(19) Some philosophers are students of mathematics.

They have **Affirmative Quality** because each *affirms* that a certain number of members of one class are included in the membership of another class. The next two sentences are Negative:

(20) No clothiers are admirals in the navy.
(21) Some navy officers are not submariners.

These sentences have **Negative Quality** because each *denies* that a certain number of members of one class are included in the membership of another class.

We now have very precise designations for our four kinds of categorical sentences. These are as follows:

Universal Affirmative
(22) All university deans are active in fund raising.

Universal Negative
(23) No logic teachers are ignorant of student needs.

Particular Affirmative
(24) Some logic teachers are cautious about what they say.

Particular Negative
(25) Some college professors are not sensitive to student needs.

The four sorts of categorical sentences have come to be known also by very short designations. The letters "A", "E", "I", and "O" are used to refer to the above types of sentences. We shall adopt the use of these letters to refer to the four categorical sentences. Their forms are:

Sentence	Quantity	Quality
A All ϕ are ψ.	Universal	Affirmative
E No ϕ are ψ.	Universal	Negative
I Some ϕ are ψ.	Particular	Affirmative
O Some ϕ are not ψ.	Particular	Negative

Exercises 2.2

A. Identify the quality and quantity of the following sentences.

1   Some multimedia designs are not user-friendly.
2   No logician can prove the legitimacy of the laws of logic.
3   All categorical sentences are true.
4   Some acoustic guitars are made with scalloped bracing.
5* Some 17th century women were accomplished writers.
6   "No 'quoted phrase' is about itself."
7   Some persons are not morally responsible for their actions.
8   All ethical relativists are cognitively limited by their biases.
9   Some smokers will not die of cancer.
10* Some contemporary scientists are not fully convinced of the truth of Einstein's special theory of relativity.

2.3 Distribution

Every normal form categorical sentence is said to either **distribute** or not distribute its subject and predicate terms. *A term is distributed if the sentence itself asserts something about every member of the class designated by the term.* For example, in

(26) All Muslims are devoted to the glory of God.

the subject term, "Muslims", is distributed, because (26) asserts something about every single Muslim and not merely one or two, or this one or that one. In fact, all **A** sentences distribute their subject terms.

E sentences also distribute their subject terms, as in

(27) No university library is maximally funded.

where the assertion has to do with every member of the class of "university libraries". Not every university library is being named here, for in fact no university library is being named; not the one in Berkeley, nor the one in Oxford, nor the one in East Lansing, Michigan. Rather, the class itself is being named and the reference is to *every member of the class*. Now, given our definition of distribution, since to say that no university library is maximally funded is really to say that all university libraries are not maximally funded, the subject term in (27) is distributed. What should clinch the fact that **A** and **E** sentences distribute their subject terms is that their quantifiers, "all" and "no", are Universal.

Contrast, now, **I** and **O** sentences, whose quantifiers ('some') are Particular.

(28) Some musk roses have white flowers.
(29) Some law suits are not settled out of court.

In neither (28) nor (29) is an assertion made about the entire classes, and hence all the members of the classes, of musk roses or law suits. (28) makes an assertion about there being "at least one" musk rose, while (29) makes an assertion about there being at least one law suit. Given our definition of distribution again, then, neither **I** nor **O** sentences distribute their subject terms. Their subject terms are said to be **undistributed**.

We turn now to predicate terms, and the question of their distribution.

In the sentence

(30) All plums are red.

one might ask, "Isn't 'red' distributed by the mere fact that the class itself of red things has been named?" The answer is "No", because though the class has been named, (30) does not make an assertion about all the many things there are, besides plums, that are red. Consider, for example, some fire engines, blood, stop signs, and so on. Sentence (30) says nothing about "all red things". A sentences, therefore, do not distribute their predicate terms.

This reasoning applies also to the predicate terms of **I** sentences. In

(31) Some jackstraws are made of cotton.

'things made of cotton', which is the full predicate term, is undistributed simply because the sentence is not saying anything about every member of the class of things made of cotton. It follows that **I** sentences do not distribute their predicate terms.

In contrast, both **E** and **O** sentences do distribute their predicate terms. Take the sentence,

(32) No whale is a fish.

What this sentence is saying is that no member of the class of whales is included in the class of fish, or that the class of whales is wholly *ex*cluded from the class of fish, or that the classes of whales and fish are mutually exclusive. Here the reference to all whales is direct, given the universal quantifier "no". Indirectly, however, every fish is being referred to by the simple fact that one could replace the word "fish" with any word denoting a fish and the result would be a true sentence, since (32) is itself true. For example, if we replace 'fish' with 'trout', we derive,

(33) No whale is a trout.

which is true. The same result would be had by replacing 'fish' with 'pike', 'bass', 'salmon', 'walleye', and so on. It must be admitted that the predicate term here is distributed though the reasoning is "round about".

The **O** sentence also distributes its predicate term. Consider,

(34) Some grapes are not green.

This sentence claims that there is at least one apple that is excluded from the class of green things. This being so, the sentence is making an assertion about the entire class of green things. Hence, on our definition of distribution, 'green' is distributed in (34).

Further examples of sentences follow:

(35) All poets are literate people.
(36) No novelists are William Shakespeare.
(37) Some surgeons are not physiologists.
(38) Some whales are not sharks.
(39) Some snowstorms are destructive to property.
(40) All emeralds are green.
(41) Some diamonds are blue.

The subject terms are distributed in (35), (36), and (40) above; the predicate terms are distributed in (36), (37), and (38); no terms are distributed in (39) and (41).

In the end we have the following: **A** sentences distribute the subject term but not the predicate term; **E** sentences distribute both subject and predicate terms; **I** sentences distribute neither subject nor predicate terms; **O** sentences do not distribute the subject term but do distribute the predicate term. In short, Universal Sentences distribute their subject terms and Negative Sentences distribute their predicate terms. It may be useful to see the symmetry sketched in the table below.

Table of Distribution

Quantifier		Subject Term	Copula	Predicate Term
A	All	*distributed*	are	**undistributed**
E	No	*distributed*	are	*distributed*
I	Some	**undistributed**	are	**undistributed**
O	Some	**undistributed**	are not	*distributed*

The concept of distribution will prove quite important when we begin evaluating arguments in Aristotelian Logic (Chapter 3).

Exercises 2.3

A. Identify only the distributed terms in the following sentences.
1 Some comedians are more boring than computer classes. U U
2 Some stereo salespersons are not completely sincere. U D
3 Some historians are wrong about Heraclitus. U U
4 All professors of Greek have been to Athens. D U
5* No microwaves are guaranteed to be free of leaks. D D
6 No free thinkers are concerned about their reputations. D D
7 All works of art have something in common with burritos. D U
8 Some works of art are unintelligible. U U
9 No person is her own sister. D D
10* Some puzzles worth solving are genuine paradoxes. U U

B. For the following sentences, 1) put each into normal form, 2) identify full subject and predicate terms, 3) identify each as either A, E, I, or O; 4) indicate which, if any, of the terms are distributed.

1 Xenophon wasn't a great philosopher.
2 The teachers at Vista High School were always watching one student.
3 "Business and ethics don't mix".
4 Not all smokers will die of lung cancer.
5* Each union is forced to accept some compromises.
6 None of the umpires wears glasses.
7 Most analogical arguments are invalid.
8 Every student except one passed the exam.
9 Gottlob Frege was the greatest logician who ever lived.
10* Some desire a reduction in teaching hours per term.
11 The history of philosophy is the history of epistemology.
12 A penny saved is a penny earned.
13 A stitch in time saver nine.
14 Anyone who laughs is liable to be happy.
15* The Hope Diamond is a blue stone.
16 All who linger are lost.
17 A few friends of liberty were imprisoned.
18 Jake always watched "M.A.S.H.".
19 Many birds have hollow bones.
20* Not all dogs have tails.

C. Which of the following are true and which are false?

✗ 1 'There are students having fun right now' is in nonnormal form.

⊤ 2 The predicate term in the normal form categorical sentence of the sentence in #1 above is undistributed.

3 The subject term in the normal form categorical sentence of the sentence in #15 in the above section of exercises is 'Hope Diamond'.

4 Every affirmative sentence distributes its subject term.

F 5* No affirmative sentence is distributed.

⊤ 6 Terms are distributed, not sentences.

7 'Lions with cubs' is distributed.

8 Universal Negative sentences distributed predicate terms.

F 9 E and O sentences do not distribute their predicate terms.

10* Every categorical sentence distributes at lease one term.

F 11 The quantifier 'each' implies that the predicate term is distributed.

F 12 Distribution is a concept having to do with the placement of copula in a normal form categorical sentence.

F 13 Sentence #4 above distributes its predicate term.

14 Some I sentences don't distribute the subject term.

15 Sentence #14 above distributes its predicate term.

2.4 The Traditional Square of Opposition

What is called the Traditional Square of Opposition is a geometrical figure showing the various logical relations that hold between, and inferences one can draw from, the four forms of categorical sentences. There are four relations that hold between the sentences: **contradictory**, **contrary**, **subcontrary**, and **subalternation**. Briefly, sentences which are contradictory can neither be both true nor both false at the same time; contrary sentences cannot be both true at the same time, but may both be false; subcontraries may both be true at the same time, but cannot both be false. The subalternation relation is somewhat different than the other three in that it is a relation of implication. **A** and **I** sentences are co-subalterns, as are **E** and **O**. The universal co-subaltern implies its respective particular co-subaltern, but the reverse is not the case. Hence, **A** implies **I**, and **E** implies **O**.

The Square, which is on the next page, indicates which relation holds between which sentences.

Traditional Square of Opposition

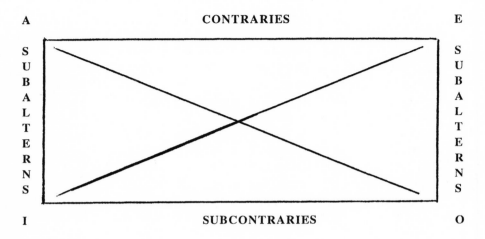

A   CONTRARIES   E

S U B A L T E R N S

I   SUBCONTRARIES   O

To restate, we define two sentences as **contradictory** if they cannot both be true at the same time *and* cannot both be false at the same time. Two sentences are said to be **contrary** if they cannot both be true at the same time but may both be false at the same time. Two sentences are **subcontraries** if both may be true at the same time but cannot both be false at the same time.

To illustrate the contradictory relation, consider the sentences

    A   All deer are shy.
    O   Some deer are not shy.
and
    E   No deer are shy
    I   Some deer are shy.

Notice that if every deer was shy (as stipulated by the **A** sentence), then it must be false that there is at least one deer that is not shy (the **O** sentence). In effect, all deer being shy would preclude any deer not being shy. Similarly, if there was a deer that was not shy (**O**), then it could not be the case that every deer was shy (**A**). Hence, we see that it is impossible for **A** and **O** to both be true at the same time.

But what if it is false that all deer are shy? That is, what if the **A** sentence is false? In that case, there would be at least one (maybe more)

deer that was not shy, i.e., the **O** sentence would be true. Similarly, if the **O** sentence is false, i.e., if there is not at least one deer that is not shy, then it would follow that all deer are shy (**A** being true). Thus, we see that it is impossible for **A** and **O** sentences to both be false at the same time.

This reasoning will suffice to show that it is impossible for **E** and **I** sentences to both be true at the same time, and also impossible for them both to be false at the same time. Briefly, if no deer is shy (**E**), it would be false that at least one deer is shy; and if at least one deer is shy (**I**), it couldn't be the case that no deer is shy. Equally, if it is false that no deer is shy, then it would have to be true that at least one deer is shy; and if it is false that at least one deer is shy, it would have to be true that no deer is shy. All of which proves that A and O are mutually contradictory and that E and I are also mutually contradictory.

To explicate the *contrary* relation, let us use the following categorical sentences:

A All computers are intelligent.
E No computers are intelligent.

Clearly, if it is true that all computers are intelligent, it is false that none are. This is one of the inferences mentioned above. The **A** and **E** sentences above are contraries because if one is true, the other cannot be. If it is true that no computers are intelligent, it can't be true that all computers are. In no case can **A** and **E** sentences both be true at the same time.

To show how **A** and **E** sentences can both be false at the same time, another example will be taken up. Consider

A All dogs are friendly.
E No dogs are friendly.

The existence of one friendly dog would prove the **E** sentence to be false, while the existence of an unfriendly dog would prove the **A** sentence to be false. "Bingo" and "Babe" are dogs I know who are friendly and unfriendly respectively. Hence, we have an example of **A** and **E** sentences being both false at once.

The *subcontrary* relation has to do with I and O sentences. For example,

I   Some dogs are friendly.
O   Some dogs are not friendly.

Bingo proves that **I** is true, while Babe proves that **O** is true. Hence, corresponding to our definition of the subcontrary relation, we see that **I** and **O** sentences *can* both be true at once.

Both cannot be false at the same time, however. For example, if the **I** sentence was false, i.e., if no dogs were friendly, then it would follow that at least one dog was not friendly (**O** being true); and if the **O** sentence was false, i.e., if all dogs were friendly, then there would be at least one dog that was friendly (**I** being true).

So far we have the following relations:

Contradictories (A & O; E & I)
{Not both true; not both false}

Contraries (A & E)
{Not both true; both may be false}

Subcontraries (I & O)
{Not both false; both may be true}

The final relation is that of *subalternation*. **A** and **I** sentences are co-subalterns. That is, **A** is the subaltern to **I** and **I** is the subaltern to **A**. Likewise, **E** and **O** are co-subalterns. The rule for subalternation is that if the Universal (**A** or **E**) is true, then the Particular (**I** or **O**) is true, but if the Particular is true, the Universal may be either true or false.

Consider the following two sentences:

A   All gymnasts are limber.
I   Some gymnasts are limber.

While it must certainly be true that if all gymnasts are limber, then there is at least one who is, it does not follow that because one is limber, all are. Maybe all are limber, but we cannot draw the inference that all are on the basis of one being limber. Hence, if the **A** sentence is true, the **I** is also true, but if the **I** is true, it is undetermined whether the **A** is true. Another example is:

A All singers are dancers.
I Some singers are dancers.

What if all singers were dancers? That would entail that there was at least one singer who was also a dancer. The subalternation relation is thus seen to hold from the **A** to the **I**. However, while it is true that there really is a singer who is also a dancer, viz., Liza Minnelli, it is false that all singers are also dancers; Neil Young is a singer but not a dancer. So, this shows that one cannot infer the truth of an **A** sentence on the basis of the truth of an **I** sentence. This is not only to say that if the Universal is true, the Particular will also be true; it is also to say that, given the truth of the Particular, one will have to examine the Universal itself to determine its truth value.

The following table shows the inferred truth values of sentences in accord with the Traditional Square of Opposition.

If **A** is true, **E** & **O** are false, **I** is true.
If **A** is false, **E** & **I** are undetermined, **O** is true.
If **E** is true, **A** & **I** are false, **O** is true.
If **E** is false, **A** & **O** are undetermined, **I** is true.
If **I** is true, **A** & **O** are undetermined, **E** is false.
If **I** is false, **A** is false, **E** is true, **O** is undetermined.
If **O** is true, **A** is false, **E** and **I** are undetermined.
If **O** is false, **A** & **I** are true, **E** is false.

Exercises 2.4

A. Give an argument, similar to that given for **A** and **I** sentences being co-subalterns, showing that **E** and **O** sentences are also co-subalterns. Use the following pairs of examples:

E No computer is completely reliable.
O Some computers are not completely reliable.

E No Spartans sailed to Troy.
O Some Spartans did not sail to Troy.

B. Use the Traditional Square of Opposition to determine the truth value of each 'b', 'c', and 'd' sentence below, where each 'a' sentence is taken to be true.

1   a   All philosophy journals are technical. *A*

  F b   Some philosophy journals are not technical. *O*

  T c   Some philosophy journals are technical. *I*

  F d. No philosophy journals are technical. *E*

2   a   Some musicians are not concerned with harmony. *O*

  U b   No musicians are concerned with harmony. *E*

  v c   Some musicians are harmony. *I*

  F d   All musicians are harmony. *A*

3   a   No Takayama surfboards cost less than $400. *E*

  F b   All Takayama surfboards cost less than $400. *A*

  T c   Some Takayama surfboards do not cost less than $400. *O*

  F d   Some Takayama surfboards cost less than $400. *I*

4   a   Some ridable waves are 30 feet high. *I*

  U b   Some ridable waves are not 30 feet high. *O*

  F c   No ridable waves are 30 feet high. *E*

  v d   All ridable waves are 30 feet high. *A*

C. Use the Traditional Square of Opposition to determine the truth value of each 'b' sentence below, where each corresponding 'a' sentence is taken to be true.

1. a. No cream sauces are delicate enough for lamb.
     b. Some cream sauces are not delicate enough for lamb.

2. a. It is false that all radishes are hot.
     b. All radishes are hot.

3. a. Some wines do not complement chicken.
     b. It is not true that all wines complement chicken.

4. a. It is false that some desserts are sweet.
     b. It is false that no desserts are sweet.

2.5 Further Inferences

This section concerns three further inferences that can be drawn from categorical sentences. To make these inferences, we use three different methods: **conversion**, **obversion**, and **contraposition**.

The rules for the *conversion* of a categorical sentence are:
1. *Replace the subject term with the predicate term.*
2. *Replace the predicate term with the subject term.*

For example, we can convert an **A** sentence:

(46) All marmots are rodents.

Simply switch the subject and predicate terms, to obtain:

(47) All rodents are marmots.

Clearly, (46) is true while (47) is false. Thus, we note that con-version does not work for **A** sentences. This is to say that there are cases where converting a *true* **A** sentence yields a *false* **A** sentence. Recall the Method of Counterexample from Chapter 1. Examples (46) and (47) constitute a counterexample to the claim that **A** sentences can be converted validly. Since not all **A** sentences can be converted validly, we say that conversion does not work for **A** sentences.

This reasoning suffices to show that conversion does not work for **O** sentences either. Consider:

(48) Some marsupials are not koala bears.
(49) Some koala bears are not marsupials.

By merely switching the subject and predicate terms here, we obtain a false sentence (49) from a true sentence (48). This counter-example shows that conversion does not always yield a true **O** sentence from a true **O** sentence.

Conversion does work for **E** and **I** sentences, however. From

(50) No Chicago Cubs are New York Yankees.

it follows that

(51) No New York Yankees are Chicago Cubs.

Whether (50) is actually true does not matter here. The strict point is that *if* (50) is true, then so is (51). Similarly for the two following **I** sentences.

(52) Some calendars give tide charts.
(53) Some things that give tide charts are calendars.

Many more examples could be enumerated here to show that conversion works for all **E** and **I** sentences. This is to say that a counterexample for **E** and **I** would be impossible. It may be instructive to think about how the terms are distributed in **E** and **I** sentences to get clearer on conversion. **E** sentences distribute both subject and predicate terms while in **I** sentences neither the subject nor the predicate term is distributed.

To obvert and contrapose categorical sentences, we need to introduce the concept of what is known as the "negation of a term". In Aristotelian Logic, to negate a term is to prefix the term, at the appropriate place, with a "non", or some other combining form. For example, to negate the predicate term in

(54) Some accomplished flutists are composers.

one simply attaches 'non' to the class term "composers" to obtain

(55) Some accomplished flutists are non-composers.

The prefix "non" wouldn't be the common choice for every negation, however, such as when negating the subject term in the following sentence:

(56) All learned people are people who study.

To negate 'learned people', we affix 'un' to 'learned', thus, obtaining

(57) All unlearned people are people who study.

One must use a bit of common sense when negating class terms, always paying attention to what is the common usage of a term. For example, care must be taken when negating subject and predicate terms in the following sentence:

(58) Some players are not winners.

To negate 'players', one must make the negated term refer to all things/people that are not in the class of players. Hence, if X is not a player, X is a non-player. Similarly with 'winners'. Given that the subject of this sentence is 'players', and is what the sentence is "talking about", we negate 'winners' with 'losers', since if X is a player, X either wins or loses (where a tie is impossible), such as in baseball or tennis. We derive the following sentence:

(59) Some non-players are losers.

However, there are cases where a person doesn't play and hence cannot be said to be either a winner or a loser. For example,

(60) No winners are ever forgotten.

To negate the subject term in (60), it would be appropriate merely to prefix 'winners' with 'non', since it is unclear that players are being referred to here. Hence, we derive

(61) No non-winners are ever forgotten.

Again, a little care and common sense will go a long way in making the right sorts of negations to the terms found in categorical sentences.

The rules for *obversion* of a categorical sentence are:

1. *Change the quality of the sentence.*
2. *Negate the predicate term.*

To change the quality of an Affirmative sentence, one makes it Negative; and to change the quality of a Negative sentence, one makes it Affirmative. The four sets of sentences below are examples of correct obversions.

(62) All weddings are happy occasions.
(63) No weddings are unhappy occasions.

(64) No loggers are playwrights.
(65) All loggers are non-playwrights.

(66) Some CIA agents are unpopular people.
(67) Some CIA agents are not popular people.

(68) Some ethicists are not ontologists.
(69) Some ethicists are non-ontologists.

Notice that the subject term as well as the quantity of these sentences remains unchanged. In (62) and (64), the quantifier was changed, since that is the proper way to change the quality of **A** and **E** sentences. However, in changing the quantifier, the quality is unchanged, since both quantifiers "all" and "no" are universal. In effect, when an **A** sentence is obverted, an **E** sentence is obtained, and an **E** sentence obverts into an **A** sentence.

In (66), change of quality is affected by adding 'not' to the copula. Conversely, in (68), change of quality is had by deleting 'not' from the copula. Subject term and quantity remain unaltered.

An important point to remember is that there is a strict ban on multiplying the number of "non's" on any term. The predicate term in (66) is "unpopular people". To negate this term, it would be improper to write "ununpopular people". Rather, common sense tells us simply to delete 'un' and write "popular people". The same is true of the following sentence:

(70) No aged humans are nonpersons.

Consider now the following sentences:

(71) No aged humans are nonnonpersons.
(72) No aged humans are persons.
(73) All aged humans are nonpersons.

(71) is incorrectly negates the predicate term of (70); (72) correctly negates the predicate term of (70); we conclude that (73) is the correct obversion of (72).

We will adopt the following rule: *At most, one "non" per term*. As you will have seen from the foregoing examples, obversion works for all of the four types of categorical sentence. This is to say that if any categorical sentence is obverted, the categorical sentence that is obtained will be equivalent to the original sentence, whence it follows that if the original sentence was true, the sentence obtained will be true, and if the original was false, so the obtained sentence will be false.

The rules for *contraposition* of a categorical sentence are:
1. *Replace the subject term with the negation of the predicate term.*
2. *Replace the predicate term with the negation of the subject term.*

The following pairs of sentences are correct contrapositions, the second sentence in each pair being the obtained sentence.

All bachelors are unmarried human males.
All married human males are non-bachelors

No turtles are mammals.
No non-mammals are non-turtles.

Some sailors are non-admirals.
Some admirals are non-sailors.

Some journals are not informative periodicals.
Some uninformative periodicals are not non-journals.

Contraposition works for **A** and **O** sentences, but does not work for **E** and **I** sentences. This is to say that there are no counter-examples to **A** and **O** sentences, whereas the second and third pair of sentences directly above are actual counterexamples, showing that it is possible to contrapose a true **E** sentence and thereby obtain a false sentence, and also that it is possible to contrapose a true **I** sentence and thereby obtain a false sentence. Another way of putting this is to say that when you contrapose an **A** or **O** sentence, you end up with an equivalent sentence, i.e., equivalent in truth value. When you contrapose an **E** or **I** sentence, you don't necessarily end up with an equivalent sentence.

The table of inferences is below:

Conversion
Replace subject term with predicate term.
Replace predicate term with subject term.
Works for **E** and **I** sentences.

Obversion
Change quality of the sentence.
Negate the predicate term.
Works for **A**, **E**, **I**, and **O** sentences.

Contraposition
Replace subject term with negation of predicate term.
Replace predicate term with negation of subject term.
Works for **A** and **O** sentences.

Exercises 2.5

A. Convert the following sentences and indicate whether the derived sentence is equivalent to the original.

1   Some 'bed & breakfast' houses are luxurious and expensive.
2   All business lunches are private meetings.
3   No IRS officers are characters on situation comedy shows.
4   Some uninvited guest are not unwelcome.
5* Some attractive models are very intelligent people.
6   No scientific theory is non-falsifiable.
7   All non-vertebrates are egg-laying creatures.
8   Some talent scouts are on the 'ten most wanted' list.
9   No sophomores with 'buzzes' are welcome at Buck House.
10* Some marijuana growers are wealthy tax evaders.

B. Obvert the following sentences and indicate whether the derived sentence is equivalent to the original.

1.   All unlucky gamblers are welcome at the Golden Nugget Saloon.
2.   No truck drivers are 'legally blind'.
3.   Some grant-proposal-writers are slick customers.
4.   Some slick customers are not grant-proposal-writers.
5* All corporate executives are yacht owners.
6.   No Rolling Stones are police officers.
7.   Some non-police officers are non-criminals.
8.   Some lawyers are not non-criminals.
9.   No non-spiders are eight-legged creatures.
10* All creatures with hearts are creatures with kidneys.

C. Contrapose the following sentences and indicate whether the derived sentence is equivalent to the original.

1. Some sheepdogs are able to count.
2. All new pennies are shiny coins.
3. Some prostitutes are not public servants.
4. No Krugerands are non-metals.
5* Some AIDS victims are opposed to mandatory testing for AIDS.
6. All Fundamentalist Christians are non-neutral about Papal power.
7. Some existentialist philosophers have not studied at Princeton.
8. No rivers in Washington are rivers that flow south.
9. All Smetana concerts are artistic and fashionable events.
10* Some sisters are not non-sister-helping-sisters.

2.6 Venn Diagrams for Categorical Sentences

The principal method for evaluating arguments in Aristotelian Logic is known as the Venn Diagram Method. However, before we move ahead with arguments themselves, it would be well to introduce the Venn method for diagraming sentences, since one always diagrams individual sentences when using the Venn method to analyze arguments.

The Venn method for diagramming categorical sentences consists in drawing two intersecting circles, as follows:

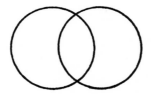

Each circle represents a class, i.e., one of the classes of objects referred to in the sentence one is diagramming. Let's say one wants to diagram the sentence

(74) All baseball players are coordinated people.

The 'B' circle represents the class of baseball players, while the 'C' circle represents the class of coordinated people.

Clearly, three classes are represented here: 1) the class of baseball players who are outside the class of coordinated people, 2) the class of coordinated people who are outside the class of baseball players, and 3) the class of baseball players who are coordinated people. These three classes are designated by the diagram below:

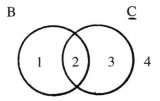

Class section '1' designates baseball players who are not coordinated; class section '3' designates coordinated people who aren't baseball players; and class section '2' designates baseball players who are coordinated *and* coordinated people who are baseball players. (Notice the '4' completely outside both circles. One might say there is a fourth class here, i.e., the class of people who are neither baseball players nor coordinated people, or, the class of everything outside the classes of baseball players and coordinated people.)

The point of diagramming is to make the diagram "say" just what the sentence itself says, i.e., to say no more and no less. There are two marks used in Venn diagrams. One is 'shading' and the other is an 'X'. For example, below is the Venn for (74):

All baseball players are coordinated people.

In effect, one "takes out", i.e., shades, the part of the diagram that represents baseball players that are not coordinated. Since (74) says that every baseball player is coordinated, if we take out all the baseball players that are *not* coordinated, we have a diagram that correctly represents what (74) says and means. Now, the only class section in the diagram representing baseball players is in the class section representing coordinated people, which indicates that all baseball players are coordinated people, which is what (74) says. Now consider the following sentence:

(75) No compact discs are monophonic.

Let 'C' represent the class of compact discs; let 'M' represent the class of monophonic things. To diagram this sentence, it suffices to shade the class section in the diagram representing compact discs that are also monophonic. Hence, we "take out" the middle class section, where the classes representing discs and monophonic things overlap. Hence the following diagram:

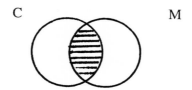

Now the only areas left unshaded in the diagram are those representing the class of compact discs that are not monophonic and the class of monophonic things that are not compact discs. This diagram correctly represents (75).

A rule: *Use shading to diagram **A** and **E** sentences.*

Diagramming **I** and **O** sentences differs a great deal from diagramming **A** and **E** sentences. This has to do with the fact that **I** and **O** sentences posit the existence of at least one individual belonging to one or more classes. To represent this obscure individual, we use an 'X'. Consider,

(76) Some right-fielders are left-handed.

This sentence says that there exists at least one individual who is a member of the class of right-fielders, and who is also a member of the class of left-handed things. It claims that at least one right-fielder is left-handed, or that at least one left-handed person is a right-fielder. (Recall that conversion works for **I** sentences.) In the diagram, then, we want to place an 'X' in the class section representing the intersection of the two classes. Let 'R' represent the class of right-fielders. Let 'L' represent the class of left-handed people. The correct diagram is:

Some right-fielders are left-handed.

R 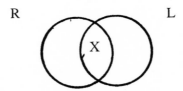 L

Notice that this sentence (76) doesn't say anything about all right-fielders, or about all left-handed people, or that one class is entirely included in or excluded from the other. And neither does the diagram. The diagram merely indicates that there is some individual who is a member of both classes.

O sentences are similarly diagrammed using the 'X'. Consider:

(77) Some evening gowns are not elegant.

Let 'G' represent the class of evening gowns. Let 'E' represent the class of elegant things. What (77) says is that there is one thing, namely a perfume, that is outside the class of elegant things. In our diagram then, we want to place the 'X' inside the class section representing evening gowns that are outside the class section representing elegant things. The correct diagram for (77) is:

G 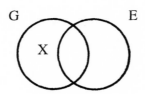 E

A rule: *Use an X to diagram I and O sentences.*

There are certain conventions which will be followed in this book. One is that the subject term of a sentence is to be represented by the left circle and the predicate term by the right circle. Another is that there is no case where either 'shadings' or 'X's' appear outside intersecting circles.

Exercises 2.6

A. Diagram the following categorical sentences.
1   All asphalt surfaces are unsuitable for tennis courts.
2   No Scots are unpatriotic people.
3   Some unpatriotic people are not Scots.
4   Some people named 'Smith' are really named 'Jones'.
5* All ancient Assyrians were tolerant of infanticide.
6   Some modern Greeks are tolerant of infanticide.
7   No books by Virginia Woolf are without literary merit.
8   Some famous poets are reclusive acrophobes.
9   All oysters are creatures that feel pain.
10* Some creatures that feel pain are not oysters.
11 No umpires are tolerant of foul language.
12 All laborers are people who should receive higher wages.
13 Some nurses are excellent diagnosticians.
14 No standing armies are engaged in productive research.
15* Some secretaries are better than others.

B. Work conversion on #2, #4, #6, and #7 in section 'A' above and diagram the converted sentence. What is noticeable about the diagram for the converted sentence in comparison with the diagram for the original sentence?

C. Show, through a series of legitimate conversions, obversions, and/or contrapositions, and the Traditional Square of Opposition, that the second sentence of the pairs (below) can be inferred from the first with which it is paired. Diagram each first sentence.

1. All obelisks are fragile objects.
    Some fragile objects are obelisks.
2. Some gay activists are not non-violent people.
    Some violent people are gay activists.
3. It is false that some microfiche are not made of plastic.
    It is false that all things made of plastic are non-microfiche.
4. Some libertarians are radical liberals.
    Some radical liberals are not non-libertarians.
5* No actors are as shy as Martin Short.
    Some people as shy as Martin Short are not actors.

3. Aristotelian Logic B

3.1 Preliminaries

The last chapter was devoted to the study of categorical sentences. The reason so much space is devoted to sentences is that if one is to study/evaluate arguments, since arguments are comprised of sentences, one must get as clear as possible about sentences. In the present chapter, we will study the nature of arguments constructed from categorical sentences, typically known as the **categorical syllogism**.

A **syllogism** is an argument with two premises and one conclusion. Hence, the following argument is a syllogism:

Darwin thought of evolution as an algorithmic process.
Darwin had the correct view of evolution.
Therefore, evolution is an algorithmic process.

This argument, however, is not a *categorical* syllogism, since none of the sentences in the argument are categorical sentences. The same is true of the following argument.

If Dylan does a concert, we'll drive to San Francisco.
If we drive to San Francisco, we'll visit Linda and Lloyd.
So, if Dylan does a concert, we'll visit Linda and Lloyd.

The argument directly above is known as a *hypothetical syllogism*, because each sentence in the argument is a "hypothetical", i.e., contains the word "if" as meant to denote a condition, as in the first sentence where Dylan's doing a concert is a condition for driving to San Francisco. These sentences are also known as "condi-tionals", and we will study them at length in Chapter 5.

As mentioned, categorical syllogisms are made up entirely of categorical sentences. Since categorical syllogisms are syllogisms, it follows that there will always be two categorical sentences as premises and one categorical sentence as a conclusion. The two arguments below are categorical syllogisms.

All weavers are environmentally conscious.
All quilters are weavers.
So, all quilters are environmentally conscious.

No science fiction writers are aliens.
Some Venusians are aliens.
Hence, some Venusians are not science fiction writers.

It will be most helpful to be able to construct categorical syllogisms, and to do that we need to know the properties common to these types of argument. Hence, we move now to the attributes of categorical syllogisms. The short designations, **A**, **E**, **I**, and **O** will be retained throughout this chapter to refer to the four types of categorical sentence.

3.2 Normal Form, Mood, Figure

We must begin with what is most simple. Each categorical syllogism contains a **major term**, a **minor term**, and a **middle term**, with each term appearing twice, and only twice, in each syllogism. The *major term* is defined as the term appearing as the predicate term of the conclusion. The *minor term* is defined as the term appearing as the subject term of the conclusion. The *middle term* is not found in the conclusion, but appears once in each premise. Consider the following categorical syllogism:

All switch-hitters are players batting over .340.
Some rookies are switch-hitters.
Therefore, some rookies are players batting over .340.

The *major term* in this syllogism is "players batting over .340", since that is the predicate term of the conclusion. The *minor term* here is "rookies", since that is the subject term of the conclusion. The term "switch-hitters" does not appear in the conclusion, but appears as the subject term of the first premise and as the predicate term of the second premise. Hence, 'switch-hitters' is the *middle term* of this syllogism.

The premise in which the major term appears is called the **major premise**. We will adopt the convention of placing the major premise as the first premise of each categorical syllogism. The **minor premise** is defined as the premise in which the minor term appears. Our convention will be to place the minor premise as the second premise of each categorical syllogism. Further, the conclusion will always appear last in each syllogism.

We will refer to any syllogism which has the major premise first, the minor premise second, and the conclusion last as a **normal form categorical syllogism**.

The **mood** of a normal form categorical syllogism is defined as the combination of the designating letters (**A, E, I, O**) of the categorical sentences, in the order of sentence appearance, com-prising the syllogism itself. Hence, the mood of the syllogism above is **AII**, since the major premise is an **A** sentence, the minor premise is an **I** sentence, and the conclusion is an **I** sentence. All moods will denote normal form categorical syllogisms, i.e., as placing the major premise first, the minor premise second, and the conclusion last. The moods of the following two syllogisms are **EOO** and **AEE**, respectively:

No T-shirts are uncomfortable.
Some T-shirts are not soft.
So, some soft T-shirts are not uncomfortable.

All postcards from Greece are colorful.
No colorful things are misplaced.
Thus, no misplaced things are postcards from Greece.

It would be a simple task, at this point, to identify the mood of any normal form categorical syllogism that was presented. However, what if a mood itself were presented? Could a syllogism be constructed simply from knowing the mood? It will be helpful to see why the answer to this question is "no". Let's take a mood, say, **EIO**. We know that the major premise will be an **E** sentence, that the minor premise will be an **I**, and that the conclusion will be an **O**. We can again adopt 'p', 's', and 'm' as letters designating major term, minor term, and middle term, respectively. This will be helpful for constructing syllogisms when we lack a specific subject matter. The conclusion of the **EIO** syllogism will be

Some s are not p.

We know this because, since 'p' designates the major term, it will appear as the predicate term of the conclusion, and since 's' designates the minor tem, it will appear as the subject term of the conclusion. We also know that we want to place the major term in the first premise and the minor term in the second premise. The bare bones, so far, for **EIO**, is:

No   are   .
Some   are   .
Therefore, some s are not p.

The problem becomes knowing where to place the 'p' in the major premise. It could be placed as the subject term or as the predicate term, and, so far, we have no directions for where to place it. The same is true of the placement of 's' in the minor premise. If we knew the location of the middle term, 'm', in each of the premises, however, that would solve our problem.

The location of the middle term is defined by what is known as the **figure** of a normal form categorical syllogism. There are only four possible figures, or placements of the middle term, in a syllogism, and they are referred to as: **First Figure, Second Figure, Third Figure**, and **Fourth Figure**. In the *first figure*, the middle term appears as the subject term of the major premise and as the predicate term of the minor premise; in the *second figure*, the middle term appears as the predicate terms of both major and minor premises; in the *third figure*, the middle term appears as the subject term of both major and minor premises; in the *fourth figure*, the middle term appears as the predicate term of the major premise and as the subject term of the minor premise.

If we add a figure to the mood, say, the second figure, with mood and figure written as **EIO-2**, we can now fill in the positions of the major, minor, and middle terms in the premises, as so:

No p are m.
Some s are m.
Therefore, some s are not p.

Two tables that might help one to remember the placement of the middle term in each figure are:

	Fig 1		Fig 2		Fig 3		Fig 4	
Major Premise	m	p	p	m	m	p	p	m
Premise	s	m	s	m	m	s	m	s
on	s	p	s	p	s	p	s	p

	Fig 1	Fig 2	Fig 3	Fig 4
Major Premise	m ⌐ p	p ⌐ m	m ⌐ p	p ⌐ m
Minor Premise	s ⌐ m	s ⌐ m	m ⌐ s	m ⌐ s
Conclusion	s p	s p	s p	s p

Below are examples of mood and figure:

AAA-1   All m are p.   AAA-3   All m are p.
        All s are m.   All m are s.
        So, all s are p.   So, all s are p.

IOI-2   Some p are m.   IOI-4   Some p are m.
        Some s are not m.   Some m are not s.
        So, some s are p.   So, some s are p.

EAE-1   No m are p.   AEA-3   All m are p.
        All s are m.   No m are s.
        So, no s are p.   So, all s are p.

AEO-2   All p are m.   OAE-4   Some p are not m.
        No s are m.   All m are s.
        So, some s are not p.   So, no s are p.

AAI-1   All rice growers are farmers.
        All grain growers are rice growers.
        Hence, some grain growers are farmers.

AOO-2   All fungi are multicellular.
        Some algae are not multicellular
        It follows that some algae are not fungi.

EIO-3   No Edgar Allen Poe poems are lighthearted.
        Some Edgar Allen Poe poems are terrifying.
        We infer that some terrifying things are not
            lighthearted things.

IAI-4   Some genes are segments of DNA molecules.
All DNA molecules are information carrying things.
We can conclude that some information carrying
things are genes.

Exercise 3.2

A. Identify the mood and figure of each of the following syllogisms. Put any sentence not in normal form into normal form prior to determining mood and figure.

1. All Disneyland characters are funny.
   No Twilight Zone characters are funny.
   So, no Twilight Zone characters are Disneyland characters.
2. No mail carriers with bunyons are in good moods.
   Some people in good moods are not on drugs.
   So, some people not on drugs are not mail carriers with bunyons.
3. No ethics books are about juggling.
   Some ethics books are concerned with epistemology.
   So, no books concerned with epistemology are about juggling.
4. All male parents are lovers of games.
   All non-female parents are male parents.
   Hence, all non-female parents are lovers of games.
5* Some even primes are less than the number 3.
   All number 2's are less than the number 3.
   We conclude that all number 2's are even primes.
6. No persons on heavy medication should drive.
   Some hospital out-patients are on heavy medication.
   Thus, some out-patients should not drive.
7. All Mille Bornes players have stamina.
   Some Bridge players are Mille Bornes players.
   It follows that some Bridge players have stamina.
8. No famous analytic philosophers read Harlequin Romances.
   All famous analytic philosophers read Bertrand Russell.
   So, some readers of Russell don't read Harlequin Romances.
9. All cities in Alaska are beautiful in winter.
   All things beautiful in winter are worth photopgraphing.
   So, some things worth photographing are cities in Alaska.
10* All Chang Dynasty vases are made of porcelin.
   All Ming Dynasty vases are made of porcelin.
   Hence, all Ming Dynasty vases are Chang Dynasty vases.

11 Some TV commercials are not tasteful.
No plays about Nazis are tasteful.
Hence, some plays about Nazis are not TV commercials.

12 Some egoists are intuitionists.
No intuitionists are hedonists.
Therefore, some hedonists are not egoists.

13 No criminal lawyers are people who can be bribed.
All people who can be bribed are untrustworthy.
So, some untrustworthy people are not criminal lawyers.

14 Some sea anemones are polyps.
All cnidarians are sea anemones.
We conclude that some cnidarians are polyps.

15* No fans of Ayn Rand are altruistically inclined.
Some fans of Ayn Rand are philosophically minded.
Thus, some philosophically minded people are not altruistic.

B. Use 'p', 's', and 'm', to designate major, minor, and middle terms when constructing the categorical syllogisms defined by the following moods and figures.

1. EEE-1	7. EEI-3	13 OIO-1	19. AAE-3
2. EEE-2	8. EEI-4	14. IOI-2	20* IAI-4
3. EEE-3	9. EIE-1	15* AEA-3	21. EAO-1
4. EEE-4	10* EIE-2	16. OAO-4	22. OEA-2
5* EEI-1	11 EIE-3	17. III-1	23. IAA-3
6. EEI-2	12 EIE-4	18. OOO-2	24. OEE-4
			25* OIO-1

C. Put the following categorical syllogisms, as well as the categorical sentences found therein, into normal form. Indicate the mood and figure of each.

1. Some Senators are good listeners, so all Senators are good notetakers, since some good listeners are good notetakers.

2. Since all Professors profess to know something, it follows that some Associate Professors profess to know something, because no Professors are Associate Professors.

3. Not all predators kill with their teeth, and not all teeth bearing animals are predators. We can draw the conclusion that not all teeth bearing animals kill with their teeth.

4. Some disaccharides are carbohydrates, because some carbohydrates are a bond of two monosaccharides and all disaccharides
are a bond of two monosaccharides.

5* Every Arctic Wolf raises its hackles when it is about to attack
and some Arctic Wolves lower their heads when they are being
playful. Hence, some animals that raise their hackles when about
to attack are animals that lower their heads when playful.

3.3 Venn Diagrams for Categorical Syllogisms

We are now at a point where it is possible to evaluate, or test,
categorical syllogisms for validity. Of the two hundred and fifty six
possible moods and figures, *only fifteen are valid.* In the present section
we will use Venn Diagrams for testing for validity. In the next section
we will introduce the notion of a formal fallacy for this purpose.

You will recall that Venn Diagrams are for sentences. When
constructing a diagram for one sentence, two intersecting circles are used,
since one sentence contains reference to two classes. In categorical
syllogisms, however, reference is made to three classes, viz., the class of
the major term, the class of the minor term, and the class of the middle
term. Since there are three classes, we need three intersecting circles for
the syllogism, as below:

Let 'S' = 'Swedish persons', 'P' = 'peasants', and 'M' = 'musicians'.
Here we will adopt the convention that a bar before a letter represents the
negation of the class designated by that letter. For example, '-S'
designates the class of "non-Swedes". The following diagrams, one with
the sections numbered 1-8, the other with various combinations of 'SPM',
are the keys to understanding the method of using Venns for syllogisms.

A

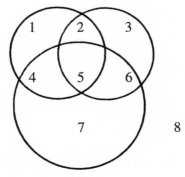

B

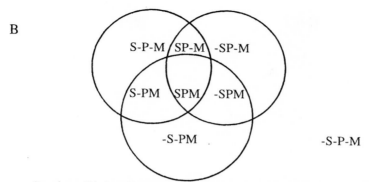

Section #1 in diagram A represents the class of Swedes who are neither peasants nor musicians, and corresponds to S-P-M in diagram B; section 2 represents the class of Swedish peasants who are non-musicians and corresponds to SP-M; section 3 represents the class of peasants who are neither Swedish nor musicians and corresponds to -SP-M; section 4 represents the class of Swedish non-peasant musicians and corresponds to S-PM; section 5 represents the class of Swedish peasant musicians and corresponds to SPM; section 6 represents the class of non-Swedish peasant musicians and corresponds to -SPM; section 7 represents the class of non-Swedish non-peasant musicians and corresponds to -S-PM; section 8 represents the class of non-Swedish non-peasant non-musicians and corresponds to -S-P-M.

Before diagramming an argument, it is necessary to lay out the method in some detail. The method of Venn Diagrams is one of the most straightforward ways of seeing what the concept of validity is all about, in practice. Here are the rules for constructing Venns for syllogisms:

1. First, diagram the Universal premise.
2. Second, diagram the undiagrammed premise.
3. If the conclusion is diagrammed, mark the argument **valid**.
4. If the conclusion is *not* diagrammed, mark the argument **invalid**.

Recall our definition of validity: it is impossible for the premises to be true and the conclusion false in a valid argument. Now, if one diagrams the premises and the conclusion is thereby also diagrammed, this is an indication that the conclusion follows from the premises. **Never diagram the conclusion!** The point here is to see whether the conclusion follows from the premises.

We can now diagram an argument.

All Swedes are musicians.
AII-3   <u>Some Swedes are peasants.</u>
Some peasants are musicians.

Since the first premise is Universal premise, diagram it first, as so:

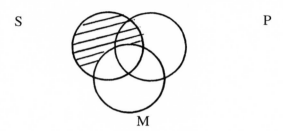

Recall that Universal sentences are diagrammed by "shading". What was done here was the "shading out" of all those Swedes that are not musicians. All the Swedes left are musicians, as denoted by the class "S" in the diagram which are not shaded, which is what the first premise says. In effect, what one wants is to make the diagram "say" what each of the premises say. When that is accomplished, if the diagram "says" what the conclusion says, the argument is valid. If not, not.

We diagram the second premise as follows:

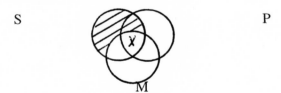

Recall that an 'X' is used when diagramming Particular sentences. Since the second premise says that there exists at least one Swede who is a peasant, we place an 'X' in that class section of the diagram representing Swedish peasants. **Never place an 'X', or part of an 'X' in a shaded class section.** The only section representing Swedish peasants that is open (not shaded) is the center section, where Swedes are peasants and musicians. The 'X' is placed in that class section.

Now the premises have been diagrammed. Does the diagram "say" that there is at least one peasant that is a musician? Or, is there an 'X' in one of the sections where peasants are musicians? The answer is yes. Hence, the conclusion has been diagrammed and the argument is valid. The reason that one diagrams a Universal premise before a Particular premise is that not doing so can make it impossible to correctly construct a diagram for some arguments. For example, if we had diagrammed the second premise, which is Particular in the above syllogism, first, it would have prevented our correctly diagramming the first premise.

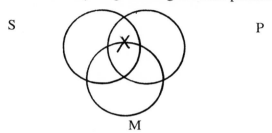

Here we have an 'X' on the line. This is because the second premise says that there is an individual who is both a Swede and a peasant, but the premise does not say whether this Swedish peasant is a musician or not. Hence we don't have enough information to justify putting the 'X' in either class section to the exclusion of the other. Nor can we place one 'X' in the class of Swedish peasant musicians and one 'X' in the class of Swedish peasant non-musicians, because that would be tantamount to affirming the existence of at least two individuals who were Swedish peasants, which is not what the second premise says.

Now, having the 'X' on the line prevents us from shading the two class sections indicated by the first premise, for a further rule is, *Never shade a section which contains an 'X' or part of an 'X'.* Hence, we are barred from completing the diagram. Also, however, given the 'X' on the line, the conclusion would not be diagrammed, because it is not clear whether the Swedish peasant is, or is not, a musician. And if the Swedish peasant is not a musician, then the peasant is not a musician, which would make the argument invalid. But we know, from the previous correct diagram, that the argument *is* valid. All of which argues for diagramming the Universal first.

If both premises in an argument are Universal, or, if neither is Universal, it does not matter which premise is diagrammed first. Consider the diagram on the following page.

No Swedes are musicians.

EEE-4   No musicians are peasants.

No peasants are Swedes.

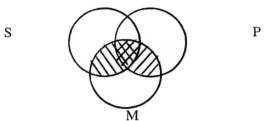

Here, since both premises are Universal, shadings are used to diagram both premises. As per the first premise, the class sections representing Swedish musicians has been "taken out". The diagram now "says" that no Swedes are musicians. As per the second premise, the class sections representing musicians who are peasants has been shaded, *with* overlapping shade in the center section. Does the diagram "say" that no peasants are Swedes? Or, are all sections representing peasants who are Swedes shaded? The answer is no. The section representing Swedish peasant non-musicians has not been shaded. So the conclusion has not been diagrammed and the argument is invalid.

Consider an argument with two Particular premises:

Some peasants are musicians.

IOO-2   Some Swedes are not musicians.

Some Swedes are not peasants.

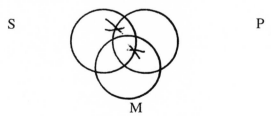

Notice that both X's are on lines between class sections. This will be true in all diagrams for syllogisms with two Particular premises. As it turns out, every normal form categorical syllogism with Particular premises is invalid.

Regarding the above diagram, to diagram the first premise, an 'X' was to be placed in the class of peasant musicians. However, two placements where peasants who are musicians are non-Swedes. The first premise says nothing about the class of Swedes at all, so we cannot but put the 'X' on the line separating the class of peasant musician non-Swedes and peasant musician Swedes.

To diagram the second premise, an 'X' was to be placed in the class of Swedes who are non-musicians. However, there are two such classes: where Swedes are non-peasants and where Swedes are peasants. The second premise fails to refer to peasants altogether and is thus no help to us in trying to decide where to place the 'X' in relation to the class of peasants. Hence, we must place the 'X' outside the class of musicians, on the line separating the classes of Swedes and peasants.

It may be well, at this point, to note a few "negative" rules:

Never place an 'X' on an
outside line of a diagram:

Never place an 'X' at the
intersection of two lines:

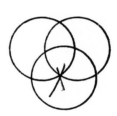

Never place more than
one 'X' on a line:

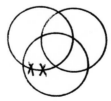

Never place more than one
'X' inside a class section:

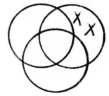

Never place an 'X' outside
of the diagram itself:

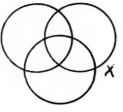

Never place an 'X' in a shaded area.

Below are examples of mood, figure, the syllogism, and the matching
diagram:

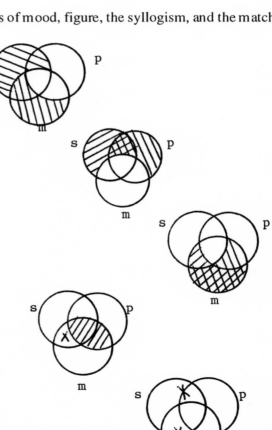

AAA-1 -- Valid
    All m are p.
    <u>All s are m.</u>
    All s are p.

AAA-2 -- Invalid
    All p are m.
    <u>All s are m.</u>
    All s are p.

AAI-3 -- Invalid
    All m are p.
    <u>All m are s.</u>
    Some s are p.

EIO-4 -- Valid
    No p are m.
    <u>Some m are s.</u>
    Some s are not p.

OOO-1 -- Invalid
    Some m are not p.
    <u>Some s are not m.</u>
    Some S are not p.

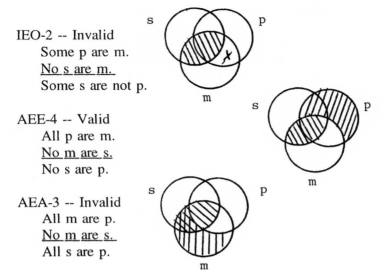

IEO-2 -- Invalid
   Some p are m.
   No s are m.
   Some s are not p.

AEE-4 -- Valid
   All p are m.
   No m are s.
   No s are p.

AEA-3 -- Invalid
   All m are p.
   No m are s.
   All s are p.

Exercise 3.3

A. Construct the arguments defined by the following moods and figures. Then construct the Venn diagram for each argument. Valid or Invalid?

1. AAA-3	7. EIE-4	13. AOO-2	19. IAI-3
2. EIO-1	8. OAO-3	14. IAI-1	20* OAE-2
3. AOO-4	9. OEE-1	15* OAI-3	21 EAE-2
4. AAI-2	10* OIO-3	16 OOO-1	22 OOI-3
5* AEE-1	11 IOI-4	17 EEE-3	23 AII-1
6. AEO-2	12 EIO-2	18 EAO-4	24 III-4
			25* AAA-1

B. Name the mood and figure, and construct a Venn diagram for the following arguments. Indicate whether each argument is valid or invalid.
   1. Some actors are not well-suited for their parts.
      Some actresses are well-suited for their parts.
      So, no actresses are actors.
   2. All librarians are people who like to read indexes.
      Some librarians are experts in Artificial Intelligence
      Hence, some AI experts like to read indexes.
   3. No brain surgeons are prize fighters.
      All neurosurgeons are brain surgeons.
      Therefore, no neurosurgeons are prize fighters.

4. All plumbers are people who make over $50,000 per year.
   Some carpenters do not make over $50,000 per year.
   Thus, some carpenters are not plumbers.
5* All unicorns are one-horned animals.
   All one-horned animals are vertebrates.
   Hence, some vertebrates are unicorns.
6. Some sheep, but no goats, are carnivorous. Hence it
   follows that some goats are not sheep.
7. Many children know the value of a buck. We know this is true
   because anyone who spends money wisely knows the value of a
   buck and many children do spend money wisely.
8. Each and every student in this class feels sad at some time o r
   other. So, since sadness is sometimes healthy, every student in
   this class is healthy at some time or other.
9. Each and every student in this class feels sad at some time o r
   other. Since sadness is never healthy, it follows that no healthy
   student is a student in this class.
10* A few automobiles are too expensive; and not one automobile is
   worth a year's wages. Hence, whatever is worth a year's wages
   it too expensive.

C. Are the following statements true or false?
1. If a categorical syllogism contains two Particular premises, one
   should diagram the first premise first.
2. All categorical syllogisms with two Universal premises are valid.
3. If, after diagramming the premises, the conclusion is not
   diagrammed, one should diagram the conclusion to show the
   syllogism to be valid.
4. It is sometimes appropriate to place an 'X' outside the diagram.
5* It is sometimes inappropriate to place an 'X' outside the diagram.
6. 'Figure' indicates the placement of the major and minor terms.
7. No non-normal form syllogism can be shown to be a valid
   syllogism.
8. The middle term is defined as the predicate term of the second
   premise
9. The major term in figure 3 is located as the predicate term of the
   conclusion and as the predicate term of the first premise.
10* In 'IAI-1', the minor premise is to be diagrammed first.

3.4 Formal Fallacies

Constructing Venn diagrams is not the only method for deter-mining the validity of categorical syllogisms. Another method, and the only other treated here, involves analyzing syllogisms to determine whether one or more fallacies are committed. To say that an argument commits a **fallacy** is to say that there is something wrong with it, e.g., that it has false premises or, for one reason or another, the conclusion does not follow from the premises. There are two kinds of fallacies: **formal** and **informal**. We will be studying informal fallacies in Chapter 4.

An argument that commits a *formal fallacy* has what we call a "defective form". The content of any argument is no factor in determining whether it commits a formal fallacy. This is to say that it does not matter what the argument is about. Hence, any argument is formally valid or invalid by virtue of its form. To elaborate on this, notice that one can determine the validity of the argument defined by the mood and figure AAA-1 without the sentences of the argument having any subject matter whatever. Using 'p', 's', and 'm', this argument can be schematized as follows:

All m are p.
All s are m.
All s are p.

The Venn diagram for this argument will prove it to be valid, without subject matter. Similarly, a Venn diagram will prove the argument defined by 'EOO-3' to be invalid.

No m are p.
Some m are not s.
Some s are not p.

Again, this argument can be shown to be invalid without subject matter by the very fact that 'p', 's', and 'm' do not have meaning. We have used them to stand for "major term", "minor term", and "middle term", respectively, but this is not to give them a meaning, like, say, 'animals as shy as brook trout' has meaning.

There are seven formal fallacies to be presented here. There are more, but these seven suffice for determining the validity of every categorical syllogism.

A. Fallacy of Undistributed Middle Term

No categorical syllogism is valid unless the middle term is distributed at least once. The following each commit **Undistributed Middle**:

(A)	(B)	(C)
All p are m.	Some m are not p.	Some m are p.
<u>All s are m.</u>	<u>Some s are m.</u>	<u>Some m are s.</u>
All s are p.	Some s are not p.	Some s are p.

In (A) the middle term is undistributed in both premises, since no **A** sentence distributed its predicate term. In (B) the middle term is undistributed in the first premise, since no **O** sentence distributes its subject term; and undistributed in the second premise in (B) because no **I** sentence distributes its predicate term. The middle term is undistributed in (C), since no **I** sentence distributes its subject term.

None of the following examples commit Undistributed Middle:

(D)	(E)	(F)
All m are p.	Some p are m.	No m are p.
<u>No s are m.</u>	<u>Some s are not m.</u>	<u>Some m are not s.</u>
No s are p.	Some s are p.	Some s are p.

In (D) the middle term is distributed in both premises, since **A** sentences distribute their subject terms and since **E** sentences distribute both terms. In (E), though in the first premise the middle term is undistributed, it is distributed in the second premise. Since the rule is that *the middle term must be distributed **at least once***, (E) does not commit Undistributed Middle. (F), conversely, since the middle term is distributed in the first premise, does not commit Undistributed Middle.

B. Fallacy of Illicit Major Term

No categorical syllogism is valid if the major term is distributed in the conclusion and not in the major premise. This is to say that if the major term is distributed in the conclusion, it must be distributed in the major premise. Each example below commits **Illicit Major**:

(G)
All m are p.
<u>No s are m.</u>
No s are p.

(H)
Some p are m.
<u>Some s are not m.</u>
Some s are not p.

(I)
Some p are not m.
<u>No m are s.</u>
No s are p.

In each of the above, 'p' is distributed in the conclusion but not in the major premise. (J), (K), and (L) below do *not* commit Illicit Major.

(J)
All p are m.
<u>Some s are not m.</u>
Some s are not p.

(K)
Some p are not m.
<u>Some m are not s.</u>
All s are p.

(L)
No m are p.
<u>No s are m.</u>
Some s are p.

In (J), the major term is distributed in the conclusion as well as in the major premise. In (K), the major term is not distributed in the conclusion, so the rule for Illicit Major does not apply. (The rule states *if* the major term is distributed in the conclusion, then it must be distributed in the major premise. The rule does not state that the major term must be distributed in the conclusion.) In (L), as in (K), the major term is not distributed in the conclusion. The difference between (K) and (L) is that the major term in the major premise is undistributed in the former but distributed in the latter. This is not a factor, however, when the term is not distributed in the conclusion.

C. Fallacy of Illicit Minor Term

This fallacy is the counterpart to Illicit Major and states that if the minor term is distributed in the conclusion, then it must be distributed in the minor premise. Each of the following arguments commits **Illicit Minor**:

(M)
All p are m.
<u>Some m are s.</u>
All s are p.

(N)
Some m are not p.
<u>All m are s.</u>
No s are p.

(O)
No p are m.
<u>Some s are not m.</u>
No s are p.

In each of (M), (N), and (O), the minor term is distributed in the conclusion, since both **A** and **E** sentences distribute their subject terms. The minor terms are undistributed in the minor premises in the above arguments, since **I** and **A** sentences do not distribute their predicate terms and since **O** sentences do not distribute their subject terms.

The following arguments do not commit Illicit Minor:

(P)	(Q)	(R)
All m are p.	No p are m.	Some m are p.
Some m are not s.	No s are m.	Some s are m.
All s are p.	No s are p.	Some s are p.

In (P) and (Q) the minor terms are distributed in both conclusions and both minor premises. In (R) the minor term is not distributed in the conclusion and, hence, does not need to be distributed in the minor premise.

D. Fallacy of Exclusive Premises

No valid categorical syllogism can have more than one negative premise. This is to say that at least one of the premises must be either an **A** or **I** sentence. We can thus see that all syllogisms with the forms **EEE, OOO, EO?, OE?**, in all figures, are invalid. The following commit **Exclusive Premises**:

(S)	(T)	(U)
No m are p.	Some p are not m.	No p are m.
No s are m.	Some m are not s.	Some s are not m.
No s are p.	Some s are not p.	No s are p.

The three following do not commit Exclusive Premises:

(V)	(W)	(X)
Some m are not p.	No p are m.	All m are p.
Some s are m.	All m are s.	All m are s.
Some s are not p.	No s are p.	All s are p.

Neither (V) nor (W) commit Exclusive Premises since in both cases only one of the premises is Negative. (X) has two Affirmative premises, so Exclusive Premises does not apply to it.

E. Existential Fallacy

No categorical syllogism is valid if both premises are Univer-sity and the conclusion is Particular. This will appear obvious if one recalls the method of constructing Venn diagrams. With two Universal premises, the diagram would contain only shadings and no 'Xs'. However, any valid argument with a Particular conclusion would have at least one 'X'. No syllogism with two Universal premises and a particular conclusion would have an 'X' in the diagram. The 'X' would denote the existence of at least one member of a class, hence the name Existential Fallacy. The three following commit the Existential Fallacy:

(Y)	(Z)	(Aa)
All p are m.	No m are p.	All m are p.
All s are m.	No s are m.	No m are s.
Some s are p.	Some s are not p.	Some s are not p.

None of the following commit the Existential Fallacy:

(Ab)	(Ac)	(Ad)
Some p are m.	No p are m.	Some m are p.
All m are s.	All m are s.	Some s are not p.
Some s are p.	No s are p.	No s are p.

In (Ab), while the conclusion is Particular, so is the major premise. In (Ac), though the premises are University, the conclu-sion is as well. In (Ad), the two premises are Particular and the Existential Fallacy cannot apply, for the Existential Fallacy is concerned with Universal, not Particular, premises.

F. Fallacy of Drawing an Affirmative Conclusion from Negative Premises

In every valid categorical syllogism with a Negative premise, the conclusion will also be negative. Hence, any categorical syllogism with a Negative premise and an Affirmative conclusion commits this fallacy. We have already seen that no valid syllogism can have two Negative premises. Some valid syllogisms do have one negative premise, e.g.,

OAO-3. Notice that in **OAO-3** both the major premise and the conclusion are Negative.

The three below commit **Affirmative Conclusion from Negative Premises**:

(Ae)	(Af)	(Ag)
No m are p.	All p are m.	Some p are not m.
<u>No s are m.</u>	<u>Some s are not m.</u>	<u>No m are s.</u>
All s are p.	Some s are p.	All s are p.

The following three do not commit this fallacy:

(Ah)	(Af)	(Aj)
Some m are p.	No p are m.	Some p are not m.
<u>Some s are m.</u>	<u>All s are m.</u>	<u>All s are m.</u>
Some s are p.	No s are p.	Some s are not p.

G. Fallacy of Drawing a Negative Conclusion from Affirmative Premises

If both premises are Affirmative, the conclusion cannot be Negative. This is not to say that no categorical syllogism with two Affirmative premises can be valid, as we know **AAA-1**, for example, is valid. This is also not to say that no categorical syllogism with a Negative conclusion can be valid, as we know that **AOO-2** is valid. We might put it this way: if the conclusion is Negative, then one of the premises must be Negative.

Each of the following commit **Negative Conclusion from Affirmative Premises**:

(Ak)	(Al)	(Am)
Some m are p.	All p are m.	Some p are m.
<u>Some s are m.</u>	<u>All m are s.</u>	<u>All s are m.</u>
Some s are not p.	No s are p.	No s are p.

None of the following commit Negative Conclusion from Affirmative Premises:

(An)
Some p are m.
All s are m.
Some s are p.

(Ao)
No m are p.
Some s are not m.
Some s are not p.

(Ap)
All p are m.
No m are s.
No s are p.

You will surely have noticed, in this section, that some of the examples used have committed more than one fallacy. This is not uncommon, as seen in the following:

(M)
All p are m.
Some m are s.
All s are p.

This syllogism commits Illicit Minor and Undistributed Middle.

(Q)
Some m are not p.
Some m are not s.
All s are p.

This syllogism commits Exclusive Premises, Affimative Conclusion from Negative Premises and Undistributed Middle.

(U)
No p are m.
Some s are not m.
No s are p.

This syllogism commits Exclusive Premises and Illicit Minor.

(Aq)
Some p are m.
Some s are m.
No s are p.

This syllogism commits four of the seven fallacies Undistributed Middle, Illicit Minor, Illicit Major and Negative Conclusion from Affimative Premises.

No argument is valid if it commits one or more of the formal fallacies. And no argument is any more invalid than another if the first commits more than one fallacy while the second commits only one. Any argument that commits none of the seven formal fallacies is a valid argument. Given the strict definition of validity we have adopted here, there are no degrees of validity or invalidity. If it is possible to provide a counterexample for some argument, whether it be a hypothetical syllogism, a categorical syllogism, or any other syllogistic or non-syllogistic argument, wherein the premises are all true while the conclusion is false, the argument is invalid. And that, as a former teacher of mine liked to say, is the end of the matter of logical validity.

Exercise 3.4

A. Which of the following moods and figures define arguments that commit one or more of the seven formal fallacies, if any? Which fallacies are committed? If no fallacy is committed, mark the argument valid.

1. IAI-3	6. AAI-3	11. EEO-2	16. IOA-1	21. AEA-4
2. EIO-1	7. EIO-2	12. EIO-3	17. EIO-4	22. EAE-1
3. IAI-4	8. AIA-1	13. OAO-1	18. EEA-3	23. IEE-2
4. IEO-1	9. IIO-2	14. AAA-3	19. IEO-4	24. AOO-4
5* III-2	10* IOO-4	15* OII-4	20* EAO-2	25* AII-3

B. Which of the following statements are true/false?

1. If any categorical syllogism has two Particular premises, it commits the Existential Fallacy.

2. No valid categorical syllogism can have more than one distributed middle term.

3. There is no such thing as "degrees of validity".

4. All categorical syllogisms with two negative premises commit the fallacy of Exclusive Premises.

5* If any categorical syllogism commits Illicit Major, it will also commit Illicit Minor.

6. Every fallacious categorical syllogism can be detected to be invalid via the method of Venn Diagrams.

7. Sometimes, when constructing a Venn Diagram, it is necessary to place an "X" at the intersection of two or three lines.   8. A sentence which refers to every member of the class designated by some term is said to distribute that term.

9. The following is a syllogism:

All clear reports are acceptable.

All acceptable reports are typed.

All typed reports are legible.

Therefore, all clear reports are legible reports.

10* The following is a syllogism:

Either Cranston or Bradley will run for governor of California.

Cranston will never run for governor of California.

Hence, Bradley will run for governor of California.

11. The following is a categorical syllogism:
Illogical people are despised.
All babies are illogical.
No one is despised who can manage alligators.
So, no babies can manage alligators.

12. The following is a normal form categorical syllogism:
Some puppies are cute and cuddly.
Some puppies are not cute and cuddly.
So, some puppies are puppies.

13. All categorical syllogisms whose middle term is distributed at least once is a valid categorical syllogism.

14. No categorical syllogism with a negative conclusion is valid unless at least one of the premises is negative.

15* If one discovers that some categorical syllogism commits none of the formal fallacies, one must also construct a Venn diagram for the argument to discover whether the argument is valid.

4. INFORMAL FALLACIES

4.1 Preliminaries

Having studied formal fallacies at the end of the last chapter, we have an idea of what it means for an argument to commit a fallacy. More needs to be said, however, since formal fallacies differ, in certain important respects, from informal fallacies. We know already that no argument that commits a formal fallacy is a logically acceptable argument. That in itself is important information. The goal of the present chapter is to get us well acquainted with informal fallacies so that we will be able to analyze an argument in terms of 1) whether or not it commits one or more informal fallacy, 2) which fallacy or fallacies it commits, if it commits any, and 3) why it commits the fallacy or fallacies it does commit. We will study sixteen of the most common fallacies (there are over two hundred), fallacies so common as to have been given names.

A **fallacious argument** is a defective argument and a **fallacy** is the defect in the argument itself. Recall the formal fallacy Undistributed Middle. Any normal form categorical syllogism that fails to distribute its middle term at least once commits Undistributed Middle. The fallacy (defect) here is that the middle term has not been distributed at least once. As with the formal fallacies, any argument committing one of the informal fallacies is an argument in which the conclusion does not follow conclusively from the premise(s). The presence of a fallacy in an argument precludes the premises leading to the conclusion in a decisive way. We call such arguments invalid, though that term is misleading at times. There are two instances of informal fallacies where the argument itself may be valid in the formal sense of the term, but the arguments are unacceptable because of the presence of the fallacy.

Informal fallacies differ from *formal* fallacies primarily in that the former do not, whereas the latter do, arise from the specific forms of arguments. To detect an informal fallacy, one needs to have a subject matter with which to deal. This is to say that the argument must have content, unlike, say, the categorical syllogism defined by the mood and figure "AAA-2", which commits a fallacy no matter what the content of the argument happens to be.

Another difference between formal and informal fallacies has to do with the psychological effect an argument committing an informal fallacy may have on the hearer of the argument. Many fallacious arguments can be quite persuasive because of the way they are presented. English is a very rich language and many people have such a command of the language that they can "make the worse argument seem the better". Whenever the worse argument does seem the better, a fallacy is being committed, because the worse can only seem the better if there is some sort of defect in our thinking about which argument *is* better. This defect in thinking about the arguments is due to our having missed the defect in the worse argument. For example, let's say Dustin Hoffman is my favorite actor. I can imagine Hoffman appearing on television in a commercial for, say, Bayer Aspirin. If the commercial is done with taste, which I probably will think it is, given that Hoffman is in it, I might think, "Well, if Bayer is good enough for Hoffman, it's good enough for me." Or, I might think, "If Hoffman takes Bayer, and says it's a good pain reliever, it must be all right, since he wouldn't say it if it wasn't true". I believe I would have missed something crucial in the argument being presented here. First, I would be thinking exactly what the Bayer company probably wanted me to think when the commercial was conceived. (That in itself is not reason for rejecting the argument, however, for many times an arguer will present an argument and will want another person to come to believe something through the argument and the argument will be a good one.)

Second, and this is the important part, I've missed the point of asking whether Dustin Hoffman is an expert in pharmacology, i.e., is Hoffman an authority in the properties of the various chemicals used in Bayer and other types of pain relievers? What I need is detailed information (that I, a layperson, can understand) about the pain relieving qualities of Bayer. Although I admire Dustin Hoffman very much as an actor, I'm not convinced of his prowess in the chemistry lab. (This, of course, is not to say that I'm right about Hoffman. Perhaps I am just ignorant of the fact that he is a highly respected person in the field of pharmaceutics. If I have jumped to an incorrect conclusion about Hoffman here, then it must be admitted that I should take the commercial more seriously.)

The point is that I should look closely at what the argument is, as well as at the motive and expertise of the arguer. But when I see Dustin Hoffman on the TV, I'm already interested in what he's going to say because of my respect for him as an actor. If I don't realize that acting skills have very little to do with skills in chemistry, then I could be led to believing that Bayer Aspirin is the best pain reliever *just because* Dustin Hoffman says it is. And this is a fallacious argument.

There are a number of different categories of informal fallacies. There are fallacies of inconsistency, fallacies of grammar, fallacies of relevance, analogical fallacies, and so on. We are not so much interested in the various classes of fallacies as we are with the fallacies themselves. However, since understanding the nature of a fallacy is helpful for understanding each particular instance of fallacious reasoning, the fallacies will be grouped in terms of the classes of fallacy.

4.2 Fallacies of Relevance

All fallacies of relevance have at least one thing in common, to wit, the premises in arguments that commit one of these fallacies are logically irrelevant to the conclusions they are intended to support. However, though these arguments are logically fallacious, they sometimes have great psychological appeal to the listener. The earlier example of Dustin Hoffman is applicable here. Even though the conclusion may seem to follow from the premises, closer attention will show that it in fact does not follow at all. In attempting to detect fallacies of relevance, it is helpful to pay attention to "why" one thinks some argument is a good one. Ask, "Is the arguer appealing to my emotions or to my sense of logic?" If the former, then it is likely that a fallacy of relevance is being committed.

A. *Argumentum ad Vericundiam (Argument from Authority)*

There are three sorts of *ad Vericundiam* fallacies. The first is the most typical and involves an arguer who cites someone as an authority on some topic who is not an authority on the topic at all. We call this type of *ad Vericundiam* **False Authority**. The Dustin Hoffman example is one of these. Consider the following argument.

Since Albert Einstein was a thoroughgoing advocate of a Zionist state, and since Professor Einstein's reputation for being an intelligent man is beyond reproach, we can only conclude that a Zionist state is something to be advocated.

There is no doubt that Einstein was a remarkable man. One needs only to read his biography to see this. But Einstein is famous for his work in physics, mathematics, and related fields. He is not known for his political or religious polemics. Einstein is considered an authority in science, not an authority in religion and/or politics, and when one uses Einstein's esteemed name to get someone to accept an argument having to do with religion and/or politics, then the arguer has committed the argument from authority.

The second kind of fallacy of authority is related to the first, but is different in that the arguer cites a person who *is* an authority and says that just because this person said X, X must be true. This sort of *ad Vericundiam* is called **Absolute Authority**. An example:

> John Stuart Mill believed that pleasure is the highest good, and built much of his ethical theory around this idea. Mill was considered a genius by many of his peers. Hence, since he believed it, pleasure must be the highest good.

In his *Utilitarianism*, Mill writes, "...pleasure and freedom from pain are the only things desirable as ends; and...all desirable things (which are as numerous in the utilitarian as in any other scheme) are desirable either for pleasure inherent in themselves or as a means to the promotion of pleasure and the prevention of pain." We see, then, that the first part of the argument is correct, i.e., that Mill did in fact think that pleasure is the highest good. We also know that Mill was, and is, considered an authority in ethics. However, being an authority in some field does not mean that one knows everything there is to know about that field, nor does it mean that one cannot be wrong. There is a great difference in being an authority and being a complete or absolute authority. There is simply no such thing as a complete authority in the sense in which it is being used in the above argument, i.e., in the sense of someone knowing everything there is to know about any given topic and being infallible about it. (I leave it to the reader to contemplate what has just been said in light of the widespread belief in the authority of some religious figures and books.)

Perhaps the best example of the use of the fallacy of Absolute Authority comes from the veneration many medieval scholars had for Aristotle. St. Thomas Aquinas cites Aristotle's *Physics* without argument when he writes,

> "And if it be said that the statue in question is endowed with some vital principle by the power of the heavenly bodies, this is

impossible. For the principle of life in all living things is the substantial form, because, as the Philosopher says, *in living things to be is to live.* Now it is impossible for anything to receive anew a substantial form, unless it lose the form which it had previously, since *the generation of one thing is the corruption of another."* (Aquinas' italics of Aristotle's text)

Note here that in this one paragraph Aquinas refers to Aristotle, not as Aristotle, but simply as "the Philosopher". Also note that Aquinas does not back up his double use of Aristotle's words with any argument at all. It's as though "just because Aristotle said it, it must be true".

The third type of *ad Vericundiam* has to do with an arguer appealing to custom or tradition as authoritative. A good example of this occurs sometimes when one takes a new job and tries to change the way things are done only to hear, "we've always done it the other way, so let's stick with that".

Few would deny the importance of custom and tradition in shaping our attitudes, practices and life styles. And many of us see the importance, the virtue of retaining cultural traditions. However, even with that said, it does not logically follow that custom and tradition are in themselves reason enough for continuing a practice. When someone does appeal to custom or tradition in this way, we call it **Authority of Custom**. Consider the following argument.

Segregation has been the way of the Southern states for generations. Hence, this practice must continue, in such forms as "white only" drinking fountains, for example, and "colored only" restaurants.

Many people are simply dumbfounded by such arguments. It is hard to believe that such reasoning could be taken seriously. Of course, what is missing from the above argument are the "real" reasons people have advocated segregation. When those reasons are brought in, the argument changes and it will no longer commit Authority of Custom. To see what fallacy or fallacies the altered argument would commit, we would need to see, and assess, the set of premises offered in support of the conclusion.

Another name for *ad Vericundiam* arguments is the general phrase "appeal to authority". It is true that we do appeal to authorities in our daily lives. These are people whom we recognize as either having an advanced degree in some field, or considerable practical experience, or both. If you want to know something about political liberalism, perhaps a good person to see would be a political scientist; if one has questions about subjunctive conditionals, see a linguist; if one has a pulled muscle, seeing a physician would seem to be a reasonable choice; and so on. We do, however, have the practice of getting a "second opinion" on matters, whether they be in medicine, history, art criticism, chemistry, or whatever. We take these authorities to be "the people most likely to know", but not as "infallible sources of information". To treat anyone (or custom) as an incontestable authority, or to cite someone as an authority who isn't one, is to commit the fallacy of authority.

B. Argumentum ad Populum
(Argument from the Populace)

This fallacy is commonly known as the "appeal to the people", and is committed when an arguer appeals to the listener's need or desire to be "one of the group" to get the listener to accept an argument. There are certain reasons people need or want to be part of a group, most of which involve the values we possess. However, appealing to those values does not establish an argument as reasonable or acceptable. It is only when the premises lead to the conclusion that an argument is reasonable or acceptable.

There are two sorts of appeal to the people. One occurs when a speaker is trying to evoke the emotions of a crowd of people, as, say, when a politician uses such phrases as "the threat of communism", or "the American way" in an attempt to get the audience heated up. When banners are flying and everyone is listening to a speech on the "evils of socialism", it is then that one need be on guard for an argument appealing to our emotions rather than our reasoning faculty.

Can we take another four years of a government bent on destroying the American Dream? Will we allow the further destruction of our children's future by continued no-growth in social reform? Will we stand for higher taxes and higher budget deficit? The answer to these questions is a resounding. "NO!" We can take back the freedom we had when this great nation offered our children the hope of a future ripe with happiness and success. We can do it and do it together -- as a people, as a community. How? There is only one way: We can vote for John Alexander Jameson!!!

This argument is like many we have heard in the past. It may be that Jameson is the best candidate. The point is that the argument itself does not present us with the facts we need to judge. This argument appeals to our patriotic and parental emotions, not to logic and not to evidence, which is what is needed for acceptable argumentation.

In the above sort of situation, the members of the audience are caught up in the words, music, and actions of the present situation. They are carried away by the scene, being led to accepting conclusions on the basis of the rise of emotion, the sense of purpose, and the fervent shouting and emotion being displayed by the other people in the audience. The speaker's words are intended to heighten these emotions, not to present a cool, calm, and rational account of why Jameson should get the vote.

The other type of appeal to the people commonly has as its audience one person. This fallacy has the same purpose behind it as the one above, except that it is not intended to stir our emotions to frenzy, but rather is supposed to work in a more subtle way. Many advertisements commit this fallacy, and though in an indirect way, they are all designed to appeal to various emotions we have about belonging to a group. For example,

Everyone here at the Center is reading the works of Maya Angelou now. You certainly don't want to be out of it, so you need to do some reading of Angelou's work.

The phrase "out of it" says it all. No one wants to be out of it, and if being out of it means one is not reading or has not read Angelou, then perhaps we should all get a copy of one of her books. There is a certain legitimate appeal here, I think. I mean that if one is to be able to converse with the members of one's community, from necessity, then perhaps one ought to get acquainted with Angelou. However, this is far from the sense of avoiding being out of it as displayed in the above passage. The argument is appealing to our *sense* of being out of it; it neither appeals to our wanting to read Angelou because there is some value in her work, nor to any supposed value the works of Angelou may possess. The appeal here is to our sense of wanting to be part of the group.

The number of examples of arguments committing *ad Populum* is vast. They range from a parent trying to persuade a child to eat liver and peas so the child can grow up to be like Wonderwoman or Superman to a computer salesperson trying to sell a customer a "state of the art" machine because that's what "computer people" use. Some of the arguments are quite direct and open, some are subtle and seductive. But the one thread running through each argument, overt or covert, is that appeal to our sense of wanting to be a member of "the" group, the "in-crowd", the "people in the know", the "gang".

Take another example, this time more indirect, but by this time not fooling many. I'm watching TV and an ad comes on with this young, attractive man driving a shiny, new sports car. (The background music is soft jazz, with a tune.) He pulls up to a stop light. Another car pulls up next to him in which there is a very attractive young woman who notices, first, the car he's driving, and then him. She gives him a sexy smile, we hear the revving of engines, the screen fades to black and the caption reads,

NOW WHAT WOULD YOU DO?

Well, the first thing I'd do is smile back. That is, *if* I had one of those sports cars. But since I don't have one, I'd better get hopping and buy one. I'd better get myself into the group of guys (young and attractive or not) who own one of those sports cars. Then I'll get the girl, right? Well, I might get the girl, if she doesn't suspect the fact that I accepted a fallacious argument. The point here is that the ad is not appealing to the quality of the car (which is what is being advertized here), but rather to my desire to be accepted as a member of a class of people. Hence, *ad Populum*.

C. Argumentum ad Misericordiam (Argument from Pity)

This fallacy, commonly known as the "appeal to pity", relies on evoking pity in the listener. The listener is then asked to accept some conclusion on the basis of this emotion. For example,

Tom: My friend Tony was abandoned by his real parents and sent to an orphanage when he was three.

Rob: I'm sorry to hear that.

Tom: He never had the money to go to college and had learned none of the ordinary skills at the orphanage because the people there didn't care about anything but themselves. He was neglected and had to fend for himself, picking up odd jobs where he could get them. He injured his hand and foot in a railroad accident and spent two years in hospital.

Rob: He's sure had a rough time of it.

Tom: So, won't you give him a job on your fishing boat?

It is obvious that Tom's story has caused Rob to feel sorry for Tony. But the relevant question is: Is that good reason, by itself, to hire Tony? Probably not, for the crew of a fishing boat is a highly skilled team of individuals. Tony, who has none of the skills required, couldn't do the job, no matter how much pity one feels for him.

Notice here, as in *ad Populum* and *ad Vericundiam*, that the premises are really irrelevant to the conclusion; they don't have anything to do with one another. From this perspective, one can accept the premises and reject the conclusion.

Another example of *ad Vericundiam* comes sometimes with the appeal for money to assist with famine relief. A television or film personality is seen crying about the deplorable circumstances of people who don't have nutritionally adequate and/or enough food to eat. Film is shown testifying to this. Is the intention to evoke pity from the viewer so he/she will send money? If so, the argument behind this commits the fallacy. However, one might detect a "moral" argument here as well. If one's moral code includes the principle that one should help other people if one can, and if that is the principle upon which the appeal is made, then *ad Vericundiam* is not committed here.

D. Argumentum ad Baculum (Argument from Force)

An "appeal to force" occurs when someone threatens another in order to get a conclusion accepted. As examples,

People who don't vote for Wayne Winger for "Senior Man of the Year" will find certain doors closed to them in Spring.

Unless you believe that the Ford Cobra is the fastest car on the road, we'll have your gas tank filled with sand.

If you don't do your homework, you'll not go to the game.

In the first case, the consequences referred to are rather vague. We ask,

What doors? Nonetheless, the threat is evident here and constitutes a clear *ad Baculum*. In the second case above, it seems absurd to try to *make* someone believe something on the basis of a threat. Beliefs are usually arrived at on evidence in favor of that which is to be believed. It may be the case that a person will "say" that the Ford Cobra is the fastest car, but that does not mean the person "believes" it. The third case is different, however. We have all done things to avoid something we consider bad happening. This does not, in itself, make the threat a *logically* good reason for doing, or not doing, the thing in question.

> This gun just might go off unless you tell me where the money is. It's got a hair-trigger, and I'm the nervous type.

Prudent advice would probably be to tell the threatener where the money is located. But this doesn't mean we take the argument to be valid, or even as acceptable, the point here being that if we feel forced to give in and tell where the money is, that is tantamount to feeling forced to "act as if" we accept the argument. The argument above, spelled out, is:

> Tell me where the money is or I'll shoot you.
> You don't want to be shot.
> Therefore, you want to, and will, tell me where the money is.

This is simply an invalid argument. If we accept it, it is because we are forced to, but not because it is acceptable "as an argument".

Argumentum ad Baculum is committed anytime a person threatens to harm another person (physically or psychologically) in order to get the other person to accept a conclusion (which may or may not lead to action on the part of the listener). It is important to note that the premises to any argument committing *ad Baculum* are *logically* irrelevant to the conclusion. This is not to say they are *practically* irrelevant, however. This should be obvious from the fact that we do sometimes feel forced to accept, and act on, an argument committing this fallacy.

E. *Argumentum ad Hominem*
   ## *(Argument to the Person)*

There are three distinct versions of the *ad Hominem* fallacy: *abusive*, *circumstantial*, and *tu quoque*. The situation in which a person commits this fallacy always involves at least two arguers. Typically, it goes like this: One person presents an argument. The second person then presents what is to be taken as a refutation of the first argument. However, the second arguer does not attack the first arguer's argument, but rather attacks the arguer her/himself. The crucial point here is that an arguer and an arguer's argument are separate entities. A very nice person can present the most invalid of arguments, as the meanest of villains can present a valid argument. An argument must be judged on its own merits, quite apart from merits or demerits of the person who puts it forth.

Ad Hominem "abusive" is committed when the second arguer makes abusive statements about the first arguer. For example,

> The Senator has made the absurd argument that we need to rewrite the legislation on campaign contributions because there are loopholes allowing tax write-offs on undisclosed amounts. It's beyond me how you could seriously consider the reasoning of a man who cannot even balance his own checkbook, who has been seen sneaking around 2nd Street late at night talking to known dope addicts, and who is simply the laugh of the town.

So the Senator has trouble with mathematics, and talks to drug addicts. Does that mean that the legislation shouldn't be rewritten? Clearly, no! What needs to be done here is to investigate the plausibility and ramifications of a rewriting the legislation. The Senator and the Senator's argument are different things; they are not, and are not to be, judged by the same criteria. The following example is much the same,

> Jack Kerouac was a marijuana smoking, beatnik bum who advocated a life of the vagabond rogue, searching for experiences having nothing to do with growth and learning. His book *On The Road*, therefore, cannot be taken as serious literature and should not be read by serious students.

What has been said about the separation of the argument from the arguer holds good here. However, there are a number of points to consider. First, we must question the nature of "abuse" in any supposed *ad Hominem*. Calling Kerouac a marijuana smoking beatnik, for example, just may not be considered abusive by everyone. The important thing here is that the one committing the fallacy "intends" to abuse.

Second, one has to wonder whether the things said about the person are in fact true. But, true or false, the things said are said about the person, not about the person's argument. And this means that the argument itself has not been refuted. Many times criminal attorneys are portrayed as people who will try to discredit a witness's testimony by calling into the question the character of the witness her/himself. This kind of ploy, whether the witness is shown to have unappealing qualities or not, is a perfect example of *ad Hominem* abusive. Attention is diverted away from the witness' testimony toward the witness proper. The idea behind such tactics is that if the attorney can show the witness in a bad light, perhaps the jury or judge will discount what the witness has said in the testimony. The fact that the witness may not be a model citizen has little to do with the truth or falsehood of the witness' testimony. Even though we will question the truth or falsehood of the testimony of a witness who is shown to be, say, a persistent liar, that in itself is not a good reason for discounting altogether the testimony. The witness may, this time, be telling the truth.

The second variant of the *ad Hominem*, the "circumstantial", is the same as the abusive except the first arguer is not abused, but rather it is pointed out that the first arguer's argument ought not be accepted because the first arguer stands to gain something if it is accepted. This is to say that the second arguer appeals to the first arguer's special circumstances to show that the first arguer's argument is to be rejected. For example,

I know your advisor, Professor Crum, said that you should take English 303. I also know why: because Professor Crum is an English teacher and will get in good with the Dean if you do take the course.

If you think about it, sometimes that's exactly how it works: the Dean will usually be happy when the enrollment increases in departments. And if the Dean is happy with a department, it can benefit that department. The faculty, students and staff in the department, then, will in turn benefit as well. Your physician recommends surgery; your mechanic advises a tune-up on your car; your stock broker recommends buying Disney stock;

your butcher recommends T-bone.... All these people make money from their services, but that does not mean that you should not invest in Disney, have surgery, a tune-up, or T-bone.

The focus in the passage above directs attention away from the idea of taking a certain course toward the advisor, who is the first arguer. No mention is made about the prudence of taking English 303. Even though the special circumstances of the advisor entitle her/him to benefit if you do take the course, it just may be a good idea to take the course anyway, given that you want to benefit from your advisor's advice.

The third version of *ad Hominem*, the *tu quoque*, is what I call the "children's fallacy". It consists in one arguer charging someone with having said or done a certain thing, and the second arguer charging the first arguer with having said or done something similar. A typical example:

Bobby: You wrecked my fort.
Rick: Well, you wrote all over my homework.

So Bobbie wrote all over Rick's homework and Rick wrecked Bobbie's fort. Rick is presenting a *tu quoque* here, in that he is not responding to Bobbie's charge that he (Rick) ruined the homework. Rick is coming back with a charge of his own. Bobbie accuses Rick of being guilty of something, and instead of defending himself against that accusation, Rick diverts attention away from himself and his supposed guilt, toward Bobbie and Bobbie's supposed guilt. This fallacy is also known as the "you, too fallacy" because the one who commits it is responding to someone's charge of guilt by saying, essentially, "you are guilty too", i.e., not denying guilt but trying to show that someone else is also guilty. No one is fooled here. Even if Bobbie is guilty, that does not mean that Rick is innocent. The point is that Rick tries to get the focus of attention away from himself, by arguing against the person of Bobbie---*ad Hominem, tu quoque.*

F. Argumentum ad Ignorantiam
(Argument from Ignorance)

The "appeal to ignorance" fallacy is committed when someone argues that nothing is/can be known about X and then goes on to make a positive statement about X. This commonly involves a denial of evidence about, or proof of, X. For example,

> Some of the greatest thinkers of our time have worked long and hard trying to find a solution to Russell's Paradox. No one has come up with a solution acceptable to everyone in the academic community. We can conclude that there is no solution.

It is clear that the conclusion of this argument does not follow from the premises. Many of the best minds had, for centuries, wrestled with Zeno's puzzles about motion, and it was only in the 20th century that they were finally put to rest. It would have been false in, say, the 17th century for someone to say that since no one had solved Zeno's Arrow Puzzle, no one ever would.

The premises in the above argument are true. But if/when someone does come up with an acceptable solution to Russell's Paradox, the conclusion will then be known to be false and the argument will be shown to have true premises and a false conclusion, which violates our definition of a valid argument.

There are many instances of this fallacy being committed. Some of the topics have been: ghosts, the soul, the claims of astrology, parapsychology, a Northern route to the Indias, extra-galactic visitors in ancient times, and so on. Some of these topics are still under close scrutiny by interested individuals, with books and articles appearing every month/year claiming "new and conclusive evidence". The crucial question becomes, What is the evidence and how was it discovered?

This question leads to a situation many believe to be a legitimate exception to the fallacy. When a group of people (or a person) is engaged in the pursuit of knowledge regarding the existence of a certain thing, and when these people are considered experts in the field in which they are studying, then if this group makes some claim to the effect that there is no evidence to show that X exists, this claim is thought to be acceptable. For example,

> Scientists for many years worked under the theory that phlogiston, a chemical supposedly released during combustion, existed. After much research, this phantom "stuff" has never been found. Therefore, phlogiston does not exist.

The conclusion here is true. But it is not the case that this is proven by the fact that many scientists were unable to discover it. Rather, it is proven by further research into combustion itself, and determining exactly in what this process consists. I believe we have a tendency to believe what those who are supposed to know, i.e. the experts, say. It seems we commit two fallacies at once here, to wit, *ad Vericundiam* **and** *ad Ignorantiam*. Just because they haven't found X does not lead to the conclusion that X isn't there to be found. It seems most likely to us, when a group of trained people are working on such a project, that if they fail to locate X, then probably X doesn't exist. This seems an acceptable argument, when the "probably" is inserted. Presumably these people know pretty much where and how to look for X. This is so if they are correct about the properties X is supposed to possess. However, we must admit that it is always possible for a group of people to overlook crucial facts in any research project.

Another accepted exception to the *ad Ignorantiam* fallacy has to do with the United States justice system, where, *in the eyes of the law*, an individual is innocent until proven guilty.

> Lawyer to jury: As you have seen, ladies and gentlemen, the prosecutor has failed to establish, beyond any reasonable doubt, that the defendant had any connection, public or private, with the deceased. Not one bit of evidence places my client at the scene of the crime, nor has anything pointed to a possible motive on her part. Therefore, in accord with the law of the United States of America, Sonia Bergson is innocent of the murder of Lawrence Railton.

In the most strict usage of *ad Ignorantiam*, this is not an exception, since if someone is guilty of a crime, whether proven so beyond a reasonable doubt or not, still the person is guilty. However, as the presumption of innocence is taken to be a basic and indispensable element in legal proceedings, we admit to the good sense of the presumption, and hence, we tacitly agree to overlook the fallacy for practical purposes. The best reason I've heard for this agreement is that the consequences of the opposite presumption would be completely disastrous for truly innocent people.

G. Accident

When a general rule is applied incorrectly to a specific instance, the fallacy of accident has been committed. The general rule referred to here is usually one thought to be a good rule, i.e., worth adhering to. For example,

> Since you promised not to disclose the nature of this case, it does not matter whether someone's life depends on the knowledge only you possess. You cannot talk about it because everyone knows that lying is wrong.

This is one of those "hard cases" we all know about. It is true that we go by the rule that one should not lie. It could be argued, and has been, that the reason we call the rule against lying a "general" rule is that it holds in many, or most, cases, but not in all cases. One might suspect that the class called "white lies" are specifically designed to override any ruling that lying is always wrong. Take another example:

> The rule of freedom of religion and worship are absolutes in this country. Hence, there is really nothing we can do about the religion that advocates sacrificing two human teenagers per year to their god.

Freedom of religion seems to be a reasonable general rule. However, when values conflict, as here and in the case above, one usually points to a hierarchy of values. If we take the value of human life to be greater than the value of freedom of religion, this argument commits the fallacy of accident.

H. Hasty Generalization

The fallacy of hasty generalization is the opposite of accident. That is, one commits hasty generalization when one reasons to a general rule from a limited number of specific instances. For example,

> Karen and Jan and Nancy each bought a 1985 Audi 5000. The clutch cable kept snapping and the crankshaft ripped apart on Karen's Audi; the fuel line repeatedly clogged up and the front

axle cracked on Jan's Audi; the carburetor valve got stuck, the gas tank leaked, and the headlights wouldn't work on Nancy's Audi. We can therefore conclude that 1985 Audi 5000s were ill-made vehicles.

Here the general rule is that 1985 Audi 5000s were ill-made. This is supposed to follow from three (3) examples of people who had trouble with theirs. The conclusion does not follow, since there is no vehicle on the road which is free from problems. It is to be suspected that everyone who bought an Audi 5000 1985 had to have it worked on by a mechanic at some time or other, even if it was something as minor as replacing a shock absorber. That Jan, Karen, and Nancy had so much trouble with their Audis does not indicate that *all* Audi 5000s were faulty/ill-made. What it indicates is that *some* were faulty. The above argument is typical of hasty generalization, going from a limited number of instances to a general rule.

Another way of representing this fallacy is to say that when one picks out a number of atypical cases and then concludes with a general rule based on the cases, one hastily generalizes. The above argument picks out three Broncos owned by three different people. Given that the Audis were each made at the same factory, along with hundreds of other Audis, the cases are not at all atypical. But, consider the following argument:

Mark spoke up in the Senate meeting yesterday for the first time since he was elected over five months ago. His comments were neither relevant nor well-spoken and Claudio drew the conclusion that Mark is not a good public speaker.

This conclusion may well be false. Add the following facts: 1. Mark was very nervous; 2. The topic of Mark's comments is very controversial and complex. In the first place, we might well say that Claudio is guilty of hasty generalization by basing his argument on an unfair sample. In the second place, we can say that it is very unusual to find Mark speaking before that particular crowd and, therefore, the argument that Claudio is using commits hasty generalization based on an "atypical case". As with the clichè regarding summers and swallows, we might say here that one ill-presented set of comments does not a bad orator make. The above characterization of Claudio's argument, then, is guilty of hasty generalization both regarding the limited number of cases as well as picking out an atypical instance and generalizing from it.

I. False Cause

When someone reasons to a conclusion on the basis of there being some causal connection between premises and the conclusion, or between certain facts about the world, *when in fact the causal relationship does not hold*, one commits the fallacy of false cause. If one suspects that some argument rests on false cause, one should be able to pick out the incorrect causal relationship referred to in the argument. For example,

> For over a year now, Harper's television picture has been fuzzy and dark. At about the same time the television started to malfunction, Harper began a rigorous program of cataloging his considerable collection of baseball cards. Every day he works on the cards and sits in a chair with his shoulders slumped forward. At the end of the day he has a great deal of back pain and uses a hot water bottle to give him comfort while he watches television. If he would just stop using that hot water bottle, Harper's television would work just fine.

So far as is presently known, there is no causal relationship between the use of hot water bottles and the operation of televisions. This should clue us in on the false cause here.

The fallacy of false cause can be quite persuasive at times, because we are often ignorant of the exact causal relationship between events, i.e., whether two or more events are in some way causally related. For example, AIDS is linked with blood transfusions, unsafe sex, and with the sharing of needles. It is not known conclusively, at present, whether these are the only methods of transmitting AIDS. HIV, the virus that causes AIDS, has been found in virtually every bodily fluid. Hence, arguments like the fictional example below may, without our knowing it, commit the fallacy of false cause.

> Maria, a periodontist for many years, recently contracted AIDS. She recalls discovering, after one of her treatments of an HIV infected patient, that one of her plastic gloves had a tear in it. She also recalls that she had two small paper cuts on one of her cuticles. She is certain that some of the saliva from her patient made contact with her cuticle. We can conclude that Maria became HIV infected as a result of the contact between the saliva and the cuticle.

Now, if AIDS cannot be transmitted through contact with an infected person's saliva, then that cannot have been the cause of Maria's AIDS and a different cause must be discovered. The point is that no one is *absolutely* sure at this point. This is much different in the case of hot water bottles and televisions. There is simply no evidence whatever to link these two things in terms of causality.

J. Ignoratio Elenchi (Irrelevant Conclusion Proper)

So far, each of the fallacies we have looked at have had arguments in which the premises are irrelevant to the conclusion. *Ignoratio elenchi* is committed when someone presents a set of premises which seem naturally to lead to one conclusion but then a quite different, and irrelevant, conclusion is drawn. For example,

The poetry and prose of D.H. Lawrence are written in a style quite different from those who preceded Lawrence. The classical literature written before Lawrence published *Lady Chatterley's Lover* displays a bias toward male dominated society, whereas Lawrence's work seems, at times, to be written from a woman's point of view. We can conclude that Lawrence was either gay or simply an incompetent writer.

The conclusion drawn above has virtually nothing to do with the premises. In fact, a wholly different conclusion was expected, i.e., something such as: We can conclude that Lawrence was sensitive to the fact that woman have a unique perspective on the world. This is perhaps not the only conclusion which follows from the premises, but the point is that the conclusion that *is* drawn above certainly does not follow from the premises because it is quite irrelevant to the premises. Consider another *ignoratio elenchi*:

The U.S. Department of Health, Education and Welfare has slowly been infested with incompetent people who care nothing about the people they are supposed to serve. This can be seen to be true from the facts that it takes over a week for a hungry family to get food stamps, two weeks for an unemployed citizen to receive the first unemployment check, and up to six weeks for a family to be reimbursed for medical costs that nearly destroy the economic basis of the family.

The conclusion that Health, Education and Welfare has been infested with uncaring, incompetent people is simply irrelevant to the premises of this argument. The conclusion that actually does follow, and the one to be expected, is this: The bureaucracy of the Department of Health, Education and Welfare has grown to such   proportions that there is significant delay in the services to the citizens which sometimes result in serious hardships for individuals and families.   Keep in mind that an argument commits *ignoratio elenchi* when you are looking for, expecting, one conclusion to be drawn from the premises when a wholly different one is drawn.

4.3 Fallacies of Ambiguity

Natural languages are, of course, very rich in meaning and nuance. Many words and phrases can be used in a number of different senses, and when used in such a way as to admit of various ways of understanding what is being said, we call that being ambiguous, or, not saying explicitly what you mean. The following fallacies each involve some ambiguity of terms and/or phrases.   The problem with arguments with ambiguous components is that different conclusions can be drawn depending on the meaning of the ambiguous terms.

K. Equivocation

When an argument is presented in such a way that one of its terms or phrases is actually used in two, or more, different senses, the fallacy of equivocation is committed. For example,

All bunnies have tails and since Christine was a Playboy Bunny, it follows that Christine has a tail.

Obviously the term "bunny" is being used here in two different senses. One sense is that of the lagomorph mammal. The other sense is that of a person who works in one of the infamous Playboy Clubs. This is a classic example of a valid argument, given its *form*. But, because of the equivocation on the word "bunny" the argument would be unacceptable. It must be noted that each premise could be true, given the different senses of 'bunny' in each premise. This is to say that it is true that all bunnies, the mammals, have tails, and it is true that there is a human person named Christine who used to be a Playboy Bunny.

It is curious to note that a great number of jokes turn on equivocation. We have a tendency to groan when the joke is very silly, for example, Q: Why did the chicken cross the road once but not twice? A: Because it didn't want to be a double-crosser". Equivocation in jokes are fun; in arguments, not.

L. Composition

The Fallacy of Composition is committed when an argument is presented which proceeds from the attributes of the parts of something, as premise(s), to the attributes of the whole of some-thing, as conclusion. We can call this the "part-to-whole-fallacy". For example,

Nelson's library contains only books that are well-known. Therefore, Nelson's library is well-known.

Let's say that Nelson owns only books that were written by famous authors, books by John Stuart Mill, Karl Marx, Stephen King, William Shakespeare, John Updike, and so on. That each book in Nelson's library is well-known indicates an attribute of the books. Many other people, however, own just those sorts of books. It does not follow that Nelson's library is special and hence well-known itself. We've gone from the attributes of the parts of Nelson's library to an attribute of the library itself. The premise may be true, but the conclusion false. This is an invalid argument; it commits the fallacy of composition. Another example is:

Each player on the team is an outstanding player. Hence, the team is an outstanding team.

Here, of course, it would be pointed out that even if each player is outstanding, unless the players play/work "as a team", then the team won't be outstanding.

One must take care not to confuse composition with hasty generalization, for though the latter may seem to go from parts to whole, two factors distinguish these fallacies: 1) composition refers to the *attributes* of the parts and the whole, not generalizing, and 2) hasty generalization relies on premises that are either atypical or of a limited scope, with a conclusion that is a generalization.

M. Division

The Fallacy of Division proceeds in the opposite direction as that of composition. We might call it the "whole-to-part-fallacy", because when someone presents an argument wherein the pre-mise(s) refer to the attributes of a whole leading to a conclusion referring to the attributes of the parts, division is committed. For example,

> Oxford University's Bodleian Library is well-known. Hence, every book in the Bodleian Library is well-known.

The Bodleian Library contains some rather obscure books, books of which even the most well-read of scholars are unaware. Of course, the locution "well-known" is relative, but generally speaking, we might say that within a certain very large circle, the Bodleian Library is well-known and attracts many more visitors than, say, a local town library. Another example is:

> The Toledo Mudhens is an outstanding team. Hence, every player on the Mudhens is an outstanding player.

It is not always true that outstanding teams have only outstanding players. Sometimes the high level of ability of some of the players will make up for the inadequacy of other players. It must also be said that there are outstanding teams and then there are *outstanding teams*, 'outstanding' being somewhat of a relative term.

As the fallacy of composition must not be confused with hasty generalization, so the fallacy of division must not be confused with accident. The reasons are parallel. While accident runs from a general rule to specific instances wherein the rule is incorrectly applied, division makes no mention of a general rule, but refers rather to attributes of some whole to draw a conclusion about the attributes of the parts of this whole.

N. Petitio Principii (Begging the Question)

Essentially there are three ways to "beg the question". One way is to more or less assume as true the very conclusion for which one is arguing. Strictly speaking, all these sorts of "petitio" arguments are valid in the sense that if at least one of the premises is true, i.e., the question-begging one, then the conclusion is also true, or, since one of the premises says the same thing as the conclusion, it is impossible for the premises to all be true and the conclusion false. For example,

> It is morally permissible for a psychiatrist to betray the confidential relationship between client and physician when the psychiatrist has information about the intentions of the client that, unless disclosed, would result in harm to a third person. This is so because a psychiatrist, even though bound by the confidentiality of the client/physician relationship, cannot be held ethically responsible for violating a trust when not doing so would cause another person to be harmed.

The first sentence is the conclusion and the second sentence the premise in the above argument. Notice that 'morally permissible' and 'cannot be held ethically responsible for' have the same connotations. These two sentences "say" the same thing. Hence, the argument begs the question. Consider the following:

> Ektelon racquetball racquets are the best racquets made. We can see that this is so because Ektelon racquets are made with only the finest materials. They are made with only the finest materials because professional racquetball players demand high performance and endurance in their racquets. These players can be sure that Ektelon racquets perform well and last long because Ektelon racquets are the best racquets made.

This is an example of an argument based on "circular reasoning", beginning and ending with the same sentence. Since *one* of the premises is precisely the same as the conclusion, this argument begs the question.

The second way an argument can beg the question is by failing to state all of the premises explicitly. That is, some arguments have "hidden" or "suppressed" premises. These premises are hidden because they are false, or, at least, questionable or arguable. For example,

> The elephant is a protected species and whoever kills one is guilty of poaching. Carleton, who works for the Krathicom Wildlife Service Program, killed an elephant. Hence, Carleton is guilty of poaching.

In this case, one hidden premise is that the elephant killed by Carleton was a rogue and had destroyed much property and killed many people. The second hidden premise is that the Wildlife Service has a policy which permits destroying rogue elephants. We can see that if these two premises were to have been included in the original argument, then no fallacy would have been committed. Another example of "hidden premise *petitio*" is below.

> Advocating the violent overthrow of the government is a crime of treason, punishable by exile or death. It follows that Bernard may be banished or executed for his riot-causing speeches about impeaching the president.

The hidden premise here is that Bernard's speeches, which cause riots, can be construed as advocating the violent overthrow of the government. This is not explicitly stated in the argument, but is obviously being used in reasoning to the conclusion. The problem is that the sort of behavior Bernard is engaging in is arguably *not* promoting the violent overthrow of the government, but is rather designed to get people angry enough to demonstrate a certain dissatisfaction with the president. The fact that the speeches cause riots may be reason enough to arrest Bernard. But the question of whether his acts are treasonous is open to interpretation. This argument begs the question in that it fails to point out the crucial premise upon which the argument relies.

The third way an arguer can beg the question is to state a controversial premise as though it is not controversial. As examples, consider the two following arguments.

> Infants born with birth defects are of little value to the society. They require a great deal of the scarce resources and therefore should be terminated and not treated.

> Research by a professor at a university specializing in teaching should always be directed toward improving her/his teaching. Ivan, who works at an institution whose primary mission *is* teaching, has an outstanding teaching record but insists on doing research in areas outside his teaching areas. Hence, Ivan will never be awarded tenure.

The first premise in each of the arguments above is controversial. To establish them as true would presumably require much argumentation.

Both premises are stated in a more or less dogmatic way, thus, closing the door on dispute. If any listener detects this, the argument could legitimately be rejected on that basis alone.

O. Limited Alternative

The fallacy of limited alternative is committed when one is given a choice between two (or more) options when there are clearly more options than are presented. For example,

> If you study Philosophy in graduate school, you can specialize either in theory of knowledge or ethics. If you concentrate on the theory of knowledge, you are in danger of losing sight of many of the most important issues facing the world today. Hence, that it would be better for you to specialize in ethics.

Like any major discipline at a university, Philosophy offers a wide range of possibilities with regard to specialization. The following are some examples: ancient Greek philosophy, philosophy of language, philosophy of science, logic, modern philosophy, 20th century philosophy, medieval philosophy, the empiricists. Clearly, then, the first premise in the argument above gives limited alternatives. Hence, the fallacy of limited alternative.

> Either you vote for a Democrat or you vote for a Republican in the presidential election. Since all the Republican candidates are equally unappealing, you can't vote for any of *them*. Hence you will vote for a Democrat.

There is one thing we can pretty much predict in an election year, and that is that there will be many more sorts of candidates for office than just Democrats and Republicans. There will be Peace and Freedom, Libertarian, and Independent party candidates, just to name a few. Hence, in the above argument, one is given a limited number of alternatives, i.e., one might not vote for a Democrat *or* a Republican, but rather one of the others. Or, one might not vote at all -- another alternative.

Note, however, that the above argument is valid. This is to say that *if* there were only Democrats and Republicans to choose from in the election, and *if* one found each of the Republicans to be so unappealing as to be unable to vote for any, then it would follow that one would vote for a Democrat. Recall one of the ways mentioned in Chapter 1 that an argument could be unacceptable was if one or more of the premises were unacceptable. This is precisely the case in the above argument. The first premise is unacceptable *because* it presents a limited alternative.

P. *Deontic Fallacy (Deriving An 'Ought' From An 'Is')*

The deontic fallacy is otherwise known as the "normative" or "moral" or "Naturalistic" fallacy, and is committed when one presents an argument in which the premises are **descriptive statements** (asserting that something *is* the case) but where the conclusion is a **prescriptive statement** (asserting that something *ought to be* the case). There is always a hidden premise in an argument that commits the deontic fallacy, and this hidden premise is always a **value statement** (asserting a value one holds). For example,

Black South Africans have been seen by White Afrikaners as second-class citizens and nonpersons for hundreds of years. This is an outgrowth of the way South Africa grew, historically, as a nation. Therefore, this is the way it should be.

The hidden premise here is that history always works out for the best, an assertion of value. This, of course, is debatable, as are all value judgments we encounter. One can attack this argument from at least two sides: 1) by attempting to show that the hidden premise is false, and/or 2) by attempting to show that the conclusion itself is false. Another way of showing its unacceptability is to present a counterexample, such as,

Jews have been considered second-class citizens and nonpersons for hundreds of years. The Third Reich's treatment of Jews was an historical outgrowth of this attitude toward the Jews. We conclude that this treatment was the way it ought to have been.

One of the distinct problems with this argument as a counter-example to the argument above is that it also relies on a value judgment, one perhaps not shared by all readers of this text. The most that can be said here is that the argument itself is simply formally invalid, which means that the conclusion does not follow from the premises.

The deontic fallacy, being one of the most common of all fallacies, is many times persuasive. The primary reason for this is that the hidden premise is many times one we would presumably accept. Consider:

Smoking cigarettes causes shortness of breath, diminishment of circulation, heart disease, bronchial infections, and lung cancer. Hence, one ought not smoke.

The hidden premise here is that one ought to avoid all of these effects of cigarette smoking. This is a case in which, if the hidden premise is added to the argument, the argument becomes more or less acceptable. However, it is possible that the hidden premise might be rejected by a person who could present an acceptable argument for doing so, say, in a situation where a number of people had agreed (having been informed of the possible consequences) to smoke cigarettes for a research project studying the effects of cigarette smoking on distance runners. The point is, again, that value judgments are open to question as to their truth. They are not simply statements of objective fact (whatever that is). That is, a value statement, such as, "New York is as beautiful as New Orleans", is not in the same category with such sentences as, "Chicago is further from San Diego than Detroit is from Toronto", in terms of discovering their truth.

When there is differing opinion about the truth value of a sentence in an argument, the acceptability of the argument is also in question. To get at the disagreement usually takes getting clear on what values are being pulled in to the arena of judgment about the argument. When the values themselves are made explicit, further new arguments will result, having to do with the acceptability or unacceptability of these values, and so on. It is only when agreement is reached on these values that the original argument itself can be agreed upon as acceptable or the reverse.

One of our jobs here is to try to discover when an argument is valid and when not. The fact that one cannot validly go from a fact to a value indicates that any argument containing only *factual* statements in the premises and a *value* statement in the conclusion is not valid, no matter whether one thinks it acceptable or not. Thus, for example, many people have argued that,

Lying, in any form, creates distrust. Literally no one wants to be distrusted. Therefore, one ought never lie.

I think it cannot be denied that anyone caught in a lie is usually thereafter, to some extent, distrusted. And it is probably true that the vast majority of people would prefer to be trusted than distrusted. Does it follow that one ought never lie? It does not, since perhaps there are cases in which one might attempt to show it *better* (a value term) to lie, be found out, and be distrusted than tell the truth and avoid the risk of being distrusted. Just from the practical point of view, it seems the above argument cannot be defended against all situations. But, further, those who heartily agree with the idea that one cannot derive an 'ought' from an 'is' ask, What could it be in the premises that might possibly lead anyone to think the conclusion follows? So smoking *is* bad for one's health. Does it logically follow that one ought to stop? So polluting the environment will kill seventy-five percent of the wildlife. Does it logically follow that we ought not pollute? The strictly logical answer to these questions is "no". So that black widow spider is crawling up the nape of your neck. Does it logically follow that you should try to remove it? No! But, behind all these "oughts" are values which influence our accepting the inferences we do accept. From the point of view of logic alone, the arguments are not valid, but from the view of one who holds the various values indicated, there is no hesitation to accept the argument. The moral here is that one must take care to make one's values explicit, so there is no confusion about the "hidden" values present in any argument that might be charged with committing the deontic fallacy.

4.4 Avoiding Fallacies

The best way to avoid committing a fallacy, which is also the best way of avoiding falling prey to someone else committing a fallacy, is simply what your mother used to say to you every time you left the house: "BE CAREFUL!" One must attempt to understand precisely what is being said in an argument; whether the conclusion actually does follow from the premises; whether there are one or more hidden (suppressed/unspoken) premises; whether the arguer is appealing to one or more of our emotions; and whether there is either ambiguity or irrelevance in the relation between the premises and the conclusion.

Consider, for example, the following argument:

If I run day-care from 8am to 4pm, with 10 children, then my own family will suffer from my not being able to spend much time with them alone. If I run day-care from 9am to 2pm, with 10 children, then I will have much more time to spend alone with my family. If I run from 9am to 2pm, I will be making less money than if I run from 8am to 4pm, money that is sorely needed by the family. Either way, the family will suffer, because if I don't spend time with my own children, they do not receive the care and attention they want and deserve, and if I don't make enough money, we will not be able to make our house payment and could lose it. For the next two years at least, the money is more important than spending time alone with my family. Hence, I'll run day-care from 8am to 4pm.

Valid or invalid? Acceptable or unacceptable? You might have guessed that the last premise is the most important here. It states a value judgment, and one perhaps not everyone would share. The argument will be unacceptable for anyone who denies the last premise. For another person, however, it may be unacceptable because perhaps there is a third alternative, say, running day-care from 9am to 2pm with 12 children, yielding shorter hours but more paying customers, as it were. In terms of strict validity, however, discounting all other factors, if the premises are true, then the conclusion will also be true.

To avoid fallacies, one needs first of all to be aware of them. One needs to be able to call on one's knowledge of the fallacies when attempting to analyze an argument, to have the fallacies in mind. But just knowing the fallacies does not always get the job done. Sometimes arguments are presented in such a way as to hinder exact analysis, usually because there is ambiguity in what is being said, or because of the inarticulation of the arguer. This can happen especially where someone is trying to slip in a value judgment unnoticed. It is very difficult to state a value judgment which would be acceptable to a great majority of people. The fact that there is a value judgment in an argument does not automatically make it invalid. Consider the following:

If "open marriage" is psychologically healthier for a couple than "closed marriage", then adultery, consented to by each married partner, is not morally wrong. But that is absurd. Adultery, in all of its many forms, is always morally wrong. Therefore, open marriage is not psychologically healthier than closed marriage.

This is a valid argument. That is, there is no possibility here that if the premises are true the conclusion is false. This is not to say that the premises *are* true in fact, but rather that *if* they are, then the conclusion is also. So, here is a valid argument with the second premise, i.e., adultery is always morally wrong, that is a value judgment. If one is unhappy with the argument, there a number of ways to analyze it. One might go through each of the informal fallacies to check whether one or more has been committed. In this case, however, I think none has been. One might ask, Is the implication of the first premise a good one? That is, does open marriage being psychologically more healthy than closed marriage *entail* that adultery is not morally wrong? One might challenge the first premise on this score.

One might also challenge the truth of the second premise. It is one thing to say that *if* the premises are true, then the conclusion is also true. It is quite another to establish the premises as true. Showing, then, that the entailment of the first premise fails to hold would be tantamount to showing the argument to be unacceptable. Showing the second premise to be false would have the same result. Hence, even when one does succeed in avoiding each of the fallacies, and even when one is able to show the argument to be valid, these things in themselves do not insure that the argument is acceptable.

Any argument that commits a fallacy is suspect. Even though some arguments that commit fallacies may be more or less acceptable to some people, that is not a good reason not to avoid fallacies. And to avoid them, read carefully and for content. Know the fallacies and know what the arguer is attempting to say, whether you are analyzing an argument of your own or the argument of another person.

Exercise 4.

A. Identify the fallacy or fallacies committed in the following arguments. Some arguments may not be fallacious.

1. The dominant view of the universe among working physicists is that the universe is expanding. Since the Empire State Building, the Tower of London, and the Clock Tower at Humboldt State University are each part of the universe, it follows that these objects (and all others as well) are expanding.

2. The dominant view of the universe among working physicists is that the universe is expanding. With the recent budget cuts that have halted any new book acquisitions, it is clear that the Fallbrook County Library is *not* expanding. Hence, the physicists of today might want to rethink their theory.

3.   Crow #1 is black, crow #2 is black, crow #3 is black...crow #2735 is black. We conclude that all crows are black.

4.   Our water is polluted, our air is polluted, the wildlife in the forests and deserts are no longer safe from the consequences of our high-tech society, sea-life has become increasingly more difficult to stabilize, and our children can no longer roam the fields and hills by themselves. These things can be changed if we will only remember our roots and "get back to nature". Hence, we have a moral duty to limit the use of automobiles, factories, and any other thing that destroys what is "natural".

5* I would recommend that you take care not to damage the reputation of our client with any of your comments in the news-paper column. Remember what happened to Adrian Lester after he wrote those lies about Kyle Anders. He got dumped in the river, wearing cement shoes.

6.   Avoid broccoli at all costs! My sister once ate three stalks of broccoli, got sick, and had to go to the hospital for an appendectomy.

7.   Plastic surgery costs are the highest in the medical profession, up to $6,000 for one-half hour of the staff's time. Hence, unless one has unlimited wealth and doesn't care how one spends it, it may be advisable to seek a second or even third opinion, and find out about prices, prior to hiring a plastic surgeon.

8.   Hegel thought he was God. Now, anyone who is such a deluded egotist cannot be taken seriously as a philosopher, and that person's writings are better left to rot on the moldy shelves in the back rooms of libraries.

9.   The United States Senate is a distinguished body of men and women. We can only conclude that every senator is a distinguished person or that senators have distinguished looking bodies.

10* My Uncle Zeb just got back from a visit to Peking. He was telling me about the way the upper class Chinese women wear their hair these days. They first part it straight down the middle, front to back. They then comb the left side to the back, with a pink or gold colored ribbon tying it to the short hairs on the nape of the neck. They comb the right side to the front with a purple or blue ribbon tied in a bow and hanging just beside the eye. Hence, if you want to be considered *chic* in the Chinese style, you might try this hair style.

11 If the industrial revolution is to be thought of as having significantly altered the lives of the common person, the entire population will have to be considered in their economic, cultural, and linguistic aspects.

12 Lyndon Johnson was as powerful a president as this country has ever known. He was powerful because he had markers (IOU's) from just about every government official during the years 1959-1965. And the reason he had all these markers was because he was the most powerful president.

13 Pierre Teilhard de Chardin, 1881-1955, is thought to have been part of the great "Piltdown Conspiracy" that occurred in the early part of the 20th Century. Letters from him to his parents and friends, as well as witnesses concerning dates, times and places of Teilhard's meetings with Charles Dawson, the originator of the hoax, point to many inconsistencies in the records. Not only that, but it appears that Teilhard attempted to cover up his own part in the hoax. At least two facts follow, to wit, 1) that Teilhard is considered part of the conspiracy, and 2) that the works of Teilhard hardly merit all the attention they've received since his death.

14 One of the greatest sportscasters of our time, Vin Scully, made some comments about the possibility that the Persian Gulf shipping lanes are perhaps the most dangerous place to be right now. If I were you, I'd take my vacation on the other side of the world this year.

15* It seems absolutely incredible that the people of California could believe in a man, and believe the things he says, who stands to gain so much my being elected governor.

16 Sociology 304, Biology 303, and Philosophy 306 each satisfy a General Education requirement at the University. It follows that if we teach those classes as essentially one class, then that one class would also satisfy the General Education requirement.

17 Each and every college in this university is headed by a person who has over fifteen years experience in administration. Each and every person on the list has a reputation for excellence in her/his respective area of specialization. We may conclude that the university as a whole shares this reputation.

18 We can choose either nuclear war or nuclear peace. If we opt for the former, billions of people will die the death of violence. If we opt for the latter, billions of people will die the death of fear, greed and starvation. In the end, then, there is no way to win.

19 There can be no doubt that each of the candidates is qualified for the job. But let me make a special plea for candidate #5. This person

has just gone through a thoroughly destructive divorce, one of her children was hurt in a bus accident three weeks ago, her self-esteem is waning, and she learned yesterday that her property in Arizona has been seized by the government for payment of back taxes, the fault of her former husband.

20* I have received notice that there has been a grievance filed against my colleague because she allegedly failed to turn in her grades on time. This is sheer harassment. I happen to know, and can prove with the documents in this folder, that the person who filed the grievance, on two occasions, destroyed student evaluations from his file which would have cast a disparaging light on his performance as a teacher.

21 The question is not whether Grape Nuts is right for you, the question is whether you are right for Grape Nuts.

22 Glenn really has no right to bring a law suit against Harry. Even though Harry secretly had Glenn's father's Will altered to give him (Harry) 60% of the company, one has to consider, Glenn and Harry have been friends since they were eight years old, and you know the old adage: Once true friends, forever true friends.

23 Every time Matt and I go to a professional baseball game, the team we want to win loses. For the sake of our favorite teams, we should stay away from the baseball park.

24 Every time Matt and I go to a professional baseball game, the team we want to win loses. We went to see the Giants and the Mets and the Giants lost. We went to see the Giants and the Cubs and the Cubs lost. We went to see the A's and the White Sox and the White Sox lost. Hence, our favorite teams lose all the time.

25* If the goal of human sexuality is procreation, then all sexual acts which one participates in that could not lead to procreation are perversions of human sexuality.

26 The goal of human sexuality is pleasure.

27 Ali promised to have the truck back here by Thursday. She therefore has an obligation to have it back by Tuesday.

28 "There's something about an Aqua Velva man."

29 "We're here for the Peace Rally! What I don't understand is why we are going to listen to such a person as Conrad Welsh. He's known to be a pro-Contra radical, a Gay activist, a liar and a back-stabber. His bit about how we should spend three million dollars on media coverage for the fight in Latin America is just another one of his shady, self-serving, tricks. His family owns fourteen television stations in seven western states."

30* The Holocaust took untold numbers of innocent lives. We have a moral duty to our children, and their children, that this devastation never happen again---and never be forgotten.

5. Sentential Logic A

5.1 Preliminaries

Beginning with the present chapter, our study will focus on what is commonly known as *sentential logic*, or *propositional*, *symbolic*, or *formal logic*. The main concern here is with sentences and arguments, which may be expressed in symbolic notation. Using the logical techniques of truth tables and truth trees, we will be able to determine the logical status of sentences. Also, we will be able to determine whether arguments are valid or invalid by truth tables, truth trees, and natural deduction.

The major difference between our subject matter in the present and later chapters and Chapters 2 and 3 is that in 2 and 3 we were dealing primarily with subject and predicate terms, whereas in Chapters 5, 6, and 7 we will be dealing with entire sentences. Hence, the name "sentential" logic. One guiding principle for this study is that *every sentence is either true or false; no sentence is neither true nor false; and no sentence is both true and false*. The principle is called **The Law of Excluded Middle**. This will be unproblematic if we adopt the definition of a "sentence" as an assertion made about the world/universe. An example here is:

(1) Dwight D. Eisenhower was the U. S. President in 1957.

This is a sentence which states something about the world. In line with the Law of Excluded Middle, we see that it is either true or false that Eisenhower was President in 1957; that it is false that Eisenhower was neither the President nor not the President in 1957; and also false that Eisenhower was and was not President in 1957.

We will be referring to the **truth value** of sentences. There are only two truth values: True and False. The truth value of (1) is True, since Eisenhower was President in 1957. It often happens, however, that a sentence changes truth value. If someone had said, in 1983, that Goodman's office is in the Annex, for example, its truth value would have been False, for at that time Goodman's office was in Morrill Hall and Morrill Hall is not the Annex. Examples abound.

There *are* things that people utter that are neither true nor false, but we do not count these utterances as sentences. For example, if you pass a friend on the street and say "Hi!", you have not uttered anything that is true or false. Truth and falsehood do not apply to salutations. Nor do they apply to commands, as "Mow the lawn" and "Tie it down securely". Nor do they apply to questions, such as "Where is your sister?" and "Do you like carne asada"? These utterances do not assert anything about the world directly and hence are not counted as either true or false.

To see the importance of the concept of truth value, and of knowing which sentences are and which are not true, recall our definition of validity. We say that an argument is valid if it is impossible for the premises to be true while the conclusion is false. Truth tables, to be encountered in Chapter 6, is the most conspicuous way to use truth values to determine which arguments are valid and which are not. We will also be able to determine, in many cases, that some given sentence is true, or false.

5.2 Truth Functional Connectives and Translations

To make the work of analyzing sentences and arguments less reliant upon the ambiguities of **natural language** (French, English, German, etc.), and to seize a bit of control over the size of the sentences and arguments to be analyzed, we use specially designated symbols to represent certain terms, phrases, and sentences. In essence we will be laying out the rules for what we will call an **artificial language**. For example, the sentence

(2) Adams is a kindergarten teacher.

could be represented by the capital letter "A". Contrast (2) with

(3) Adams is a kindergarten teacher and Baker is a student.

We can represent 'Baker is a student' with 'B' and derive the following partial symbolization for (3):

(4)   (A and B)

We call (2) a **simple sentence** because it expresses essentially one idea. We call (3) a **compound sentence** because it contains two simple sentences as components, namely, "Adams is a kindergarten teacher" and "Baker is a student". Any sentence that contains two or more simple sentences as components is a com-pound sentence. The parentheses around (4) are to be understood as representing punctuation marks. They are also used as "groupers", as in (6) below:

(5) Mary and Tony must both arrive late, or the party will be ruined.
(6) [(M and T) or R]

where 'M' stands for 'Mary must arrive late', 'T' for 'Tony must arrive late', and 'R' for 'the party is ruined'. Parentheses ('( )'), Brackets ('[ ]'), and braces ('{ }') will also be used as punctuation and for grouping. It can be seen that the symbolizing of sentences greatly reduces the size of the sentence. This is a singular benefit when one is working with many sentences at once, as we will be doing further along. It will also help when the sentences we work with in natural language are large and complicated.

At this point, the notion of a **sentence connective** can be introduced. Connectives are symbols used in place of specific words and phrases found in natural language. There are five connectives. Consider the following sentences:

(7)   Seven is less than ten and greater than five.
(8)   Bruce got the sabbatical but turned it down.
(9)   The road was flooded, yet passable.
(10) Baby seals are hunted; however, they should be protected.

Each of the sentences (7)-(10) is called a **conjunction**. A conjunction is a compound sentence in which the word "and" (or some variant such as 'yet' or 'but') *connects* the simple sentences.

To symbolize the conjunction, we use the "dot", which has the same shape as a period but appears in the middle of the line rather than at the bottom. The dot in the translated (symbolized) sentence is located between the **conjuncts** of the conjunction. The conjuncts in a conjunction are the simple sentences which are "conjoined". Thus, (7)-(10) are translated as follows:

(7a)	(T • F)	The conjuncts are "T" and "F"
(8a)	(S • T)	The conjuncts are "S" and "T"
(9a)	(F • P)	The conjuncts are "F" and "P"
(10a)	(H • P)	The conjuncts are "H" and "P"

We may now introduce the notion of a **translation dictionary** to specify the exact designations of the component sentences found in the original sentences. Dictionaries are to be constructed on the following models for (7)-(10):

(7)   Seven is less than ten and greater than five.

Dictionary: 'T' = 'seven is less than ten'.
                          'F' = 'seven is greater than five.
Translation: (T • F)

(8)   Bruce got the sabbatical, but turned it down
Dictionary: 'S' = 'Bruce got the sabbatical'.
                          'T' = 'Bruce turned the sabbatical down'.
Translation: (S • T)

(9) The road was flooded, yet passable.
Dictionary: 'F' = 'the road was flooded'.
                          'P' = 'the road was passable'.
Translation: (F • P)

(10) Baby seals are hunted; however, they should be protected.
Dictionary: 'H' = 'baby seals are hunted'.
                          'P' = 'baby seals should be protected'.
Translation: (H • P)

In constructing a dictionary, the letter one chooses to represent each simple sentence is arbitrary. However, it is useful to pick some letter that can readily identify the sentence being represented. The translation dictionary must contain only simple sentences, stated in the affirmative or positive. There must never occur any term in a translation dictionary which would be translated with one of the five truth functional symbols. Hence, for example, the word "and" would never appear in a translation dictionary. More on this as we proceed.

Note how in the above translations the dot replaces the words "and", "but", "yet", and "however". Other *conjunctive words* are: "moreover", "also", "still", "nevertheless", and "although". These words are normally translated with the dot.

Not every occurrence of the word "and" can be straight forwardly translated with the dot, because some sentences containing 'and' are not straightforward conjunctions. For example,

(11) Oil and vinegar make a great tasting salad dressing.

This sentence is not an ordinary conjunction. This is where the dictionary comes to be very important. In (11), if our dictionary is 'O' = 'oil makes a great tasting salad dressing'; 'V' = 'vinegar makes a great tasting salad dressing', we derive the following:

(11a) (O • V)

When we translate (12) back into English, we get

(11b) Oil makes a great tasting salad dressing and vinegar makes a great tasting salad dressing.

Sentences (11) and (11b) do not have the same meaning. Nor do they necessarily have the same truth value. (11b) is an inadequate reworking of (11). As it turns out, (11) is a very complicated sentence which cannot be adequately translated using the limited number and variety of symbols we have here. To do it justice, we would have to move into *predicate logic* (Chapter 8). Nonetheless, it is instructive to see that there are some sentences having 'and' in them that are not straightforward conjunctions. Examples:

Oil and water don't mix.
Oxygen and hydrogen comprise breathable air.
January and June are two of the twelve calendar months.

There are other sentences which, with a little thought, can be seen to be conjunctions. For example, take the following sentence:

(12) Stephanie and Tim are wife and husband.

With the proper translation dictionary, we will be able to translate this sentence quite easily. Let 'S' = 'Stephanie is the wife of Tim'; 'T' = 'Tim is the husband of Stephanie'. We derive

(12a) (S • T)

Other examples of these sorts of sentence are:

Michael and Mary are siblings to one another.
Janice and David are sister and brother.
Michelangelo and Magellan were contemporaries.

To *negate*, or deny, any simple or compound sentence, we use the symbol known as the bar (-). The resulting sentence is called a **negation**. These are quite easily dealt with as long as it is kept in mind precisely what is being negated. There are numerous ways of negating sentences in English by merely placing the negative term in the correct position in the sentence. For example, to negate the sentence "Angela will spend the year in Madrid", each of the following would suffice,

It is not the case that Angela will spend the year in Madrid.
Angela will not spend the year in Madrid.
Angela won't spend the year in Madrid.
It is false that Angela will spend the year in Madrid.
It is not true that Angela will spend the year in Madrid.
Angela isn't going to spend the year in Madrid.

If 'M' = 'Angela will spend the year in Madrid', then the sentences above would each be translated as "-M".

Now that we have a symbol for negation, it is important to not that the dictionary may not contain any word or phrase that indicates a negation. That is, the translation dictionary must not contain a sentence that would be translated using the bar. In fact, one's dictionary may not contain any word or phrase that indicates any of the truth functional connectives.

To negate a compound sentence, groupers are needed, and it is vital that the bar be placed at the proper location. Consider, for example,

(13) Lon rented the tiller and Bob paid for it.

This sentence may be translated as (L • B). To negate the entire sentence, we place the bar in front of the first parenthesis, thus ranging over the entire formula, yielding -(L • B). Translating back into English, we derive the following sentence:

(14)   It is not the case that Lon rented the tiller and Bob paid for it.

Below are five sentences, each with dictionary and translation following.

(15)   Rita and June will not both skate. [R = Rita will skate; J = June will skate]   -(R • J)

(16)   Both Ronnie and Lennie are not as casual in their dress as Hayward. [R = Ronnie is as casual in his dress as Hayward; L= Lennie is as casual in his dress as Hayward]   (-R • -L)

Note the difference between the phrases "not...both" and "both...not", as exhibited in the translations of (15) and (16). The term "both" indicates that a conjunction is present in each sentence. However, whereas (16) says that neither Ronnie nor Lennie is as casual in his dress as Hayward, (15) does not say that neither Jack nor Rene will go fishing. In effect, what (15) says is that either one or the other won't go fishing. We will see how to translate sentences containing 'or' directly below.

(17)   Training in the military can develop a sense of discipline as well as comradeship between trainees, but not a sense of egoism. [C = training in the military can develop a sense of comradeship between trainees; D = training in the military can develop a sense of discipline; E = training in the military can develop a sense of egoism]   [(D • C) • -E]

(18)   Sisley's paintings of reflections on water are good, but they're not as good as Monet's. [M = Monet's paintings of reflections on water are good; S = Sisley's paintings of reflections on water are good]
        (S • -M)

(19)   Tom, Kathy, Jantz and Veden went skiing together, and so did Dustin, Nathan, Greg, and Henry. [D = Dustin went skiing; Greg went skiing;...]   {[(T • K) • (J • V)] • [(D • N) • (G • H)]}

The grouping of the **sentence letters** in the translation of (19) is arbitrary. Sentence letters are the letters we use to designate sentences in the translation of a sentence from English into symbolic notation. A different translation of (19) might be:

$$\{[((T \bullet K) \bullet J) \bullet V] \bullet [(D \bullet N) \bullet (G \bullet H)]\}$$

What matters here is that 'T', 'K', 'J', and 'V' are located within the same grouping. This should be obvious from the presence of the word "together" in the sentence. There is usually some indication of which letters are to be grouped together, though there are instances where it is not clear. This is where actual punctuation is important. Note that every parenthesis has a matching paren-thesis, every bracket a matching bracket, and every brace a matching brace.

The third type of sentence to be treated here is called the **disjunction**. Disjunctions are sentences containing some form of the word "or", and are translated with the **wedge** (v). As the sentence components in conjunctions are called "conjuncts", so the sentence components in disjunctions are called **disjuncts**. Consider the following disjunction:

(20)   Either England or France imports the most rice.
(20a) (E v F)   The disjuncts are "E" and "F"

There are actually two sorts of disjunctions, one called *inclusive* and the other called *exclusive*. The inclusive sense has the meaning "either one or the other and perhaps both", while the exclusive sense has the meaning "either one or the other, but not both". Since England and France cannot both import the most rice at the same time, (20) is an example of an exclusive disjunction. A fuller, more precise translation of (20), as an exclusive disjunction, would be:

(20b) [(E v F) • -(E • F)]

The English sentence for (20b) would be:

(20c) Either England or France imports the most rice, and it is not the case that both England and France import the most rice.

In general, we take the disjunction as having the inclusive sense in sentential logic. The reasoning behind this practice will become apparent when we get to truth tables. Suffice it to say, at this point, that it is sometimes very difficult to determine the intention of someone who utters a disjunction, whether it is to have the inclusive or exclusive sense. For example, in the following sentence, the intention is ambiguous.

(21) This insurance policy covers you if you are ill or unemployed.

It seems clear that the policy covers you if you are get sick. And it seems that it covers you if you lose your job. The question is: Does the policy cover you if you are ill *and* unemployed? (21) is not clear on this question and it would be well to ask the insurance agent to provide a precise translation of the sentence before signing anything.

The word *unless* is at times troublesome. It can be translated in two different, though equivalent, ways. Consider (21):

(22)   Unless it rains, we'll go to the beach.

We can reword this sentence in at least two ways:

(22a) If it doesn't rain, then we'll go to the beach.
(22b) It will either rain or we'll go to the beach.

Sentence (22a) is what we call a **conditional sentence**, because it contains the word 'if' (next on our list of sentences to be studied). (22b) is a disjunction. For the sake of simplicity and economy, we will adopt the convention of translating all sentences with 'unless' as disjunctions. Hence, where 'R' = 'it rains', and 'B' = 'we'll go to the beach', the proper translation of (22) will be:

(22c) (R v B)   The disjuncts are "R" and "B"

Below are further examples of disjunctions, with translations. Note the various forms in which disjuncts may appear.

Either the general will move the troops into position or retreat.
    (M v R)
Martha will vacation in either Vienna or Athens, or in both Florence
    and Naples.   [(V v A) v (F • N)]
Murderers either have rights or they don't.   (R v -R)

California will divide into two states, unless the issue of water resources isn't resolved and a Democrat is elected to the governorship.   [C v (-W • D)]

Neither the owners nor the players have a good historical record of compromise. -(O v P)

Not either the National Hockey League or Major League Baseball will accept binding arbitration. -(N v M)

Either Colleen or John won't set up a river boat guide service on the Red River in Shreveport.   (-C v -J)

Christian will go to either the University of Chicago or Fordham, but not Indiana University.   [(C v F) • -I]

Mark will become a Senator and a Democrat, or a Libertarian Marxist.   [(S • D) v L]

Eileen will donate huge amounts of money to the Georgetown University and become a trustee of the University, or, either move to Washington D.C. or not endow Rochester with a chair in marketing.   [(G • T) v (W v -R)]

James thought he would major in either Economics or Finance, or either Wildlife Management or Biology.   [(E v F) v (W v F)]

Shawn will either travel to the orient or open a bookstore in London, but not both.   [(O v L) • -(O • L)]

As mentioned above, a **conditional sentence** is a sentence containing the word "if".   However, there many variants of 'if', i.e., words that involve the same sort of operation within a sentence. The symbol used for conditionals is the *right-hand arrow* (→), or simply the "arrow". The sentence components in a conditional are called the **antecedent** and the **consequent**. The antecedent is the component that appears *before* the arrow and is the sentence that "implies" or "conditions" the consequent, which appears *after* the arrow. Each of the following sentences is a conditional and is translated in the same way:

If Plato dealt with ethics, *then* Plato was a philosopher.
Plato was a philosopher, *provided that* he dealt with ethics.
Plato's dealing with ethics *implies that* he was a philosopher.
Plato's dealing with ethics *entails that* he was a philosopher.
Plato dealt with ethics *only if* he was a philosopher.
Plato's dealing with ethics is a *sufficient condition* for his being a philosopher.
Plato's being a philosopher is a *necessary condition* for his dealing with ethics.

Each of the *italicized* words and phrases above is known as a **conditional indicator**. To translate any sentence containing any one or more of these indicators, an arrow is used. For the translation of these sentences, let 'E' = 'Plato dealt with ethics', and let 'P' = 'Plato was a philosopher'. The translation of each is:

(E → P)   Antecedent = E; Consequent = P

It is vitally important to achieve the correct order of the antecedent and consequent in the translation. That is, '(P → E)' would be an incorrect translation of the sentences above. To translate conditionals, always ask, "Which sentence is entailed by which sentence?" Always place the entailed sentence after the arrow. Always place the entailing sentence before the arrow.

Further examples:

(23)   If Oriel College hosts the conference and Cambridge sends a Dean, then Edinburgh will send its most renown mathematician. [(O • C) → E] Notice here that the antecedent is "(O • C)" and the consequent is "E". There is no rule saying that the antecedent or consequent must be a simple sentence. In this case, the antecedent is a conjunction.

(24)   Provided that either Illinois or Michigan agree to fund the expedition, then either the Gold Coast or the Cape of Good Hope will be the jumping off point. [(I v M) → (G v C)] In this case both antecedent and consequent are disjunctions.

(25) The present condition of politics in Washington D.C. being so unstable is a sufficient condition for either the Speaker of the House and the Minority Whip or the Secretary Pro Tem and the Senator from Utah resign. [H = the Speaker of the House will resign; P = the present condition of politics in Washington D.C. is stable; M = the Minority Whip will resign; S = the Secretary Pro Tem will resign; U = the Senator from Utah will resign] {-P → [(H • M) v (S • U)]} In this sentence the antecedent is a negated simple sentence, while the consequent is a disjunction, each disjunct of which is a conjunction.

(26)   If the Democrats push the health care plan, then if the Independents don't side with the Republicans, then either unemployment or welfare clients will suffer. {D → [-I → (U v W)]} Here a simple sentence is the antecedent, while the consequent is a conditional, of

which the antecedent to this *sub*-conditional is a negated simple sentence, while the consequent is a disjunction.

(27)   Human adults are moral persons only if they are capable of rationality, self-consciousness, and complex communication.
$\{P \rightarrow [(R \bullet S) \bullet C]\}$ In this case, the consequent is a conjunction in which one of the conjuncts is also a conjunction.

The above sentence contains the conditional indicator "only if". It may be thought curious that when translating 'only if', the consequent follows rather than precedes the 'if'. The standard way of explaining this is that 'only if' is another way of indicating a necessary condition. For example,

(28) The key will work only if it is clean.

After what has been said above, it may look as though this sentence should be translated as "$(C \rightarrow W)$", where 'C' = 'the key is clean' and 'W' = 'the key will work'. This is incorrect, however. For a key to work, it is usually a necessary condition that it be clean. But being clean is not a sufficient condition for a key to work. It also has to be cut for the specific lock, it has to be cut correctly, i.e., with no rough spots or extra ridges, etc., the lock itself has to be clean, and so on. What (28) actually says is that if the key works, then the key is clean; it does not say that if the key is clean, then it works. Hence, the proper translation of (28) is:
    (28a) $(W \rightarrow C)$

The following will be a useful rule to adopt: When translating a conditional sentence containing the word "if", the antecedent follows directly after 'if', except in the case of "only if", where the consequent follows 'if'.

Another common conditional indicator phrase is "is entailed by". Consider these two sentences:

(29)   Full civil rights entails having voting privileges.
(30)   Having voting privileges is entailed by full civil rights.

Both (29) and (30) are translated as $(R \rightarrow P)$. (29) has the antecedent at the beginning of the sentence, while (30) has the consequent at the beginning. The order of antecedent and consequent in the English sentences makes no difference to the translation itself. What is important is that one understands the function of the phrases "entails" and "is entailed by", because these indicate the order of implication, and it is only where one can say what is doing the implying and what is being implied that one can translate conditional sentences correctly. The term "implies" acts in the same way as 'entails'. Hence, in (29) and (30), 'implies' and 'is implied by' can replace 'entails' and 'is entailed by' with no loss of meaning or truth value and without change of translation. A different example follows:

(29a)   Natural selection implies diversity. $(N \rightarrow D)$
(30a)   Diversity is implied by natural selection. $(N \rightarrow D)$

The last class of sentence is called the **biconditional**. As the name implies, a biconditional is comprised of two conditionals. Since we already know how to translate conditionals, translating biconditionals will cause no problems. What must be remembered are the "biconditional indicator phrases". There are essentially three of them, as indicated in the following set of biconditional sentences:

(31)   One enjoys reading *if and only if* one learns something.
(32)   John will move *just in case that* the rent increases.
(33)   Your being eighteen years old is a *sufficient and necessary condition* for your being able to vote.

Whereas in the conditional, the arrow is used as the connective sign, in the biconditional, since we have two conditionals, the sign is the **double arrow** $(\leftrightarrow)$, indicating a two-way implication. (31)-(33) are translated as,

(31a) $(E \leftrightarrow L)$
(32a) $(M \leftrightarrow R)$
(33a) $(E \leftrightarrow V)$

What (31) is saying, in the long form, is this: If you are enjoying this book, then you are learning something, and if you are learning something, then you are enjoying this book. This sentence would be translated as '$[(E \rightarrow L) \cdot (L \rightarrow E)]$'. Hence, you might think of the biconditional as a short-cut way of expressing two conditionals in a conjunction. The biconditional indicator phrases are each treated as different ways of expressing the same thing. And, though the standard phrase is "if, and only if", each of the others, including "necessary and sufficient condition", "entails, and is entailed by", and "implies, and is implied by" is translated in the same way, i.e., with the double arrow. Consider the following sentence.

(34)   That the safari will be dangerous entails, and is entailed by, the fact that there will be wild animals along the way. Let 'S' = 'the safari will be dangerous', and let 'W' = 'there will be wild animals along the way'. Translation for (34): (S ↔ W)

If one replaces the biconditional indicator phrase in (34), i.e., "entails, and is entailed by", with any of the other biconditional indicator phrases, the translation will *not* thereby be altered. This is because all biconditional indicator phrases operate in the same fashion in a sentence. The same may be said for all "indicator" terms and phrases. That is, all conjunction indicator terms and phrases "match" in the sense of being interchangeable whenever they occur.

As noted above, each of the compound sentences are made up of simple sentences. These simple sentences are said to be components in the compound sentences, and have a name, e.g., the components in a disjunction are called disjuncts. There is no formal name for the components in biconditionals.

Let us note once again that an important point to remember about translation dictionaries is that they should never contain any occurrence of an indicator term, either conjunctive, distunctive, negative, conditional or biconditional. Each sentence letter should represent a simple sentence, without a negation.

Table of Connectives

Name of sentence:	Components:	Symbol:	Example:
Conjunction	conjuncts	dot (•)	(P • Q)
Negation	---------	bar (-)	-P
Disjunction	disjuncts	wedge (v)	(P v Q)
Conditional	antecedent/ consequent	arrow (→)	(P → Q)
Biconditional	---------	double (↔) arrow	(P ↔ Q)

Table of Indicator Terms

Conjunction: and, yet, but, moreover, nevertheless, however, although, also.

Negation: not, didn't, won't, haven't, it is false that,....

Disjunction: or, unless, either...or..., neither...nor....

Conditional: if...then, if, only if, implies that, entails, sufficient condition, necessary condition, provided that, on condition that.

Biconditional: if and only if, just in case that, necessary and sufficient condition, entails and is entailed by, implies and is implied by.

Exercise 5.2

A. Translate the following sentences into symbolic notation, providing your own dictionary for each sentence.

1   Stubby cannot fail this class if he will practice.

2   Either the St. Francis or the Mark Hopkins will prove unsuitable for the conference, although the Mark Hopkins is large enough to accommodate a party of 300.

3   If the University expands, then, since it has to add two more departments and not just one, Russian and either Advertizing or History of Science will be added.

4   On the condition that the United Nations takes action in the Orkney Islands, Commander Johnson will get a ship.

5*   The Orkney Islands will become an independent state provided that Scotland is willing to grant independence and England sees no threat to its own economic security.

6   If either England or Scotland has a long range plan to set up a nuclear research center in the Orkneys, then the Orkneys will remain a county of Scotland.

7   If Carla doesn't score high on the Graduate Record Exam (GRE), but scores in the top 5% on the Law School Exam (LSAT), then either she will change her major to Pre-Law and cut back on the number of units she's taking, or she'll stay with her present major and attempt to secure a position as a legal researcher for Thomson, Turner & Tutwell.

8   Carla's scoring high on the LSAT is a necessary condition for her getting the assistantship next year, but it is not a sufficient condition.

9   Carla will score high on the GRE if, and only if, Janet remembers to return Carla's notes before leaving for Berkeley.

10* Janet won't remember to return Carla's notes, but she'll apologize profusely and never borrow Carla's notes again.

11   One either believes David Hume to be the most important philosopher to ever write in English and agrees with his reasoning concerning causality, or one criticizes Hume's redundancy and finds the arguments naive and uninteresting.

12   No one will believe what Hume said about the future being like the past unless one can show his arguments to be valid.

13   Journal publications should be a necessary and sufficient condition for any university teacher getting tenure.

14   It will either rain or shine today, but not both.

15* It will rain tomorrow only if either a high pressure front or a cold front moves in with the jet stream tonight.

16   Anne Rice will either write one more vampire book or she won't; however, she won't both write another and not write another.

17   It is false that Ronald Reagan's administration will be judged by history as having been good to the poor.

18   If #17 is true, then if Thomas Jefferson's administration won't be so judged, then John Kennedy's administration will be.

19   Martin makes the finest acoustic guitars, while either Fender or Gibson makes the finest electric guitars.

20* Understanding Einstein is a necessary condition for obtaining a PhD in physics, unless understanding Bohr is a sufficient condition and understanding Einstein is not a necessary condition for understanding Bohr.

B. Use the dictionary below in translating the following sentences into standard English from the symbolic notation.

C = Brahe rejected the Copernican theory
D = Galileo's works are full of important philosophical insights
E = Kepler's Third Law is still in use today
F = Kepler was Brahe's assistant
G = Galileo contradicted himself
H = Ptolemy was contradicted by Copernicus
K = Kepler admired Brahe

L = Ptolemy was the father of astronomy
P = Shakespeare was born in 1564
R = Galileo was born in 1564
S = Galileo and Shakespeare were contemporaries
T = Galileo proved Aristotle wrong about planetary motion
U = Copernicus held a heliocentric theory
Z = Copernicus was the father of astronomy

1   [(P • R) → S]   2   [L → (H → U)]
3   (L v Z)   4   -(G ↔ D)
5* (C → -K)   6   [C • (U → -F)]
7   [(T v -T) • -(T • -T)]   8   [(Z v L) v H]
9   -[L • (U • H)]   10* {Z → [U → (-L • -K)]}
11 (-H v -E)   12 -[(T • G) • D]
13 [(U → Z) • (T → -Z)]   14 -(F → E)
15* [(C → U) → -H]

C. Create your own dictionary and translate the following sentences into standard English from the symbolic notation. Create sentences that make sense, and attempt, through the dictionary, to make each sentence true. Note any problems in constructing a consistent dictionary.

1   [(S → -I) → (E v -S)]   2   -[(-G • P) → -(B • P)]
3   -(-Y → -R)   4   {[(B • M) • -A] → -X}
5* [(R ↔ L) → R]   6   [(G v -G) v -X]
7   ((J → -L) v I)   8   [A → -(P • -B)]
9   --(-D ↔ B)   10* [(S → E) ↔ K]

D. Which of the following sentences are true; which are false?
1   A sentence translated with a wedge is called a conditional.
2   No sentence translated with a dot can contain another sentence which is not translated with a dot.
3   The components of sentences translated with an arrow are called "disjuncts".
4   No false sentence can be translated into symbolic notation.
5* One translates a sentence with a dot if, and only if, the sentence contains any one of the conjunction indicator terms.
6   It is proper to include connective indicator terms and/or phrases in a translation dictionary.

7   It is impossible for a sentence to contain three or more disjuncts.

8   The consequent is always implied by the antecedent.

9   The proper translation of 'Patti Page sings like a bird only if Herb's opinion of Patti Page is correct', where 'B' = 'Patti Page sings like a bird', and 'H' = 'Herb's opinion of Patti Page is correct', is: $(H \rightarrow B)$.

10* The following sentences are translated in the same way:

   Teresa's good mood implies that she bought a new car.

   Teresa's good mood is entailed by her having bought a new car.

11 One proper translation of 'the Governor of Alabama will not seek another term in office unless the Crimson Tide wins the national championship', where 'G' = 'the Governor of Alabama will seek another term in office' and 'C' = 'the Crimson Tide will win the national championship', is: $(G \rightarrow C)$.

12 There is no exception to the rule that the antecedent always follows the word "if" when one translates.

13 There is no exception to the rule that the necessary condition always follows the arrow in translations.

14 Where 'L' = '*Love and Death* is a Woody Allen film' and S = '*Sleeper* is a Woody Allen film' and 'F' = 'Woody Allen is a funny guy', '$[(L \cdot S) \rightarrow F]$' could be translated as 'If *Love and Death* and *Sleeper* are Woody Allen films, then Woody Allen is a funny guy'.

15* Only conditionals can be translated with an arrow.

6. Sentential Logic B

6.1 Preliminaries

With this chapter we begin our study of techniques for determining both the truth value of sentences and the validity or invalidity of arguments. These techniques are made possible in part by the creation of the special logical symbols in the artificial language we have sketched in Chapter 5. The present chapter treats two techniques, viz., **Truth Tables** *and* **Truth Trees**. These are purely mechanical devices, each with a set of rules that must be learned through practice if one is to work efficiently and effectively within each system. The key, as always, is *practice*. A further word is due on the subject of acceptability at this point. The primary goal in the next two chapters is the determination of the logical status of sentences and arguments. This is to say that we will be attempting to see which sentences are true, which are false, and which arguments are valid and which invalid by appealing to certain logical rules. This is part of the work of logic, but it is not sufficient in itself to determine that some sentence or argument is to be accepted by a given individual.

A sentence is acceptable if it is true, or if there is good evidence to show that it is true. An argument is acceptable if there is good evidence to show that each premise is true *and* if the conclusion either follows from the set of premises with a high degree of probability or is guaranteed to be true by virtue of the premises being true, i.e., follows conclusively. In a vast number of cases, one cannot determine, by the systems of logic alone, whether a sentence is indeed true or false. We see then that the techniques to follow only go so far in assisting the individual in determining the acceptability of arguments. One important thing one can determine, via the techniques of logic alone, is whether some conclusion really does follow from the premises offered in its support. If someone tries to persuade you, say, to vote against a certain legislative proposition, that person will present an argument. Through applying your knowledge of logic, you will be able to tell whether the conclusion actually follows. If the conclusion does not follow from the premises presented, that does not mean that you should not vote against the proposition. What it means is that the arguer has not presented *decisive* evidence for the conclusion. There may still be a better argument, one that *will* be decisive. On the other hand, there may not be a better argument, in which case, it may well be that you should vote for the Proposition.

We may now proceed to the techniques of sentential logic, beginning with a study of the logical status of sentences, moving into a treatment of arguments themselves.

6.2 Truth Tables for Sentences

We will be concerned, in this section, with a method for determining the truth or falsity of sentences containing one or more occurrences of the truth functional connectives. The method we will use is called *The Method of Truth Tables.*

To begin, recall mention of The Law of Excluded Middle. This "law of thought" says that every sentence is either true or false, and is preeminent for the method of truth tables. While there are many facts about the world the truth about which we are ignorant, still, any sentence expressing a fact about the world is either true or false, and not neither, and not both. This is to say that just because we may not know the actual height of Mt. Baldy, for example, it does not follow that the sentence "Mt. Baldy is 5,342 feet high" is neither true nor false. Mt. Baldy has height and it is either true or false that Mt. Baldy is 5,342 feet high.

We are working in a **two-valued logic**, the values being *truth* and *falsehood*, where every sentence is said to have one or the other value. For example,

(1) Goodman's computer has an amber monitor. [A]

is a simple sentence, translated as **A**. **A** is either true or false, and its full, objective truth table is:

```
A
t
f
```

A truth table is essentially a diagram showing the truth value possibilities for any given sentence. If you've never seen Goodman's computer, you won't know whether the monitor is amber or not. Hence, you won't know the actual truth value of **A**. As the truth table for **A** shows, it may be either true or false, and it has to be one or the other. Similarly for,

(2) Goodman's computer has a green monitor. [G]

```
G
t
f
```

What one needs to do, to discover the truth values of **A** and **G**, is have a look at Goodman's computer monitor. If you find, as I believe you would, that the monitor is neither amber nor green, you will know that **A** and **G** are both false.

Now, since compound sentences, with which we are most concerned, are made up of simple sentences, to discover the truth value of any compound sentence, it suffices to lay out the possible truth value combinations of the component simple sentences and determine the truth functional nature of the connective occurring in the compound sentence.
Consider the following sentence:

(3) Goodman has a color monitor and it was made by IBM.

Let 'A' = 'Goodman has a color monitor' and 'I' = Goodman's computer monitor was made by IBM'. The occurrence of 'and' in (3) indicates that we have a conjunction here. Our translation of (3) is: (A • I). To construct a full truth table for '(A • I)', we need to consider the number of different combinations of truth values for **A** and **I**. That is, **A** and **I** could both be true; **A** could be true while **I** is false; **A** could be false while **I** is true; or **A** and **I** could both be false. Each combination of truth values is called a **row**, or an **interpretation**. We can construct the following partial table:

```
                (A  •   I)
     Row 1       t      t
     Row 2       t      f
     Row 3       f      t
     Row 4       f      f
```

Every possible combination of the truth values for **A** and **I** are found in the above table. [We are not concerned, at this point, with the actual truth value of (3).]

Whereas (2) is a simple sentence, and hence, requires only two possible truth values, (3) is a compound sentence, has two different components, and requires four possible combinations of truth value. If we were to add one more component, say, **R**, we would need eight possible combinations of truth value, e.g.,

```
                  [ (A  •  I)  •  R]
Interpretation 1     t     t      t
Interpretation 2     t     t      f
Interpretation 3     t     f      t
Interpretation 4     t     f      f
Interpretation 5     f     t      t
Interpretation 6     f     t      f
Interpretation 7     f     f      t
Interpretation 8     f     f      f
```

The number of truth value combinations (rows, interpretations) doubles with each added component. Hence, if there are 4 com-ponents, 16 interpretations are needed; 5 components, 32 interpretations; and so on.

A convention we shall adopt at this time is that when assigning truth values to components, begin with the component letter closest to the letter "Z" (in the alphabet) and assign 't' and 'f' alternating by one's; then proceed to the next component letter closest to 'Z' and assign 't' and 'f' alternating by two's; and so on. This is what was done in constructing the truth table directly above, where **R** is closest to 'Z', **I** is next closest to 'Z', and then **A**. Each compon-ent has the same number of "t's" and "f's", but **R** gets "t,f,t,f...", **I** gets "t,t,f,f...", and **A** gets "t,t,t,t,f,f,f,f", which is a long way of saying that the number is the same while the order is different.

Conjunctions. Now, with these preliminaries, we are in a position to construct a full truth table for '(A • I)'. The crucial factor here is the truth functional nature of the dot (conjunction). That is, given that we have the interpretations under **A** and **I**, what remains is to assign a truth value, under the dot, for every interpretation, according to a rule. The rule here will be the truth table for conjunctions, and will be a guide for every occurrence of a conjunction in the method of truth tables. (Each of the five connectives has a truth table.)
The truth table for the conjunction is:

```
        (p  •  q)
         t  t  t
         t  f  f
         f  f  t
         f  f  f
```

(We shall be using the lower case letters 'p', 'q', 'r', 's', and 't' to designate simple **sentence forms**. Any string of these letters, in any combination, with one or more occurrences of the connectives, and the appropriate number and arrangement of groupers, will be designated a sentence form. Sentence forms are not sentences, because sentences are "about the world", i.e., have meaning. Sentence forms have no meaning because 'p', 'q', etc., have no meaning. Notice that the truth table for the conjunction is given in a sentence form. This is done to show that it does not matter what letters appear in the conjunction itself. We could easily substitute 'A' for 'p' and 'I' for 'q'. The point is that whereas 'p' has no meaning, 'A' means 'Goodman has a color monitor'. And this matters to the actual truth value of the sentence.)

Given, then, someone who is ignorant about Goodman's computer monitor, that person would have to construct a full truth table for '(A • I)', which would be the following:

```
(A  •  I)
 t  t  t
 t  f  f
 f  f  t
 f  f  f
```

And from this truth table alone, it is impossible to tell the actual truth value of '(A • I)'. This is so because one cannot determine here which interpretation is the *actual* interpretation of '(A • I)'. However, if one knows that Goodman's is a color monitor, and if one also knows that Goodman's monitor was not made by IBM, then one is able to determine, through consulting the truth table for the conjunction, the actual truth value of '(A • I)'. So, where **A** is true and **I** is false, '(A • I)' is false. Thus,

```
(A  •  I)
 t  f  f
```

which corresponds to Interpretation 2 in the truth table for the conjunction. In justifying the truth table for conjunctions, i.e., why the truth table for conjunctions is as it is, consider what is really taking place in a sentence expressing a conjunction. A person who utters a conjunction is saying that both of the conjuncts are true. If I say, "I went downtown and bought ice cream", I'm saying 1) that I went downtown and 2) that I bought ice cream. If it is true that I went downtown, and if it is true that I bought ice cream (**A** and **I** being both true), then what I've said is true. But what if I went downtown but didn't buy ice cream (**A** true, **I** false)? Then what I've said is false. Or, what if I didn't go downtown but bought ice cream, say, from the ice cream truck (**A** false, **I** true)? Then, again, what I've said is false. Lastly, what if I neither went downtown nor bought ice cream (both **A** and **I** false)? The result is a false sentence. In English, we can say: A conjunction is true if, and only if, each of its conjuncts is true; a conjunction is false if, and only if, at least one of its conjuncts is false.

Negations. Our next truth table is for negations, and is:

```
-p
ft
tf
```

This is as much as to say that the truth value of a negated sentence is the opposite to that of the non-negated sentence. Hence, where 'p' is true, '-p' is false, and conversely. This rule applies as well to compound sentences that are negated. For example,

(4) Jill and Colin won't both apply for the job.

may be translated as: -(J • C). We lay out the partial truth table for this "symbolic sentence" as before, holding to the convention of beginning with the letter closest to 'Z'. Thus,

```
- (J  •  C)
     t     t
     f     t
     t     f
     f     f
```

Now we can assign truth values to (under) the dot and the bar. We must begin with the dot, because to determine the truth value of the negated sentence one must know the truth value of the sentence itself. Another way of saying this is to point to the bar as the **primary/major connective**, i.e., the connective with the largest scope, and note that the major connective is always the last connective to be assigned truth values. The dot, in this case, is called the **subordinate/minor connective**. The two truth tables below show the two further steps in constructing a full truth table for '-(J • C)':

```
         1                    2
  - (J  •  C)          - (J  •  C)
     t  t  t            f  t  t  t
     f  f  t            t  f  f  t
     t  f  f            t  t  f  f
     f  f  f            t  f  f  f
```

Table (1) above is the penultimate stage in constructing the full truth table. It does not contain any assignment of truth values under the bar. Table (2) is the proper full truth table for '-(J • C)'. Since we don't know whether it is true or false that Jill will apply for the job, and since we don't know whether it is true or false that Colin will apply for the job, we cannot determine the actual truth value of this sentence (4). At most, what we can say is this: Where **J** and **C** are both true, the sentence is false; in all other cases, the sentence is true. Let us say that we do know that Jill will but Colin will not apply for the job. We now know the truth value of the sentence, as all we have to do is consult the full truth table, check the 3rd interpretation, where **J** is true but **C** is false. This is so, because the sentence says, essentially, that one or the other of them will not apply for the job.

Let us take a look at a more complicated sentence, and its corresponding series of truth tables. Let 'E' = 'Eggers will sign a contract with the Canadian Football League'; 'F' = 'Farley will...'; 'G' = 'Gustaf...'; 'H' = 'Holbrook will...'.

(5) It is false that both Eggers and Farley and both Gustaf and Holbrook will sign contracts with the Canadian Football League.

$$-[(E \cdot F) \cdot (G \cdot H)]$$

Note again here that the primary connective is the bar. Hence, it will be the last of the four occurrences of connectives to receive the assignment of truth values. Clearly, since there are four com-ponents in this negated conjunction, we will need sixteen different interpretations.

1a
-[(E • F) • (G • H)]

E	•	F	•	G	•	H
t		t		t		t
t		t		t		f
t		t		f		t
t		t		f		f
t		f		t		t
t		f		t		f
t		f		f		t
t		f		f		f
f		t		t		t
f		t		t		f
f		t		f		t
f		t		f		f
f		f		t		t
f		f		t		f
f		f		f		t
f		f		f		f

2a
-[(E • F) • (G • H)]

E	•	F	•	G	•	H
t	t	t		t		t
t	t	t		t		f
t	t	t		f		t
t	t	t		f		f
t	f	f		t		t
t	f	f		t		f
t	f	f		f		t
t	f	f		f		f
f	f	t		t		t
f	f	t		t		f
f	f	t		f		t
f	f	t		f		f
f	f	f		t		t
f	f	f		t		f
f	f	f		f		t
f	f	f		f		f

```
                          3a
            -[(E • F)  •  (G • H)]
                t t t      t t t
                t t t      t f f
                t t t      f f t
                t t t      f f f
                t f f      t t t
                t f f      t f f
                t f f      f f t
                t f f      f f f
                f f t      t t t
                f f t      t f f
                f f t      f f t
                f f t      f f f
                f f f      t t t
                f f f      t f f
                f f f      f f t
                f f f      f f f

            4a                        5a
-[(E • F)  •  (G • H)]     -[(E • F)  •  (G • H)]
   t t t  t  t t t          f  t t t  t  t t t
   t t t  f  t f f          t  t t t  f  t f f
   t t t  f  f f t          t  t t t  f  f f t
   t t t  f  f f f          t  t t t  f  f f f
   t f f  f  t t t          t  t f f  f  t t t
   t f f  f  t f f          t  t f f  f  t f f
   t f f  f  f f t          t  t f f  f  f f t
   t f f  f  f f f          t  t f f  f  f f f
   f f t  f  t t t          t  f f t  f  t t t
   f f t  f  t f f          t  f f t  f  t f f
   f f t  f  f f t          t  f f t  f  f f t
   f f t  f  f f f          t  f f t  f  f f f
   f f f  f  t t t          t  f f f  f  t t t
   f f f  f  t f f          t  f f f  f  t f f
   f f f  f  f f t          t  f f f  f  f f t
   f f f  f  f f f          t  f f f  f  f f f
```

When constructing a truth table for any sentence, after assigning truth values to the sentence components, begin to assign truth values under the connective with the smallest scope. Table (2) above shows this. Actually, since the dots have equal scope in the formulas "(E • F)" and "(G • H)", it does not matter which dot is assigned truth values first. When continuing with the truth table, assign truth values to formulas with connectives of ever-increasing scope. Finally, as in (5a), one will reach the primary connective, which will have the widest scope of all the connectives in the sentence. (5a) is the full truth table for (5) symbolized.

At this point, it is well to point out once again that truth values are assigned to sentence components in accord with the adopted convention, and assigned to any sentence connective only in accord with the truth table for that connective. Hence, when assigning truth values to conjunctions, consult the truth table for the conjunction; when assigning truth values to negations, consult the truth table for the negation, and so on.

Disjunctions. As noted previously, disjunctions have two senses, i.e., the inclusive and the exclusive. However, there is only one truth table for the wedge. We use the truth table for the inclusive sense, which is:

```
(p  v  q)
 t  t  t
 t  t  f
 f  t  t
 f  f  f
```

We say that the truth table for disjunctions defines the wedge symbol in truth functional terms (as the truth table for conjunctions defines the dot). The reason one truth table is sufficient for all disjunctions is that all disjunctions have at least one thing in common, i.e., each asserts that at least one of its disjuncts is true (as all conjunctions have in common the assertion that both con-juncts are true). And, if you check the table for the wedge, you will see that whenever at least one of the disjuncts is true, the entire sentence is true. Consider the following sentence, dictionary, translation, and truth table.

(6) Either the Blackfoot tribe will continue its fight to save the paintings and not attend the gathering in Tulsa, or they will learn that the paintings are of recent origin and they will not continue their fight for the paintings. [B = the Blackfoot tribe continues its fight to save the ancient paintings; L = they will learn that the paintings are of recent origin; T = the Blackfoot tribe will attend the gathering in Tulsa]

```
[(B  •  -T)  v  (L  •  -B)]
  t  f  ft   f   t  f  ft
  t  t  tf   t   t  f  ft
  t  f  ft   f   f  f  ft
  t  t  tf   t   f  f  ft
  f  f  ft   t   t  t  tf
  f  f  tf   t   t  t  tf
  f  f  ft   f   f  f  tf
  f  f  tf   f   f  f  tf
```

Examples, like the above, have been given of truth tables. Let's try another step by step explanation.

1) **B**, **L**, and **T** are the sentence components here, i.e., they are the sentence letters designating the simple sentences out of which the compound sentence is constructed. The truth values assigned to (under) these letters are determined by the relative proximity of each letter to the letter "Z" in the alphabet (recall our convention for assigning truth values to sentence letters). These letters are the smallest units to which truth values are assigned. Therefore, we start with them. There are three different letters. Thus, eight interpretations are required to show every possible combination of truth values for this sentence.

2) The next smallest units are '-T' and '-B'. This is to say that a bar ranges over the 'P' and over the 'B' and nothing else. Truth values are assigned under the bar in accord with the truth table for negations, but are determined by the truth values under 'T' and 'B'. Thus, for example, when 'B' is true, '-B' is false, and vice-versa.

3) The next smallest units are '(B • -T)' and '(L • -B)'. Strictly, as with '-P' and '-B', it does not matter which formula you deal with first here. What does matter is that you understand that the scope of these formulas is determined by the dots. The point here is to understand where the truth values under the dots come from. The truth values under the dot in '(B • -T)' come from the truth values under 'B' and '-T' in accord with the truth table for conjunctions, because '(B • -T)' is a conjunction. Hence, to find the truth value under the dot for this formula in, say, interpretation 5, one consults the truth table for conjunctions to determine what the truth value of a conjunction is when the conjuncts are both false. A conjunction is false when one or both of the conjuncts is false and true only when both conjuncts are true. So we assign 'f' to '(B • -T)' in row 5 of the above truth table.

It must be understood that the conjuncts in the conjunction '(L • -B)' are 'L' and '-B'. 'B' is not a conjunct here; '-B' is a conjunct. This means that when assigning truth values to the dot in this formula, one looks at the truth values under 'L' and '-B' rather than at 'L' and 'B'. The same reasoning applies to the conjunction '(B • -T)'. That is, the conjuncts in this conjunction are 'B' and '-T'.

4) Since sentence (6) is a disjunction, the major connective is the wedge. It ranges from the left-hand bracket to the right-hand bracket, and over all formulas between the brackets. To determine the truth value assignments under the wedge, one looks at the truth values under the two dots of the conjunctions, assigning truth values under the wedge in accord

with the truth table for disjunctions. Now, when one has determined the truth values under the major connective, one is in a position to say whether the sentence is true, false, or, when one is not sure of the *actual* truth values of the components, indeterminate. Sentence (6) seems a sentence the components of which are of unknown truth value to us. That is, we can't really say whether it is true or false, for example, that the British government will wipe out academic tenure. Hence, sentence (6) is indeterminate. At most, then, we can merely enumerate the various combinations of truth values in the different rows, as follows: Sentence (6) is *true* when **B** and **L** are true (row 2); when **B** is true and **T** and **L** is false (row 4); when **B** is false and **T** and **L** are true (row 5); and when **B** and **T** are false and **L** is true (row 6). Otherwise, it is *false*.

    Conditionals. As there are different senses of disjuctions, so there are different sorts of conditional sentences. As examples, consider the following conditional sentences:

    (7) If the match is struck, then the sulfur will ignite.
    (8) If '(R • S)' is a true sentence, then 'S' is a true sentence.
    (9) If Nip is a porpoise, then Nip is of the genus *Phocaena*.
    (10) If the Mad River waters clear, then we'll go fishing.

We can name these different sorts of conditionals as follows: (7) is an example of a *causal conditional*, pointing to one event as the cause of another event; (8) is an example of an *inferential conditional*, stating that one sentence can be inferred from another sentence; (9) is an example of a *lexical conditional*, stating the definition of 'porpoise' as 'of the genus *Phocaena*'; (10) is what we will call a *material conditional*. In each of these conditionals there is a relation of implication between the antecedent and the consequent. In each of the first three, the relation seems to be as follows: if the antecedent is true, then the consequent is also true. The last, however, does not exhibit this sort of relation explicitly. If the Mad River waters do indeed clear, still, we might not go fishing; other things may intrude in our lives preventing our going fishing.   There seems to be no definiteness about the implication relation from the antecedent to the consequent in (10).

    There is one commonality between each of these conditionals, however. This is that each "expresses" a relation of implication from the antecedent to the consequent. Just as a conjunction "says" that both conjuncts are true, the conditional "says" that the antecedent implies the consequent. If I say, "if the Sockeye Salmon isn't the most beautiful fish in the river, then I'm a monkey's uncle", no one seriously thinks that the Sockeye not being the most beautiful fish in the river implies that I'm a monkey's uncle. But, equally so, no one can doubt that that is precisely what the sentence expresses.

There is only one truth table for conditionals, and only one is needed, because the arrow is defined in truth functional terms for all conditionals in terms of what is common for all conditionals, which is, again, that each expresses a relation of implication from antecedent to consequent. From this consideration, it follows that all conditionals have a second thing in common, and that is that there is only one interpretation under which a conditional is false, i.e., when the antecedent is true and the consequent is false. Look at it this way: what a conditional "says" is that if the antecedent is
true, then the consequent is true. Now, when it turns out that the antecedent is true but the consequent is false, this goes against what the conditional itself expresses. In other words, where the antecedent is true and the consequent is false, what the conditional expresses is false. Hence, in the truth table for the conditional below, it is false in only one instance.

$$
\begin{array}{ccc}
(p & \rightarrow & q) \\
t & t & t \\
t & f & f \\
f & t & t \\
f & t & f
\end{array}
$$

Another way of understanding why the truth table for the conditional is the way it is is to think of the arrow as something of an abbreviation for a specific sort of negated conjunction. Consider the following:

$$
\begin{array}{cc}
1 & 2 \\
-(p \; \bullet \; -q) & (p \; \rightarrow \; q) \\
t \; t \; f \; ft & t \; t \; t \\
f \; t \; t \; tf & t \; f \; f \\
t \; f \; f \; ft & f \; t \; t \\
t \; f \; f \; tf & f \; t \; f
\end{array}
$$

Since the truth values in (1) and (2) are identical under the primary connectives, and have the same sentence components, (1) and (2) express the same thing. (1) expresses something such as: "not both p and not q", which is as much as to say "if p, then q". Other examples of tables are:

```
[ (R → E) •  (E → R) ]        (R ↔ E)
   t  t t t   t t t            t t t
   t  f f f   f t t            t f f
   f  t t f   t f f            f f t
   f  t f t   f t f            f t f


[ (C v -D)  →  (E •  -C) ]    { [ (G → J)  v -G]  →  -B}
   t t ft   f   t f ft           t t t   t ft   f  ft
   t t ft   f   f f ft           t f f   f ft   t  ft
   t t tf   f   t f ft           f t t   t tf   f  ft
   t t tf   f   f f ft           f t f   t tf   f  ft
   f f ft   t   t t tf           t t t   t ft   t  tf
   f f ft   t   f f tt           t f f   f ft   t  tf
   f t tf   t   t t tf           f t t   t tf   t  tf
   f t tf   f   f f tf           f t f   t tf   t  tf


              [L •  -(-K →  M) ]
                t f f ft t t
                t f f ft t f
                f f f ft t t
                f f f ft t f
                t f f tf t t
                t t t tf f f
                f f t tf t t
                f f f tf f f
```

Biconditionals. The last of the five truth functional connectives is the biconditional. Its truth table is deducible from the truth tables for the conditional and the conjunction, because the biconditional is simply two conditionals conjoined.

```
               1                   2
[ (p → q)  •  (q → p) ]        (p ↔ q)
   t t t   t   t t t            t t t
   t f f   f   f t t            t f f
   f t t   f   t f f            f f t
   f t f   t   f t f            f t f
```

A biconditional is true whenever the components have the same truth value, whether 't' or 'f', and false otherwise. Sentence (2) above *is* the truth table for the biconditional. The double arrow symbol may be understood as defined by the truth table, and as an abbreviation of the sentence '[(p → q) • (q → p)]'.

For another way of explaining how to assign truth values to the various units in a symbolized sentence, consider the truth table on the following page. Each column is numbered there, but this is only for purposes of explanation.

```
           1 2 3   4   5 6 78
         [ (B • P)  v  (L • -B) ]
           t t t   t   t f ft
           t f f   f   t f ft
           t t t   t   f f ft
           t f f   f   f f ft
           f f t   t   t t tf
           f f f   t   t t tf
           f f t   f   f f tf
           f f f   f   f f tf
```

Truth values for the units under numbers 1, 3, 5, and 8 are determined by the convention of beginning with the letter closest to 'Z' and alternating truth values by one's, and so on. The truth values under 7 are determined by the truth values under 8, in accord with the truth table for negation. The truth values under 2 are determined by the truth values under 1 and 3 in accord with the truth table for conjunctions. The truth values under 6 are deter-mined by the truth values under 5 and 7 in accord with the truth table for conjunctions. The truth values under 4 are determined by the truth values under 2 and 6 in accord with the truth table for disjunctions.

Exercise 6.2

A.   Identify each of the following symbolized sentences as conjunctions, negations, conditionals, disjunctions, or biconditionals? If any sentence is a negation, say what kind of negation it is, e.g., negated disjunction.

1 -(-L v -K)   2 ((D → N) → E)
3 [-(B • -H) v -J]   4 {[-(C ↔ F) →W] v Y}
5* [(W v -D) v (-A → -W)]   6 (-T • -(U • -O))
7 -[-(-C v -U) → -T]   8 --[K ↔ (-L • -D)]
9 [-(-S → -M) → -S]   10* [-(Ar ↔ Si) ↔ -Bp]
11 -{[G v (-X → -I)] → I}   12 -(Ljm • -Lmj)
13 [(F • R) v (-R v -F)]   14 -(-(-R → R) v --R)
15* (E → (-H → -O))   16 [-(I v O) v U]
17 {[(T → -G) • (R ↔ G)] → G}   18 {[(-H → I) → -J] v (-I v J)}
19 [(E ↔ -D) → (D ↔ -Q)]   20* -{[(V v K) → -V] ↔ O}

B. In this section, let the truth value of 'A', 'B', and 'H' be known to be true; let 'O', 'J', and 'K' be known to be false; and let the the truth value of 'L', 'M', and 'N' be unknown. Can the truth value of the following sentences be determined? If so, indicate the truth values. If not, explain why not.

1 (B → -M)   2 [L → (-A • M)]
3 [L ↔ -(B → H)]   4 (M v -K) v (M ↔ -N)
5* [(-M • M) v (H • -H)]   6 [(J → K) ↔ -B]
7 (-(-(N → -M) v L) • --M)   8 [J v (O v -H]
9 [(-L ↔ N) → (B ↔ L)]   10* [(A → -K) • (J → -K)]
11 [(-O v J) ↔ (-J → -O]   12 [(-B • -J) v -(J v B)]
13 [(-H v B) ↔ (-B v -H)]   14 [-(-M v N) ↔ (-N → -M)]
15* -{[M • (-N → -M)] → N}   16 {H ↔ [H • (H → -B)]}
17 {[O • (L v A)] ↔ (O • -D)}   18 --[(O • -O) • (-O • O)]
19 [(A → -J) v (J → -A)]   20* -{[(-K ↔ L) • -N] • -H}
21 (-((B → (-L → O)) v -K) → B)   22 [(-A v A) • (N v -N)]
23 {[-((A → -M) ↔ (-A v K)) • -B] → A}
24 -{(M → L) ↔ [(L → M) • (-L → -M)]}
25 [(A → -K) • (J → -O)] → [J v (H v -O]

6.3 Truth Functional Classes of Sentences

As we have said, sentences, i.e., assertions about the world, are either true or false (exclusive "or"). The method of truth tables allows us to determine the truth value of a compound sentence, given that we know the truth values of the simple sentences making up the compound sentence. However, if the truth value(s) of the simple sentences is/are *un*known, then usually the truth value of the compound sentence is also unknown. I say "usually" here because there are two cases in which the truth value of the com-pound sentence can be known even when the value(s) of the simple sentences remain unknown. These cases are when a sentence is either **logically true** or **logically false**.

A sentence is logically true (**L-true**) if it is true under every interpretation. These sorts of sentences are also called **tautologies**. For example, '(p v -p)' is L-true. This is to say that '(p v -p)' is true no matter what the truth value of 'p' happens to be. You will no doubt notice that it is the *form* of the sentence that determines its classification here. In the examples below, all values under the primary connectives are 't', which is to say "true under every interpretation". So, each sentence form below is L-true.

```
(-p → -p)        (p ↔ --p)        [p → (p v q)]
ft t ft          t t tft           t t   t t t
tf t tf          f t ftf           t t   t t f
                                   f t   f t t
                                   f t   f f f
```

```
{[(p → q) •  (q → r)] →  (p → r)}
   t t t   t   t t t   t   t t t
   t t t   f   t f f   t'  t f f
   t f f   f   f t t   t   t t t
   t f f   f   f t f   t   t f f
   f t t   t   t t t   t   f t t
   f t t   f   t f f   t   f t f
   f t f   t   f t t   t   f t t
   f t f   t   f t f   t   f t f
```

A sentence is logically false (**L-false**) if it is true under no interpretation. These sentences are also called **self-contradictions**. For example, '(p • -p)' is L-false. Again, it is the *form* of the sentence which determines the class of the sentence. Denying (placing a bar in front of) an L-true sentence yields an L-false sentence. Each of the following is an example of an L-false sentence, i.e., true under no interpretation.

```
-(-p → -p)      -[(p → q) ↔   (-p v q)]
f ft t ft       f  t t t   t   ft t t
f tf t tf       f  t f f   t   ft f f
                f  f t t   t   tf t t
                f  f t f   t   tf t f
```

```
{(p → q) • -[-q → (p → -r)]}
   t t t   f f ft t   t f ft
   t t t   f f ft t   t t tf
   t f f   f t tf f   t f ft
   t f f   f f tf t   t t tf
   f t t   f f ft t   f t ft
   f t t   f f ft t   f t tf
   f t f   f f tf t   f t ft
   f t f   f f tf t   f t tf
```

A sentence which is neither logically true nor logically false is termed logically indeterminate (**L-indeterminate**). These sentences are also called **contingent**. A sentence is logically indeterminate if the sentence is true under some, but not all, interpretations. For example, all simple sentences, as well as their negations, are L-indeterminate. What 'logically indeterminate' means is that one cannot determine the truth value by using the methods of logic alone; it does not mean that the sentence is neither true nor false, or that it has no truth value. As stipulated, all sentences are either true or false. Each of the sentence forms below is L-indeterminate.

```
p        -q       (p v q)      -[(r • -p) → r]
t        ft        t t t        f  t f ft   t t
f        tf        t t f        f  f f ft   t f
                   f t t        t  t t tf   f f
                   f f f        f  f f tf   t f
```

In each of the above sentence forms, there is at least one occurrence of 't' under the primary connective and at least one occurrence of 'f' under the primary connective. The simple sentence form 'p', of course, has no connective. Hence, under 'p' itself, 't' and 'f' each occur once. Since each of these sentence forms is true under at least one interpretation and false under at least one interpretation, each is L-indeterminate.

Now, if one substitutes 'B' for 'p' and 'C' for 'q' in the sentence form '(p v q)', one gets the following sentence: (B v C). Let 'B' = 'the Boston Red Sox used to be called the Boston Americans' and let 'C' = 'the Chicago Cubs used to be called the Chicago Blues'. Since 'B' and 'C' stand for actual sentences, which make assertions about the world, the sentence "(B v C)" has a determinable truth value. In accord with the table for disjunctions, we see that the sentence is true, since one of its disjuncts is true, viz., the first disjunct. The truth value of '(B v C)' cannot be determined simply by the methods of logic. Rather, one needs to know the truth values of the components, i.e., 'B' and 'C'. And, when one knows the truth values of the components of any given sentence, one can determine the truth value of that sentence.

There is another set of characteristics sentences have. These are relations sentences have with respect to one another. If any two or more sentences with the same components have the same truth values under each interpretation, these sentences are said to be **equivalent**. For example,

```
(p v -q)        (-q v p)
 t t ft          ft t t
 t t tf          tf t t
 f f ft          ft f f
 f t tf          tf t f
```

Since these two sentence forms are both true under the first, second, and fourth interpretations, and both false under the third interpretation, these two sentence forms are equivalent. (If one makes a biconditional from these two sentence forms, one will derive a sentence form that is L-true.)

Any two sentences with the same components having opposite truth values under every interpretation are said to be **contradictory**.

```
      1                    2
 (p  v  -q)          - (p  v  -q)
  t  t  ft            f  t  t  ft
  t  t  tf            f  t  t  tf
  f  f  ft            t  f  f  ft
  f  t  tf            f  f  t  tf
```

Since (1) is true under every interpretation under which (2) is false, and false under every interpretation under which (2) is true, (1) and (2) are contradictory sentence forms.

Sentences with the same components which are neither equivalent nor contradictory are **incompatible**. These sentences will have the same truth values under some interpretations and different truth values under other interpretations.

Below you will find the truth tables for the five connectives represented in both schematic form as well as explained in English. These will be helpful references as you work through the exercises throughout. Following the truth tables you will find the table of truth functional classes. These will also be useful for reference while working exercises.

Table of Truth Tables

Conjunction

True when both conjuncts are true; false otherwise.

```
(p  •  q)
 t  t  t
 t  f  f
 f  f  t
 f  f  f
```

Disjunction

True when at least one disjunct is true, false otherwise.

```
(p  v  q)
 t  t  t
 t  t  f
 f  t  t
 f  f  f
```

Conditional

False when antecedent is true and consequent is false;
true otherwise.

```
(p → q)
 t  t  t
 t  f  f
 f  t  t
 f  t  f
```

Biconditional

True when components have same truth values; false otherwise.

```
(p ↔ q)
 t  t  t
 t  f  f
 f  f  t
 f  t  f
```

Negation

True when non-negated sentence is false; false otherwise.

```
-p
ft
tf
```

Table of Truth Functional Classes

Logically True
True under every interpretation.

Logically False
True under no interpretation.

Logically Indeterminate
True under some, but not all, interpretations.

Equivalent Sentences
True under the same interpretations.
False under the same interpretations.

Contradictory Sentences
Opposite truth values under every interpretation.

Incompatible Sentences
Same truth values under some interpretations.
Different truth values under some interpretations.

Exercise 6.3

A. Determine whether the following sentences are L-true, L-false, or L-indeterminate using the method of truth tables.

1   (-U v -U)
2   (-U → -U)
3   [R • (G v -R)]
4   [(J ↔ O) → -J]
5* [A → (A → --A)]
6   -[-(--S → S) → S]
7   [(D v C) v (D → C)]
8   [(K → M) → (M v -K)]
9   -[(B ↔ L) → (-B v L)]
10* {P • [(E → W) • -P]}
11 [(L → R) • -(R → L)]
12 {[E • (-I v E)] ↔ [-I v (E → E)]}
13 {[S → (G → W)] ↔ [-(-W → -G) → -S]}
14 [(-D v -C) ↔ --(C • D)]
15* {[[(K → G) v (P ↔ G)] • (K • P)] → (G → G)}
16 -{[(R → S) ↔ (S v -R)] ↔ [(R → S) ↔ (-S → -R)]}
17 {[(-X v Y) ↔ (X → Y)] → [-(X • -Y) → -(-Y • X)]}
18 -{{[(L • A) v D] → [-A v (D → -L)]} v (L → L)}
19 {[(-B v B) → (B → B)] v (B v -B)}
20* -{[(Hrr → -Hrg) • (Hrr → Hrg)] → [(Hrr → Hrs) • -Hsr]}

B. Determine whether the following pairs of sentences are equivalent, contradictory, or incompatible using truth tables.

1   H   (J • -H)
2   (S → L)   (-L → -S)
3   (G • -I)   [I ↔ -G)

4   (D v P)   (-D v -P)
5* (C → -C)   (-C v M)
6   (R ↔ O)   [(R v O) → R]
7   -(Z → X)   -(-X • Z)
8   (W • -A)   -(A ↔ - - W)
9   [(E • L) v (B • E)]   [B v L) • E]
10* [E → (J → G)]   [-(J • E) v G]
11 [(I • M) → D]   [D v -(M • I)]
12 [Q v (D v V)]   [-Q v (-D v -V)]
13 [(W → W) v -W]   (W v -W)
14 [(O ↔ C) → R]   [-R → (-C → O)]
15*-(N • J)   -(-N v -J)
16 [H → (Y v H)]   [-H v -(-Y • -H)]
17 [(G • P) • E]   [G • (-P v E)]
18 {L v -[((J → I) • (-J → -I)) v -S]}   {[S → (J ↔ I)] → L}
19 [(Lii • Kup) → Frj]   -[Frj v (Kup → -Lii)]
20* {[Bt v (Ie → Cc)] v [Ie • (Bt → Cc)]}   [(-Cc • -Ie) • -Bt]

C. Which of the following are true, which are false?

1 Two sentences are incompatible only if the truth values under the primary connectives in each sentence are opposite.

2 It is false that the negation of a self-contradiction is a tautology.

3 Equivalent sentences imply one another.

4 '(p v -p)' entails '(p • p)'.

5* If any sentence is true under some, but not all, interpretations, then that sentence is L-indeterminate.

6 A valid argument is one for which it is impossible to assign 't' to all the premises and 'f' to the consequent under any interpre-tation.

7 A necessary and sufficient condition for any sentence to be L-true is that it be true under at least one interpretation.

8 No two sentences are contradictory unless the truth values under the primary connectives of each sentence are opposite.

9 No two sentences are contradictory if one sentence is L-true and the other is L-indeterminate.

10* Given any three sentences, if the first sentence affirms exactly what the third sentence affirms and denies exactly what the third denies, and if the second sentence affirms exactly what the third denies while denying exactly what the third affirms, then the first and second sentences are contradictory.

6.4 Truth Tables for Arguments

We may now begin to analyze arguments by the method of truth tables. In this section, we will study full truth tables for arguments in sentential logic. In the next section we will outline a short-cut method. Here, of course, we are interested in *validity* rather than truth value, though to determine validity via truth tables, one uses the truth values in accord with the truth tables. To that extent, truth values are essential.

Recall, once again, our definition of *validity*: An argument is valid if, and only if, it is impossible for the premises to be true while the conclusion is false. For our purposes, we can add to this definition the phrase "under any interpretation", and capture the sense of validity required by the method of truth tables. Below is an example of an invalid argument. Its premises are '(G → H)' and '-G'; its conclusion is '-H'. To analyze it by truth tables we set it up as follows, with '⊢' as our symbolic conclusion indicator:

(G → H)	-G	⊢	-H
t t t	f t		f t
f t t	t f		f t
t f f	f t		t f
f t f	t f		t f

Notice that in Interpretation 2, the premises are both true, but the conclusion is false. This shows that it is possible for this argument to have true premises and a false conclusion under at least one interpretation. Other arguments may have more than one interpretation under which the premises are true and the conclusion false, but one is enough to show invalidity. Since there are no degrees of validity or invalidity, one argument is not more invalid because it may have true premises and a false conclusion under two interpretations while another has true premises and a false conclusion under just one. Both arguments would be equally invalid. Likewise with arguments that have true premises and a false conclusion under no interpretation. They are equally valid. Consider the following argument:

(G → H)	-G	⊢	-H
t t t	f t		f t
f t t	f t		t f
t f f	t f		f t
f t f	t f		t f

In this argument, there is no interpretation under which the premises are true while the conclusion is false. Hence, the argument is valid.

And that is all there is to it. The arguments may be long or short, with as many components in the sentences making up the premises and conclusion as you please. As long as every combina-tion of truth values has been exhibited, one cannot fail to determine the validity of the argument. The reason this is so is because the concept of validity is like a grading system for *forms* of sentences purporting to entail a further sentence form. It does not matter which letters are present, whether capital letters from "A" to "Z", or 'p', 'q', 'r', and so on.

Take the form of the argument directly above, "plug in" any letters designating any sentences whatever, and it is guaranteed that *if* the premises of the argument are true, the conclusion will also be true. Further examples of valid and invalid arguments, analyzed via the method of truth tables, are:

```
(D • C)  ⊢   C          (K ↔ R)   R  ⊢   K
 t t t       t           t t t    t       t
 t f f       f           t f f    f       t
 f f t       t           f f t    t       f
 f f f       f           f t f    f       f

      Valid                    Valid
```

```
(S → B)  (W v -B)  ⊢  (-W → -S)       [ (-P v -O)  →  M]   -P  ⊢  M
 t t t    t t ft      ft t ft           ft f ft    t t     ft      t
 f t t    t t ft      ft t tf           ft f ft    t f     ft      f
 t t t    f f ft      tf f ft           ft t tf    t t     ft      t
 f t t    f f ft      tf t tf           ft t tf    f f     ft      f
 t f f    t t tf      ft t ft           tf t ft    t t     tf      t
 f t f    t t tf      ft t tf           tf t ft    f f     tf      f
 t f f    f t tf      tf f ft           tf t tf    t t     tf      t
 f t f    f t tf      tf t tf           tf t tf    f f     tf      f

           Valid                                    Valid
```

```
(V → F)  (-V → T)  ⊢  (T • -F)      -(Q → Z)  (-Z v O)  ⊢  --Z
 t t t    ft t t      t f ft         f t t t    ft t t      tft
 t t t    ft t f      f f ft         f t t t    ft f f      tft
 t f f    ft t t      t t tf         f f t t    ft t t      tft
 t f f    ft t f      f f tf         f f t t    ft f f      tft
 f t t    tf t t      t f ft         t t f f    tf t t      ftf
 f t t    tf f f      f f ft         t t f f    tf t f      ftf
 f t f    tf t t      t t tf         f f t f    tf t t      ftf
 f t f    tf f f      f f tf         f f t f    tf t f      ftf

          Invalid                             Invalid
```

(Y • S)	⊢	[(Y v N) • S]		-(A → Z)	(A v X)	(-X • -W)	⊢ Z
t t t		t t t	t t	f t t t	t t t	ft f ft	t
t t t		t t f	t t	t t f f	t t t	ft f ft	f
f f t		f t t	t t	f t t t	t t t	ft f tf	t
f f t		f f f	f t	t t f f	t t t	ft f tf	f
t f f		t t t	f f	f t t t	t t f	tf f ft	t
t f f		t t f	f f	t t f f	t t f	tf f ft	f
f f f		f t t	f f	f t t t	t t f	tf t tf	t
f f f		f f f	f f	t t f f	t t f	tf t tf	f
				f f t t	f t t	ft f ft	t
Valid				f f t f	f t t	ft f ft	f
		Invalid		f f t t	f t t	ft f tf	t
				f f t f	f t t	ft f tf	f
				f f t t	f f f	tf f ft	t
				f f t f	f f f	tf f ft	f
				f f t t	f f f	tf t tf	t
				f f t f	f f f	tf t tf	f

Exercise 6.4

A. Which of the following are true and which are false?

1 Equivalent sentences are always true under the same interpretations.

2 Incompatible sentences have differing truth values under all interpretations.

3 To analyze '[-(R v L) ↔ G]' using the truth table method will require eight rows or interpretations.

4 It is never proper to write two negation signs in a row since they would cancel each other out.

5* Disjunctions are false in one case only, that is, when both disjuncts are false.

6 It is false that an argument with five sentence components, to be analyzed via truth tables, needs thirty-two different interpretations.

7 To show an argument to be invalid using truth tables, one needs to locate at least two interpretations under which at least one of the premises is false while the conclusion is true.

8 Two arguments, one valid and one invalid, are said to be incompatible.

9 It is not true that a conditional is true when either the antecedent is false or the consequent is true.

10* A conditional is true whenever the antecedent is false.

11 A sentence form differs from a sentence in that the former is made up of components having no meaning while the latter contains only components designating sentences in natural language.

12 If 'A' = 'Alice is on the hill' and 'B' = 'Bill is on the hill', then the proper translation of 'Not both Bill and Alice are on the hill' would be: -(B v A).

13 In #7, if 'B' is known to be false but the value of 'A' is unknown, then it is impossible to logically determine the truth value of '-(B v A)'.

14 The one thing all conjunctions have in common is that they are true when at least one of the conjuncts is true.

15* One thing all self-contradictory sentences have in common is that when they are denied (negated), they become L-true.

B. Show which of the following arguments are valid, which invalid, by the method of truth tables.

1   (-R • R)   ⊢   G
2   (-R v R)   ⊢   G
3   (E • -W)   -(S ↔ -E)   (W v -E)   ⊢   S
4   {[(A → Q) • -(M → J)] → -Q}   ⊢   (J → A)
5* [(D → F) → O]   (D • -O)   ⊢   (F • -F)
6   (L → K)   (B v L)   (-B v P)   ⊢   -(-P • -K)
7   {(C → C) v [(C → C) • (C → C)]}   ⊢   -C
8   -T V -U   -(V → U)   ⊢   (-T v -U)
9   (G → -Y)   (-Y → H)   (H → G)   -(Y → -G)   ⊢   (H v -G)
10*[(E → J) • (I → I)]   E   [(J v -J) → (I → E)]   ⊢ [(E v -I) v -J]
11 [(D • X) ↔ -N]   (-X v -D)   ⊢   -N
12 [(E v G) • (E v F)]   ⊢   -[E • (G v F)]
13 (Z → -P)   [P → (K • Z)]   ⊢   (K v -Z)
14 (M → -I)   -(R v M)   [-R → (-M v I)]   ⊢   -I
15*{(B → A) → [B → (B• C)]}   -(-B → -B)   ⊢   (A v C)
16 [(D v R) → (R • E)]   [-(R v D) • E]   ⊢   -(E • R)
17 {[(K v W) v Z] v (-W • -Z)}   Z   ⊢   [W v (K v Z)]
18 -[(Y → U) • (U → Y)]   ⊢   [(Y • U) v (-U • -Y)]
19 (T → H)   (F → -H)   ⊢   [(F → T) → -H]
20*[(Gj → Gp) v (-Gj v Gg)]   --(-Gp • Gj)   ⊢ [(Gg v Gp) v -Gj]

C. Translate the following passages into symbolic notation. Each contains an argument. Determine which arguments are valid, which are invalid. Provide your own dictionary.

1   University fees will increase only if the Governor decides to reduce funds for welfare programs.   The Governor will make that decision if crime increases in San Diego.   Hence, university fees won't increase unless crime increases in San Diego.

2   It is false that big waves hitting the North Shore implies and is implied by high winds coming from the direction of Japan.   So, the waves will be small on the North Shore just in case there are no high winds coming from Japan.

3   Voting a Democratic ticket does not imply that one is a member of the pro-choice campaign.   Being a member of the pro-choice campaign doesn't imply that one believes abortion is morally permissible in all cases.   Hence, voting a democratic ticket doesn't imply that one believes abortion is morally permissible in all cases.

4   If one gives money to beggars, then the beggars will be encouraged to beg; and if one doesn't give money to beggars, then the beggars will not eat.   It is better that beggars eat than not eat.   Therefore, it is all right to give money to beggars.

5*   If truth is impossible to obtain, then we should give up the search and concentrate on more down to earth matters.   But, if it is possible to secure the truth, and if securing the truth would help us solve many "down to earth" matters, then we should pay people to search for the truth.   It is possible to know the truth and it is the job of the philosopher to seek it.   Hence, we should pay philosophers to search for the truth.

6   If Colleen enrolls in Romantic Literature, Renaissance Philosophy, and Survey of World War II, then she won't enroll in History of Science.   And since we know she won't enroll in the World War II course, it follows that she will enroll in the History of Science course.

7   Either Jane or Susan is in the warehouse.   But, they're not both in the warehouse.   If Susan is in the warehouse, then Christine is also in the warehouse.   If Jane is not in the warehouse, then neither is Chris. We know that Jane isn't in the warehouse, and so conclude that Susan is, though Chris isn't.

8   The sun will rise tomorrow just in case the earth continues to rotate on it axis.   The sun will not rise tomorrow only if the sun novas during the next twenty-four hour period.   The earth will continue on its axis and the sun will not nova.   Hence, the sun will rise tomorrow.

9   No artist will agree to show her/his work unless he/she can be assured that a suitable number of critics will be invited and asked to comment on the showing in the next issue of some popular magazine. It is a sufficient condition, to get any critic to show up at an art exhibit,

to provide free wine and cheese. Therefore, if any artist agrees to show her work, he/she also agrees to provide free wine and cheese.

10* Provided that the cost of the hotel in London is not too expensive and that the Britrail pass is good for eleven days, we will take our vacation in mid-October. If we cannot get away in October, then if the London hotel is too expensive, then we'll just stay in Edinburgh. We won't stay in Edinburgh unless we can visit Hume's birthplace. But, since no one knows exactly where Hume was born, we won't visit his birthplace. Hence, we'll take our vacation in October.

11 Jack and Art both believe there are ghosts. They are right if there really are ghosts. Now, neither Jack nor Art has ever seen a ghost, since ghosts, if they do exist, aren't the sorts of things that can be seen. Ghosts do exist, and hence, though Jack and Art are right about this, they believe without seeing.

12 A fetus conceived from human parents is a not a person but it is a human being, because a fetus conceived from human parents having a human genetic code is a sufficient condition for its being human and its being self-conscious is a necessary condition for its being a person. A fetus conceived from human parents is not self conscious, although it does have a human genetic code.

13 Carmen is one of the best staff persons at the university. We know this is so since if Carmen is one of the best, she can type well, file well, can answer important questions about who to contact about special problems, and inform the professors about curriculum deadlines; and Carmen can do all of these things.

14 If Jerry takes Intermediate Logic, and gets an "A", then if Pat takes Beginning Logic, then Terry will tutor Pat. If Jerry spends a lot of time with Pat, then Jerry and Pat will fall in love. Jerry will take Intermediate Logic and Pat will take Beginning Logic, and both will get "A's". Now, Jerry will tutor, and spend a lot of time with, Pat. Thus, Jerry and Pat will fall in love.

15* Either a conditional sentence is true when the consequent is true, or our truth table is incorrect. No reputable publisher of a logic book would let the truth table for the conditional be incorrect; the truth table is not incorrect. This leads to the conclusion that a conditional is true when the consequent is true.

6.5 Truth Tables: The Short-Cut Method

As we have seen, the method of truth tables can be quite effective for determining validity of arguments. This is especially so when the arguments we are working with are fairly simple, i.e., if the arguments contain, say, five components or less. But, as the number of components increases, so, the number of interpretations increases. If ten different components occur in an argument, the number of interpretations needed would be 1,024. Consider the following argument:

1 [(M v N) v (O v P)]
2 [(I • J) • (K → L)]
3 [(U • -V) v W]
4 [(E v F) • (G • H)]   ⊢   [(U v W) → -J]

If we were to attempt to determine the validity of this argument using full truth tables, we would employ literally thousands of interpretations. We need a method of proving its validity, or invalidity, that will allow us to accomplish the task in a reasonable length of time. Gladly, there is such a method.

Since all methods of using truth tables for determining validity rely on our conception of validity itself, let me state the principle of validity we have been using: *An argument is valid if, and only if, it is impossible for the premises to be true (under any given interpretation) while the conclusion is false (under the same interpretation).* The truth table short-cut method makes use of this principle, and no other.

The short-cut method is this: Attempt to assign truth values to the components in such a way which shows the argument to be *in*valid. First, assign truth values to the components in the conclusion which render the conclusion false. Second, assign consistent truth values to the components of the premises in an attempt to render each premise true. If there is any interpretation under which all the premises are true and the conclusion false, the argument is invalid. Conversely, if there is no interpretation under which the premises are true and the conclusion false, the argument is valid. In short, 1) show all the possible ways the conclusion is false, and 2) attempt to make each premise true. If you succeed for any interpretation, the argument is invalid.

Regarding the argument above, the conclusion is false under the following assignments of truth values to 'J', 'U', and 'W':

```
[ (U v W)  →  -J]
   t    t     ft
   f    t     ft
   t    f     ft
```

Notice that only premises (2) and (3) contain components found in the conclusion. Premise (2) can be rendered true by assigning 't' to each of the components as follows:

```
[ (I • J) • (K → L) ]
   t   t     t   t
```

Premise (3) is rendered true by assigning 't' to 'W', since if one disjunct in a disjunction is true, the disjunction is true. Here we see that the third interpretation in the conclusion above cannot now be used, since one must be consistent in the assignment of truth values and 'W' is assigned 'f' in that interpretation. At this point, as they say, it's academic. You simply assign 't' to each of the components found in each of the other premises.

On the assignment of the truth values that I have suggested for this complex argument, the argument is shown to be invalid. This is to say that we've found an interpretation in which each of the premises is true and the conclusion is false.

The following argument, and assignment of truth values, may help to clarify the method and the result. First, I state the argu-ment with the possible way(s) in which the conclusion is false. The conclusion is false in only one case, i.e., where 'R' is true.

```
[ (R → S)  v  -G]   (-S v G)   ⊢    -R
                                     ft
```

Second, begin attempting to render each premise true. The second premise is true where both 'H' and 'G' are true.

```
[ (R → S)  v  -G]   (-S v G)   ⊢    -R
                     ft t t           ft
```

[There are other truth value assignments that would make the second premise true, e.g., where 'S' is false and 'G' is true, but notice that this assignment would render the first premise false, which is contrary to what we're after. Also, assigning 'f' to both 'S' and 'G' would yield a true second premise, and it would also yield a true first premise.]

Third, the same truth value must be assigned to any given component at every occurrence of the component in a given interpretation. For example, if we were to assign 'f' to 'R' in the first premise, that would render the premise true, which is what we desire. However, this is an illicit move since 'R' was assigned 't' in the conclusion. The point is this: Since 'R', 'S' and 'G' have been assigned the value 't' in the second premise and the conclusion, these components must be assigned 't' in the first premise.

```
[(R → S) v -G]   (-S v G)   ⊢   -R
  t t t   t ft    ft t t         ft
```

Hence, we have found an interpretation under which each of the premises is true while the conclusion is false. The argument is invalid.

If we take the same argument, but replace the wedge in the second premise with a dot, we have a valid argument.

```
[(R → S) v -G]   (-S • G)   ⊢   -R
  t f f   f ft    tf t t         ft
```

Notice that there is only one assignment of truth values that will render the second premise true. That assignment of truth values necessitates a consistent assignment of truth values to the first premise, rendering it false. Hence, there is no interpretation under which the argument has all true premises and a false conclusion. Hence, the argument is valid.

Exercise 6.5

Determine whether the following arguments are valid or invalid using the truth table short-cut method.

```
1   (R v -D)   D      ⊢    R
2   (C → H)        ⊢      (H v -C)
3   (B • -N)       ⊢      (B → N)
4   [(S • Y) v (-S • X)]   ⊢    (Y • X)
5*  (O • K)    ⊢    (O ↔ K)
6   (O ↔ K)    ⊢    (O • K)
7   (L → G)   (G → I)    ⊢    (-L v I)
8   (K ↔ A)    ⊢    [(K → A) v C]
9   [(E v W) → -W]    ⊢    [E v (W → -W)]
10* [M → (D • -S)]   -M    ⊢    -(D • -S)
11  (K ↔ W)   -(-C → W)   ⊢ -K
12  [-(L → Q) • -(N → Q)]   -(-L • -N)   ⊢ (-Q v N)
```

13 [(-Z v -E) • -P]   (J → P)   (J v E)   ⊢ (Z • -J)
14 (F → Y)   [Y → (N → -U)]   -(D • R) → U   ⊢ [-Q • (U • L)]
15* (A → B)   [B → (C → E)]   ⊢   [(F ↔ C) → (I → E)]
16 [(G → R) • (U → H)]   (N → U)   [(R → N) • -H]   ⊢ -G
17 {[F → (T → F)] v [-F • (T → F)]}   ⊢   [(T • F) • (-T v -F)]
18 [(I ↔ J) ↔ (L ↔ P)] ⊢ -[(I → J) • (-I → -J)] ↔ (-L → -P)
19 (C → J)   [(J • E) → (L → P)]   (-E • -U)   ⊢ -C
20* (Sa → Se)   (Sc → Sr)   [(Se • Sr) → (Sg → Sn)]   -Sn
     ⊢ [-Sc v (Se → -Sg)]

6.6 Truth Trees

Thus far, we have examined two methods of testing arguments for validity. The first had to do with categorical propositions and with syllogisms. Our method involved appealing to rules and formal fallacies as well as with constructing Venn Diagrams. The second way of testing for validity concerned truth-functional sentences, connectives, and sentence components. The method we employed, i.e. truth tables, allowed us to determine whether any given argument had true premises and a false conclusion under at least one interpretation.

We saw, however, that while the truth table method is a purely mechanical and effective device, it can be laborious when the number of sentence letters contained in an argument is large. For instance, the following argument *could* be shown to be valid by constructing thirty-two rows (interpretations) and checking each row for all true premises and a false conclusion:

{-R → [(S v H) v E]}
[(S v E) v -P]   ⊢   (E • -S)

If there were ten letters, then 1,024 rows would have to be examined; the number of rows doubles with each new letter introduced. Even the truth table short-cut method would involve the quite lengthy process of examining each interpretation in which the conclusion is false.

The method of truth trees, for testing validity, works according to the same principle as all truth-functional methods for proving validity of arguments. The principle is this: *An argument is valid if, and only if, it is not possible for the premise(s) and the denial of the conclusion to be true at the same time (or under the same interpretation, in the same row...).* This amounts to saying that the premises cannot be true while the conclusion is false, or, that the conclusion is necessitated by the premise(s).

It suffices, then, to deny the conclusion and work for (try to derive) a contradiction, since a contradiction (p • -p) asserts that both conjuncts are true, which is impossible. (Recall that contra-dictions are false under all interpretations.) For truth trees, specifically, the objective is to derive a contradiction on each and every branch of the tree, according to the rules. If, after denying the conclusion, this can be accomplished, the original argument is said to be *valid*, and if not, *invalid*.

The premises and conclusion are listed in a single column. This column may be thought of as the "trunk" of the tree, from which the "branches" will grow. The growth of the tree is deter-mined by the nine rules below. Notice that there is but one rule for each type of sentence, i.e., the conjunction, the conditional, etc. *The rules require only a single application to any given formula found in an argument.* Hence, to remind yourself that a formula has had a rule applied to it, and to avoid unnecessary duplication, put a check [✓] beside each formula to which you apply a rule.

It should be noted that each sentence presented in an argument is given as true, i.e., is assumed to be true for the purpose of attempting to determine the validity of the argument itself. This is to say that there is never a question about a premise being true or false in actuality, but rather one is to keep in mind the definition of *validity* and ask: could the premises be true while the conclusion is false? If so, the argument is invalid.

Truth Tree Rules

Conjunction: If a conjunction [•] appears on a branch of the tree, put both conjuncts, in a line, on that branch.

Disjunction: If a disjunction [v] appears on a branch of the tree, divide the branch into two branches; put one disjunct on one branch and the other disjunct on the other branch.

Conditional: If a conditional [→] appears on a branch of the tree, divide the branch into two branches and put the negation of the conditional's antecedent on one branch and the consequent on the other branch.

Biconditional: If a biconditional [↔] appears on a branch of a tree, divide the branch into two branches, putting both components of the biconditional on one branch and their negations on the other branch.

Double Negation: If a double negation [--] appears on a branch of a tree, put the formula that is doubly negated on that branch.

Negated Conjunction: If a negated conjunction [-•] appears on a branch of a tree, divide the branch into two branches and put the negation of one conjunct on one branch and the negation of the other conjunct on the other branch.

Negated Disjunction: If a negated disjunction [-v] appears on a branch of a tree, put the negations of both disjuncts on that branch.

Negated Conditional: If a negated conditional [-→] appears on a branch of a tree, put both its antecedent and the negation of its consequent on that branch.

Negated Biconditional: If a negated biconditional [-↔] appears on a branch of a tree, divide the branch into two branches and put the first component together with the negation of the second compon-ent on one branch and put the negation of the first component together with the second component on the other branch.

Schemata for, and justification of, the rules

Conjunction:

$$(p \bullet q)$$
$$p$$
$$q$$

There is only one case where a conjunction is true, viz., when *both* of its conjuncts are true. Hence, where '(p • q)' is true on any branch, 'p' is true and 'q' is true on that branch.

Notice the correspondence between the truth tree rule for con-junction and the truth table for the conjunction. Recall the table:

$$(p \bullet q)$$
t t t
t f f
f f t
f f f

When a conjunction appears on a branch, it is given as constituting a true sentence. That is, the conjunction itself is presumed to be true and hence both conjuncts are presumed true. Again, there is only one instance where the entire conjunction is true, and that is shown in row #1 in the table above. Since both conjuncts must be true for the conjunction itself to be true, the truth tree rule records each conjunct as true on the same branch.

Negated conjunction:

A conjunction is false whenever at least one of its conjuncts is false. Note that in the truth table for conjunction above, there are three instances wherein the conjunction itself is false. Since in truth trees we are not assigning truth values to the components of our formulas, we cannot say which component is true, which is false. For a negated conjunction, dividing the branch into two branches is as much as to say that at least one of the components *is* false. Where '(p • q)' is true, either '-p' or '-q' is false, and perhaps both are false.

Disjunction:

A disjunction is true whenever at least one of its disjuncts is true. For the disjunction, dividing the branch into two branches is as much as to say that at least one, if not both, of its disjuncts is true. Where '(p v q)' is true, either 'p' or 'q' is true, and perhaps both are true.

$$(p \ v \ q)$$
$$t \ t \ t$$
$$t \ t \ f$$
$$f \ t \ t$$
$$f \ f \ f$$

Note the correspondence between the truth tree rule for disjunc-tion and the truth table above. The table shows the disjunction to be true in three instances, i.e., rows #1, #2, and #3. Dividing the branch into two branches tokens each of the three possible inter-pretations under which the disjunction may be true.

Negated disjunction:

$$-(p \ v \ q)$$
$$-p$$
$$-q$$

There is only one case where a negated disjunction is true, namely, when both disjuncts are false. A negated disjunction is true in the one instance where the disjunction itself is false. Where '-(p v q)' is true on any branch, '-p' and '-q' are both true on that branch and hence should be written on the branch. The appearance of '-(p v q)' in a tree is to be construed as constituting a true occurrence of '-(p v q)'. This is so for each occurrence of any formula appearing in an argument, as well as for each occurrence of any formula in a proof that is derived by applying appropriate rules. This will become apparent as we proceed.

Conditional:

A conditional is true just in case its antecedent is false or its consequent is true. Compare the truth tree rule with the table below. For a conditional, dividing the branch into two branches is as much as to say that either the antecedent 'p' is false *or* the consequent 'q' is true, and perhaps the antecedent is false *and* the consequent is true, as in row #3 of the table for the conditional.

```
(p → q)
 t  t  t
 t  f  f
 f  t  t
 f  t  f
```

Negated conditional:

```
-(p → q)
    p
   -q
```

As we know, there is only one instance where a conditional is false, viz., when the antecedent is true and the consequent is false. Note row #2 in the above truth table. Hence, where '-(p → q)' is true on any branch, 'p' and '-q' will both be true on that branch.

Biconditional:

A biconditional is true when the components have the same truth values. Note the table below. In rows #1 and #4, 'p' and 'q' have the same truth values, as do rows #2 and #3. Dividing the branch into two branches is as much as to say that either both com-ponents are true or both components are false. Where '(p ↔ q)' is true, either 'p' *and* 'q' are true, or '-p' *and* '-q' are true.

```
(p ↔ q)
 t  t  t
 t  f  f
 f  f  t
 f  t  f
```

Negated biconditional:

A biconditional is false just in case the components have opposing truth values. Note the table above. In rows #2 and #3, 'p' and 'q' have opposite truth values, rendering the biconditional itself false. Where a biconditional is false, the negated bicon-ditional is true. Dividing the branch into two branches is as much as to say that where '-(p ↔ q)' is true, either 'p' *and* '-q' are true, or '-p' *and* 'q' are true.

Double Negation:
$$--p$$
$$p$$

The truth table for the double negation is:
$$--p$$
$$tft$$
$$ftf$$

Where '- -p' is true, 'p' is also true, and where '- -p' is false, 'p' is also false. The rule for double negation is very convenient although in some cases it is, strictly speaking, unnecessary. Take the following example: (- - -G → - -N).
Applying the rule for the conditional here yields:

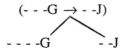

Now, '- - -G' contradicts '- -G' and is contradicted by '- - - -G'. So, if '- - -G' were to occur by itself under some interpretation connected with '- - - -G', that branch *could* be closed. But don't close it, because 1) we have the rule for double negation, and 2) every attempt should be made to simplify formulas to allow for convenient inspection. The rule for double negation applies to the formula '- - - -G' in the following way:

$$- - - -G$$
$$- -G$$
$$G$$

One further point of form may be helpful. It is strictly illicit to move from '(- - -G → - -J)' to '(-G → - -J)' or to '(- - -G → J)' or to '(-G → J)'.

This is because '(- - -G → - -J)' is a conditional, and only the rule for the conditional may be applied to it.

It may be convenient to think of a divided branch as indicating that there is more than one instance (case, interpretation) in which the given formula is true (or false, where applicable). When a branch extends undivided, the indication is that a given formula is true (or false) in one case only. The two trees below illustrate this.

```
    [(-P • A) • -N]    ✔1
      -(-P v N)        ✔2
         -P           D.C.
       (-P • A)        ✔3
         -N
         --P
         -N                    Valid
         -P
         A
         X
```

```
    -(R → G)  ✔1
    -[(L • O) → J]  ✔2
         -O     D.C.
         R
         -G
      (L • O)  ✔3
         L
         O                    Valid
         X
```

Now let us walk through a more detailed truth tree.

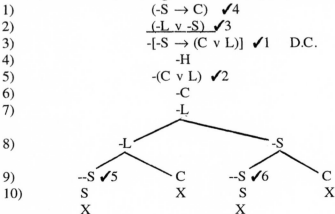

```
1)              (-S → C)   ✔4
2)              (-L v -S)  ✔3
3)              -[-S → (C v L)]  ✔1    D.C.
4)              -H
5)              -(C v L)  ✔2
6)              -C
7)              -L
```

The above steps have been numbered solely for convenience of explanation. The premises are located in (1) and (2).

As indicated by 'D.C.' to the far right in (3), the conclusion, which is '-S → (C v L)', has been denied. It would not suffice to deny the conclusion by writing '--S → (C v L)', because the conclusion is a conditional, not a negation. Hence the brackets.

Strictly speaking, it does not matter which formula you apply the rules to first, second, third, etc. I have chosen to work with the denial of the conclusion first because, upon examining the argu-ment, I saw that I could extend the trunk of the tree rather than make new branches. The end result, i.e., your discovery of the validity or the invalidity of the argument, is independent of the order in which the rules are applied. The correctness of your applications is primary.

Lines (4) and (5) are the result of one step, i.e., the rule for negated conditional was applied to the denial of the conclusion (3). Since a negated conditional is true only when the conditional's antecedent is true and its consequent false, I continued the "trunk" of the tree by writing the antecedent, '-S', in (4), and by also writing the denial of the consequent, '-(C v L)', in (5). At this point, since the formula in line (3) has had a rule applied to it, a check (✓) was written beside the formula.

When a formula is checked, assign the appropriate numerical subscript to the checkmark. Since the denied conclusion is the first formula to which a rule was applied, it is checked with the number '1', i.e., [✓1].

Questions: Does a contradiction appear on any branch? No. Are there formulas to which rules have yet to be applied, that is formulas which can be checked but which have not been checked? Yes. Then continue to apply the rules.

Lines (6) and (7) have resulted, again, from one step, viz., the rule for negated disjunction has been applied to the formula in (5). Since a disjunction is false only when both disjuncts are false, the trunk has been once again extended, but this time by denying each disjunct in the negated disjunction. Line (5) was checked, with the appropriate number, since a rule was applied to it.

Are there any contradictions yet? No. Have all formulas containing connectives been checked? No. Then continue.

Line (8) is the result of applying the rule for disjunction to line (2). Since a disjunction is true if at least one of its disjuncts is true, we divide the branch into two branches and write one disjunct, '-L', on one branch, and the other disjunct, '-S', on the other branch. Line (2) is now checked and numbered.

Contradictions? No. All formulas checked? No. Continue.

Line (9) is the result of applying the rule for the conditional to line (1). [It is important to note that any result of applying a rule must extend to *every open branch* of the tree under the interpretation with which you are working.] Since a conditional is true if either the antecedent is false or the consequent is true, (9) consists in four branches which stem from the two branches in (8), with each set of two branches in (9) consisting in the negation of (1)'s antecedent, '--S', and with consequent of (1), i.e., 'C'. (1) is checked and numbered.

There are now contradictions on the tree. In (9), 'C' appears on two branches, albeit in different interpretations. But '-C' appears in (6). Since 'C' and '-C' are contradictories [cannot both be true at the same time *and* cannot both be false at the same time], we can *close* both branches in (9) where 'C' appears alone. To close a branch, place an 'X' directly below the last formula (sentence letter) appearing on that branch.

Strictly speaking, we can close all the branches in (9). However, since we have the convenient rule for double negation, we replace every occurrence of '--S' in (9) with 'S' in (10). Check, with the appropriate numbers, each occurrence of '--S' in (9).

There are only two branches in (10), each containing 'S'. Since '-S' appears in (4) and (8), there are contradictions found on both branches in (10), which can be **closed** by putting an 'X' directly below the last formula (in this case "sentence letter" 'S') in each.

We see that there are now no open branches in the tree. Hence. the original argument is *valid*.

The steps to follow in constructing truth trees are as follows:

1   List formulas in order
2   Deny the conclusion
3   Search for trunk extension
4   Apply a rule to a formula
5   Check and number the formula
6   Search for contradictions
7   If no contradictions are found, and if there are one or more formulas unchecked, return to #4 and proceed.
8   If one or more contradictions are found, close each branch on which one *is* found.
9   For each remaining open branch, return to #4 and proceed.

10 When all formulas are checked and numbered, search for open branches.
11 If there are no open branches, designate the argument valid.
12 If there is at least one open branch, write a ring under the last letter appearing on the branch and designate the argument valid.

Further examples of truth trees are below. It is easier to "read" a tree if you will go by the numbers. As indicated above, check-1 (✔1) marks the place where the first rule was applied to a sentence in the argument.

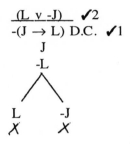

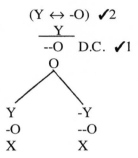

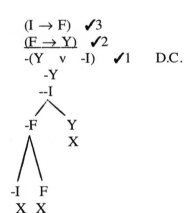

[(-E v H) • -J] ✔2
[-H • (B v E)] ✔3
--E   ✔1   D.C.
E
(-E v H)   ✔4
-J
-H
(B v E)

-E   H
X   X

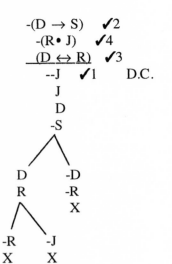

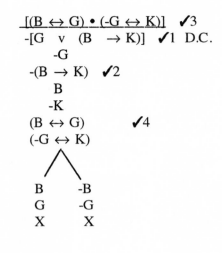

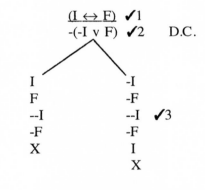

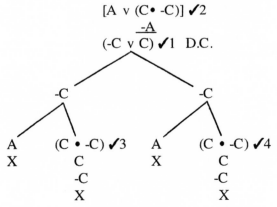

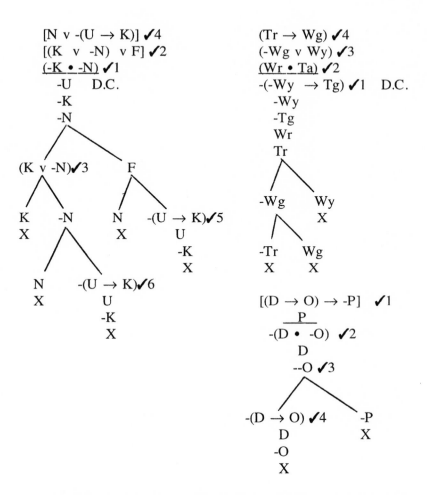

[N v -(U → K)] ✓4
[(K v -N) v F] ✓2
(-K • -N) ✓1
   -U   D.C.
   -K
   -N

(K v -N)✓3   F

K   -N   N   -(U → K)✓5
X   X   U
                  -K
                  X

   N   -(U → K)✓6
   X   U
        -K
        X

(Tr → Wg) ✓4
(-Wg v Wy) ✓3
(Wr • Ta) ✓2
-(-Wy → Tg) ✓1   D.C.
   -Wy
   -Tg
   Wr
   Tr

  -Wg   Wy
          X

-Tr   Wg
X   X

[(D → O) → -P] ✓1
   P
-(D • -O) ✓2
  D
  --O ✓3

-(D → O) ✓4   -P
  D   X
  -O
  X

The following truth tree shows the invalidity of an argument:

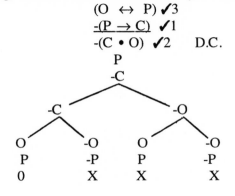

(O ↔ P) ✓3
-(P → C) ✓1
-(C • O) ✓2   D.C.
   P
   -C

   -C   -O

O   -O   O   -O
P   -P   P   -P
0   X   X   X

The result of applying the truth tree rule for the biconditional to the formula in line (1) led to four branches (interpretations) in lines (7) and (8). Three of these branches are closed. The other branch is said to be **open** because all the rules that *can* be applied to the formulas *have been* applied and no contradiction is found on that branch. To indicate an open branch, write a ring, '**0**', directly below the last formula appearing on the branch.

We will count any argument to be *invalid* just in case at least one branch remains open when all formulas containing connectives have been checked. Further examples of truth trees follow:

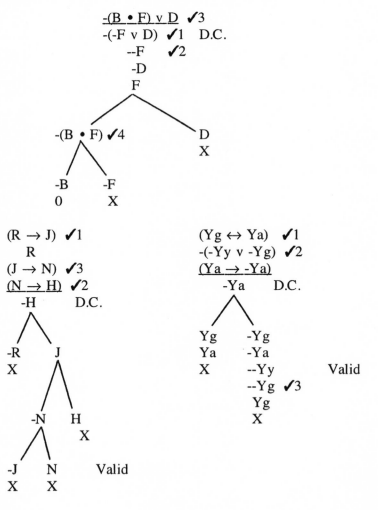

[-L → (S v E)] • [(-L • -E) → -S]
(H v S) • -(S • -E) ✓2
-[(E v S) v (E v L)] ✓1   D.C.
   -(E v S) ✓3
   -(E v L) ✓4
   (L v S) ✓5
   -(S • -E)
     -E
     -S
     -E
     -L

Valid

    L   S
    X   X

*Note here that not all formulas that can be checked have been checked. This is all right since all the branches close.

6.7   THE LOGICAL STATUS OF SENTENCES

As noted in Chapter 5, sentences are either logically true, or logically false, or logically indeterminate. This section is designed to show you how to determine, via truth trees, the logical status of sentences. To determine that a given sentence is a truth of logic, i.e., L-true, construct a tree for the negation of the sentence. The sentence is L-true just in case the tree closes (each of its branches closes). 'S.D.' indicates that the sentence has been denied. Examples:

<u>Zero premises</u>
-(-R → -R) ✓1   S.D.
   -R
   --R ✓2
    R
    X   L-true

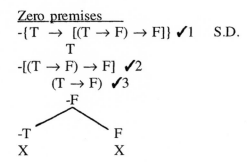

L-true

The above tree is sufficient to show that 'T → [(T → F) → F]' is a logical truth. The writing of 'zero premises' is merely a convention used to augment the formality of the proof.

The vital first move in the proof is the denying of the sentence to be shown to be tautologous. The essential reasoning is this: If some sentence 'S' is L-true, then if 'S' is denied, then '-S' will prove to be self-contradictory. This is precisely what has been achieved in the above tree, since all (both) branches close. Consider '-[(-A v B) • -(-B → -A)]'.

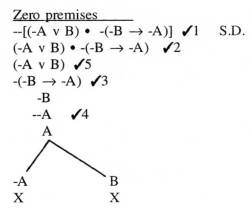

To determine whether a given sentence is L-false, construct a tree for the sentence itself. That is, do a tree without denying the sentence. It is L-false just in case the tree closes. Example:

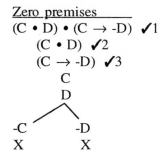

The above tree suffices to show that '[(C • D) • (C → -D)]' is self-contradictory, since contradictions have been found on all branches without denying the sentence itself.

To show that some sentence 'S' is neither logically true nor logically false, construct two trees, one for 'S' and one for '-S'. If neither tree closes, 'S' is said to be L-indeterminate. The following two truth trees will show '[(P • Q) ↔ (Q v P)]' to be neither L-true nor L-false. The first tree will prove the former; the second tree will prove the latter. If a sentence is neither L-true nor L-false, then it is L-indeterminate.

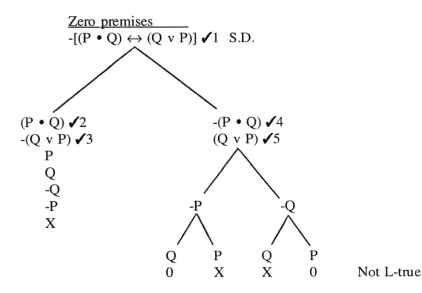

The major connective in the sentence '[(P • Q) ↔ (Q v P)]' is the double arrow, so the sentence is a biconditional. In the first tree, the sentence was denied, rendering the sentence a negated biconditional. The rule for the negated biconditional must be applied as the first move.

In the second tree, the sentence is not denied. Hence, the first move of the second tree is to apply the rule for the biconditional to the sentence itself. Here is that tree.

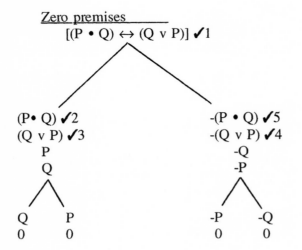

Zero premises
[(P • Q) ↔ (Q v P)] ✓1

(P• Q) ✓2   -(P • Q) ✓5
(Q v P) ✓3   -(Q v P) ✓4
    P   -Q
    Q   -P

  Q   P   -P   -Q
  0   0   0   0   Not L-false

Further examples of truth trees are below.

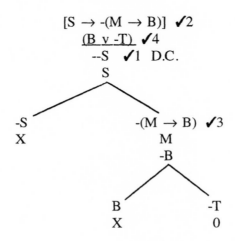

[S → -(M → B)] ✓2
(B v -T) ✓4
--S ✓1 D.C.
S

-S   -(M → B) ✓3
X   M
                      -B

                  B   -T
                  X   0

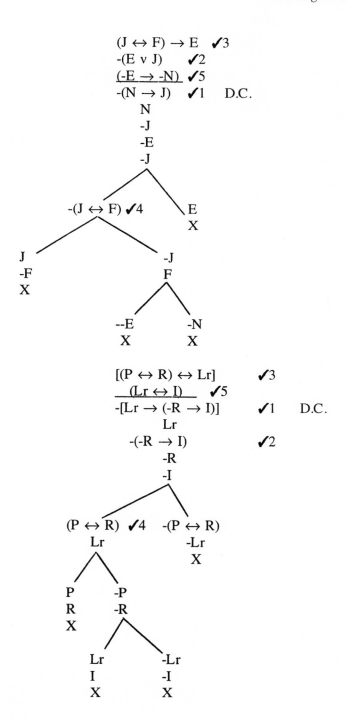

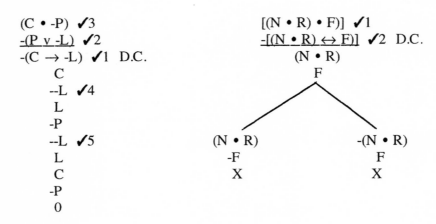

(C • -P) ✓3
-(P v -L) ✓2
-(C → -L) ✓1 D.C.
  C
  --L ✓4
  L
  -P
  --L ✓5
  L
  C
  -P
  0

[(N • R) • F)] ✓1
-[(N • R) ↔ F)] ✓2 D.C.
  (N • R)
  F

(N • R)   -(N • R)
-F   F
X   X

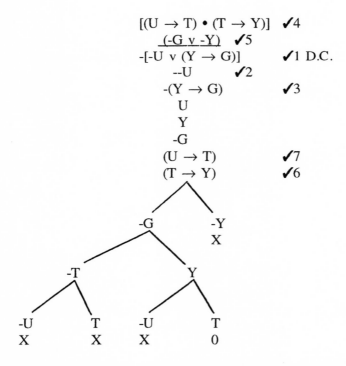

[(U → T) • (T → Y)] ✓4
  (-G v -Y) ✓5
-[-U v (Y → G)] ✓1 D.C.
  --U ✓2
  -(Y → G) ✓3
  U
  Y
  -G
  (U → T) ✓7
  (T → Y) ✓6

-G   -Y
      X

-T   Y

-U T -U T
X   X   X   0

The tree above is a good example showing that if even one branch is open, then the argument is invalid. To reiterate, the conclusion was denied and contradictions were not found on *every* branch. Hence, it is possible that the premises may be true and the conclusion false.

Exercises 6.6 and 6.7

A. Use truth trees to determine whether the following arguments are valid or invalid.

1 (R v T)
   (-R → T)

2 (L • -U)
   (U → I)

3 (-F → C)
   (C → F)

4 (J → E)
   (-E → -J)

5* (D • O)
    (D v O)

6 (A ↔ W)
   (A → W)

7 (K ↔ L)
   (K v L)
   (L • K)

8 (B • T) → Y
   (-B → M)
   L → (M v N)

9 S • (-F v G)
   (-F → -S)
   (F → F)
   F

10* (U → C)
     (C v P)
     (-U → P)
     (-P → -C) v U

11 (R v S) → Z
    (Z v R)

12 O v (Y • G)
    (-G v -Y)
    O

13 (B ↔ D)
    -D
    B → (C v -E)

14 -(K → -L) → M
    -L v (M v -K)

15* (I → F)
     (P → -Q)
     (Q v -I)
     -(U ↔ P)
     -[(P • -Q) ↔ (-U • P)]

16 -[(V • N) v T] → -S
    (V • N) → -S
    (E → -T)
    -(S → -E)

17 (A v B) → (C • D)
    (D v F) → G
    (A ↔ G)

18 (C → J)
    J → [(L → --L) → K]
    --C → --K

19 Ra → (Rb • Rc)
    Rd → (Ra v Re)
    <u>-Rc</u>
    (Rd → Rb)

20* (-Raa → Rcg) v -Rc
    (Rc → Rd) v Rcg
    <u>(Rcg → -Rd) ↔ -Raa</u>
    (-Rc v Raa)

B. Use truth trees to determine the logical status of the following sentences.   Some are L-true, some are L-false and some are L-indeterminate.

1   N → -(C → -N)
2   S → (-S → S)
3   ((S → -S) → S)
4   (H v -H) • (-H • A)
5* -(M ↔ T) ↔ (-M ↔ T)
6   (F → -T) → (-T → -F)
7   (-T → F) • (-F v -T)
8   [W v (W • Z)] ↔ W
9   -[(-P → P) • -(P → -P)]
10* -[-(E • E) → -E]
11 {[(R → U) • R] ↔ U}
12 (K → -B) ↔ (B • K)
13 (J ↔ -D) ↔ [-D ↔ (J v -W)]
14 -{(O → F) → [-F → (O → -Y)]}
15* (J v -C) → (C → -J)
16 -{[(-S → E) • -Z → (Z → -E)}
17 -[-(W v Y) v -(Y → -W)]
18 (Hr → Vw) → [(Hr • Vn) → (Vw • Vn)]
19 [B → (D • F)] → {[(F v G) → K] → (B → K)}
20* (A ↔ (-Z v -N)) ↔ (-Z → (N • -A))
21 ((E ↔ T) • -M) → (M → (T • -E))
22 (Q → (P → L)) → ((Q → P) → (Q → L))
23 (J • -J) → ((T → J) → (-T → -J))
24 (-(Y → I) • (D • -A)) • ((I v -Y) v ((D • R) → A))
25* -[(-M → -N) v O] ↔ {[(O → -N) → (M → O)] → -M}
26 (((G v S) • (I v -G)) • (((-I • -C) • -C) • -S))
27 {(B → -E) • [E → (T • B)]} → (T v -B)
28 -((--K ↔ --J) → ((-Q v (-K → -J)) • (K → J)))
29 [(Cy v Cc) → Rn] ↔ [(Rn • -Ws) v -Cy]
30* (Rs ↔ -Sr) ↔ [Rs ↔ (Sr ↔ Ri)]

C. Provide a dictionary for each of the following arguments and translate the arguments into symbolic notation. Use the method of truth trees to determine validity or invalidity.

    1   Oahu's North Shore attracts the world's best surfers if, and only if, the North Shore has the world's biggest rideable waves. The waves on the North Shore are definitely the biggest rideable waves in the world. Hence, if the North Shore attracts the world's best surfers, then the best surfers in the world are also attracted to the surf in California.

    2   If compact discs provide the best possible listening enjoyment, then cassettes will slowly lose market shares. If cassettes lose market shares, then the car stereo business will be turned on its head. Therefore, either the car stereo business will be turned on its head or compact discs do not provide the best possible listening enjoyment.

    3   Taylor Payne's seeking another term in office entails that a Republican won't be elected. But if another Democrat wants to be Senator of California, then it certainly won't be Rick Arno. If no other Democrat seeks office, Payne will seek another term. It follows that a Republican being elected implies Arno's not wanting to be Senator.

    4   Either Sisley was a great artist or half of the art critics in the Western world aren't very critical. If R.C. Gorman isn't a great artist, then Sisley wasn't a great artist. Hence, Gorman is a great artist provided that half of the critics are critical.

    5*   The physics major learns much about the ultimate constituents of matter and the literature major learns much about the constituents of fine poetry and prose, unless the physics and literature teachers are unhappy with their jobs. If a physics teacher is happy at work, then the physics teacher's colleagues will be happy and the physics majors will learn much. If the college president is neither a physics teacher nor a literature teacher, then both the physics and literature teachers are happy. The president is a physics teacher. Hence, the literature majors learn much.

    6   If Jed Towne retires next year and Ernie Semeck completes over 43% of his passes, the Cossacks will lose in the Super Bowl. The Cossacks winning is implied by Semeck's completing less than 43% of his passes. Semeck never completes 43% of his passes. So, Semeck won't complete 43% and Towne won't retire.

    7   Hindu mystics believe either in God or in a nonpersonal Unity. If the Hindu mystic has had a religious mystical experience, then the mystic believes in God; however, if the mystic has never had a religious

mystical experience, then the mystic won't believe in God but a nonpersonal Unity. No Hindu mystic has ever had a religious mystical experience. We can conclude that no Hindu mystic believes in God.

8   If Rodin's "Balzac" is the most beautiful statue in existence, then Rodin was the greatest sculptor who ever lived. Its not being the case that both Rodin was the greatest sculptor and that Michelangelo wasn't the greatest sculptor who ever lived implies that "Balzac" is indeed the most beautiful statue in existence. It follows that Rodin was the greatest sculptor.

9   One's being an ethical relativist entails one's believing that any ethical theory is as good as any other. One's being an ethical absolutist implies that one believes there are actions which are right independent of how anybody perceives the world. If anyone views the world from a moral perspective, then that person is a relativist or an absolutist. Everyone views the world from a moral perspective. Hence, everyone believes either that any theory is as good as any other, or that there are no actions which are right no matter how anyone perceives the world.

10*   If Fredricka is either a Republican or a Libertarian, then if Fredricka is a feminist, then she is a liberal. If she is not a feminist or is a socialist, then if she is Republican, she is either a moderate or a conservative. Fredricka is either a feminist or a Republican. But, she isn't a feminist. Thus, Fredricka is a liberal, and either a moderate or a conservative.

11   If Jess has much leisure time and likes to watch game shows on T.V., then Jess is either unproductive or is a fast worker. If Jess is productive or independently wealthy, he has much leisure time. If Jess is productive or has a very limited taste for fine entertainment, then he likes to watch game shows. Jess is not only productive, but the best judge of his own entertainments. It follows from the above that Jess is a fast worker.

12   If London continues to sink one-half inch per year, then by the year 2050 Picadilly Circus will be under water. If the River Thames continues to rise, London will continue to sink. If something is done about the blockages at the mouth of the Thames, London won't continue to sink. If Picadilly goes under water, tourism in London will be destroyed. But we know that tourism in London will never be destroyed. Thus, London will not continue to sink.

13   If the antecedent to this conditional is false, the conditional is true. The conditional's being true implies that language is paradoxical. But language is not paradoxical.   The antecedent to this conditional is

false provided that it is true that English is whimsical. Either English is whimsical or the antecedent to this conditional is false. Therefore, either language is paradoxical or language is paradoxical.

14 If it rains for more than three days, Highway 299 will be closed. If a high pressure ridge rolls in and the wind blows from the southwest, then it will rain for more than three days. If 299 closes, Highway 101 will close. But Highway 101 won't close. Hence, either no high pressure ridge will come in or the wind won't blow from the southwest.

15* Either the U.S. Ambassador to Ireland won't both reside in Dublin and import British goods for use at the embassy, or will win the hearts of the Irish people. If she wins the hearts of the Irish people, then if the ambassador does import British goods, the Irish Republican Army will demand her removal as ambassador. If the ambassador doesn't care what the IRA thinks, she will live in Dublin and buy British goods. She really doesn't care what the IRA thinks. Thus, the IRA will demand her removal.

16 If logic is necessary for adequate thinking, then good thinkers use logic. If good thinkers use logic, then logic is useful. Either logic is necessary or good thinkers use logic. Therefore, not only is logic necessary or useful, but if it is necessary, then it is also useful.

17 If the laws of science are merely probable, then the safety of home appliances is doubtful, since appliances have arisen from technology based on sets of laws of science. If science is progressive or always changing, then the laws of science are only probable. Science *is* always changing, but some things never change. We can conclude that the safety of home appliances is doubtful.

18 The President will go to Congress and praise them or the President will go to Congress and scold them. If the President goes to Congress or proposes a "*New* New Deal", Congress will laugh at the President. Therefore, Congress will laugh at the President.

19 Either California's secession from the Union implies that its leaders believe it to be financially equipped for such a move, or California's movie moguls will continue their lobbying in Sacramento and will finally win the battle for lower taxes for film companies. The moguls won't both continue their lobbying and win the battle for lower taxes. However, California leaders do not believe California is financially stable enough to leave the Union. Hence, California won't secede from the Union.

20* Being morally responsible for one's actions implies both that one is rational and that one has free will. If one's not being rational implies that one is a nonperson, then one will certainly have no moral rights. Therefore, one has no moral rights only if one is not morally responsible for one's actions.

7. Sentential Logic C
Natural Deduction

7.1 *Preliminaries*

The final method for showing arguments to be valid is known as the method of Natural Deduction. This method involves deriving a conclusion on the last line of a proof, from a specified set of premises, using a specified number of rules.

We have used various schema to set up arguments up to this point. In syllogistic logic the format we used was:

All roses are flowering plants   Premise
All flowering plants contain chlorophyll.   Premise
So, all roses contain chlorophyll.   Conclusion.

In working out truth tables, the format was:

$(R \rightarrow S)$ $(-S \vee T)$ $(R \vee T)$ $\vdash$ $-R$
  ↑   ↑   ↑   ↑
Premise   Premise   Premise $\vdash$ Conclusion.

For truth trees, we set up arguments in this fashion:

$(-B \vee -R)$ Premise
$(--H \vee -N)$ Premise
<u>$(R \bullet --B)$</u>   Premise
   H   Conclusion

In natural deduction our schema is:

  1. Premise
  2. Premise
  3. Premise $\vdash$ Conclusion.

Each premise is numbered. The conclusion appears in two places in a proof in natural deduction, viz, once on the same line as the last premise of the argument, and once as the formula appearing on the last line of the proof itself. The following symbolized valid argument is represented in the method of natural deduction:

1. (B v -E)
2. [B → (C → D)]
3. [(B • C) → D]   ⊢   [(E • C) → D]

One of the curious things about the method of natural deduction is that it does not allow one to show any argument to be invalid. Since one is trying to derive a conclusion from a set of premises using some rules, and since the rules do not allow for drawing an illegitimate inference by their use, it follows that, using the rules correctly, one could never make an illegitimate inference, which is what an invalid argument does. The practical moral here is that if one spends a great deal of time attempting to prove some argument to be valid using natural deduction, and if one is having trouble showing it to be valid, it may be wise to check its validity via some other method, e.g., truth tables or truth trees. The person who tries to show that some invalid argument is valid is engaged in a task that cannot be completed. Natural deduction is a method for showing arguments to be valid, it is not a method for showing arguments to be invalid. For all that, however, one must not count as wasted the time one worked on the invalid argument trying to show it to be valid. At very least, one will have been attempting to use the rules to derive the conclusion, and to that extent will have become just that much more acquainted with the rules themselves and their possible uses. To work well in natural deduction, it is requisite that one have a ready apprehension of and an ability to apply the rules to the formulas presented. To that end, practice is indispensable.

7.2 Rules of Inference

The primary rules are typically called "rules of inference". We will follow this practice. In what follows, the rules of inference are stated first in English, then in schematic form.

The rule **Modus Ponens** states that 1) when a conditional statement exists on a separate line and 2) when the antecedent to the conditional exists alone on a separate line, then 3) the consequent may be written on a further line.

The rule **Modus Tollens** states that 1) when a conditional statement exists on a separate line, and 2) when the negated consequent to that conditional exists alone on a separate line, then 3) the negated antecedent may be written on a further line.

The rule **Hypothetical Syllogism** states that 1) when two conditionals each exist on separate lines and 2) when identical statements comprise the antecedent of one of the conditionals and the consequent of the other conditional, then 3) a third conditional statement may be written on a further line comprised of the two components in the original conditionals which are not the original identical components, the antecedent of the third conditional being the antecedent in one of the original conditionals and the consequent of the third conditional being the consequent of the other original conditional.

The rule **Disjunctive Syllogism** states that 1) when a disjunction exists on a separate line, and 2) when the negation of the first disjunct exists on a line by itself, then 3) the second disjunct may be written on a further line.

The rule **Constructive Dilemma** states that 1) when a conjunction, having as its conjuncts conditional statements, exists on a separate line and 2) when a disjunction, the disjuncts of which are identical to the antecedents of the conditionals in the conjunction, exists on a separate line, then 3) another disjunction may be written on a further line, the disjuncts of which are identical to the consequents of the conditionals in the conjunction. The rule Addition states that when any statement (atomic or molecular) exists on a line, then a further statement may be written, on a separate line, in the form of a disjunction in which the original statement appears as the first disjunct.

The rule **Simplification** states that when a conjunction exists on a separate line, then the first (left-hand) conjunct may be written on a further line.

The rule **Conjunction** states that when any two statements exist on separate lines, then a further statement may be written, on a separate line, in the form of a conjunction in which the original two statements appear as conjuncts.

In schema for the primary rules of inference are as follows:

Modus Ponens (MP):

$(p \rightarrow q)$
p ⊢ q

Modus Tollens (MT):

$(p \rightarrow q)$
-q ⊢ -p

Hypothetical Syllogism (HS):

$(p \rightarrow q)$
$(q \rightarrow r)$ ⊢ $(p \rightarrow r)$

Disjunctive Syllogism (DS):

$(p \vee q)$
-p ⊢ q

Constructive Dilemma (CD):

$(p \to q) \cdot (r \to s)$
$(p \lor r)$ $\vdash$ $(q \lor s)$

Addition (Ad):

$p \vdash (p \lor q)$

Simplification (Si):

$(p \cdot q) \vdash p$

Conjunction (Con):

p
q $\vdash$ $(p \cdot q)$

The first rule of natural deduction is usually said to be *modus ponens*. The following arguments each have the form of MP.

If Matthew plays golf at Torrey Pines Golf Club, then Matthew is a good golfer. Matthew will play at Torrey Pines. Therefore, Matthew is a good golfer.

$(T \to G)$
T $\vdash$ G

Anna will be happy only if she studies literature or biology. Anna will be happy. Hence, she'll study literature or biology.

$[A \to (L \lor B)]$
A $\vdash$ $(L \lor B)$

Jay's traveling through the Milky Way only if he becomes an astronaut implies that he doesn't get space-sickness very easily. Jay will travel through the Milky Way only if he becomes an astronaut. It follows that Jay doesn't get space-sick easily.

$(M \to A) \to -S$
$(M \to A)$ $\vdash$ $-S$

That Moira won't both become a Supreme Court Justice and President of the American Civil Liberties Union (ACLU) is implied by the fact that being a Supreme Court Justice and being President of the ACLU each takes all of one's time and energy. Being a Supreme Court Justice and being President of the ACLU does take all of one's time and energy. We can conclude that Moira won't both become a Supreme Court Justice and President of the ACLU.

$$[(Ti \bullet En) \to \text{-}(Scj \bullet Pac)]$$
$$(Ti \bullet En) \qquad \vdash \quad \text{-}(Scj \bullet Pac)$$

The above four examples are to show that *modus ponens* is really an *argument form* with many instances that don't look exactly like *modus ponens*. The same is true for each of the other rules of inference as well. The symbolized argument directly above can be seen to have the same form as *modus ponens* if one thinks of '(Ti • En)' as 'p' and '-(Scj • Pac)' as 'q'. It will be helpful for the reader to attempt to construct a few complex arguments with the forms of each of the other rules of inference. This will not prove difficult if one begins with the *forms* of the inferences, for example, the rule for simplification: $(p \bullet q) \quad \vdash \quad p$.

7.3 Incorrect Applications

If one follows the rules as shown in schematic form above, one will, for the most part, have little trouble applying such rules as *Modus Ponens*, *Modus Tollens*, Hypothetical Syllogism, and so on. However, it is worthwhile, at this point, to note some common mistakes made by students of logic.

One of the canons of working in natural deduction is that when attempting to derive a certain formula on a given line by the rules, the formulas one uses to derive the further formula must "match" or "fit" the form of the formulas as found in the rules to be used. For example, the following set of formulas matches the set of formulas of the rule *modus tollens* precisely:

1.	$(F \to G)$	Except for the fact that 'F' and 'G' have
2.	-G	replaced 'p' and 'q' in this case, the inference
3.	-F	matches *modus tollens*, and is, hence, a
		valid inference.

Compare now the following alleged use of the rule Simplification on the left with the actual rule, as schematized on the right.

1.   [D → (B • N)]   (p • q)
2.   B   p

As can readily be seen, these two sets of formulas do *not* match. It follows that the first set is not an instance of the rule of Simplification and can not have that rule cited as part of its justification. It is an invalid inference. While it is true that '(B • N)' is a conjunction, in order to "simplify" out of a conjunction, the conjunction must appear on a line by itself, which '(B • N)' does not, since it appears as the consequent to the conditional in line 1.

Each of the following six inferences is either invalid or incorrect, owing to a misuse of one of the rules.

1. (R → J) ↔ S	It may appear that 'J' has been derived from
2. R	'L' on line 2 and '(R → J)' on line 1 from
3. J	*modus ponens*. This is an error, since '(R → J)' does not exist on a separate line, as *modus ponens* requires.

1. (H • I)	This is an incorrect use of the rule Addition,
2. H • (I v C)	as the inferred proposition is not a disjunction, as is required by Addition.

1. (A → K)	This is an invalid inference and if one tries
2. (A → K) • P	to justify it by Addition, it would be pointed out, as above, that when one uses the rule of Addition, the inferred proposition must be a disjunction.

7.4 Proofs

As with many other things, perhaps it is best if we simply launch into a sufficiently detailed argument, work the proof, and then explain the details. Recall that when one attempts to prove the validity of any argument in natural deduction, the conclusion is to appear in two places; once on the same line as the last premise, and once as the last line of the proof itself. Consider the following valid argument and proof.

1. $[D \rightarrow (L \rightarrow X)]$
2. $(X \rightarrow E)$
3. $D \qquad \vdash \quad (L \rightarrow E)$
4. $(L \rightarrow X)$ 1,3, MP
5. $(L \rightarrow E)$ 2,4, HS

Lines 1, 2, and 3 are what we can call the **argument lines**. Each consists of the line number, and one or more formulae (e.g., '$(X \rightarrow E)$' in line 2 is a formula). Line 3 contains two formulae; the first is a premise and the second is the conclusion of the argument, as will be noted by the symbol '⊢', the conclusion indicator. Each formula in an argument line is a premise, except the formula appearing to the right of the last premise, which is the conclusion. Lines 4 and 5 we can call **proof lines**, and contain the formulae and justifications of the inferences drawn. For example, line 4 contains the line number, the formula derived from lines 1 and 3 by the rule *Modus Ponens*, and the justification itself (i.e., '1,3, MP'). Consider another argument and proof:

1. $(O \lor R) \rightarrow -T$
2. $G \rightarrow (O \lor R)$
3. $T \lor -F$
4. $G \qquad \vdash \qquad -F$
5. $(G \rightarrow -T)$ 1,2, HS
6. $-T$ 4,5, MP
7. $-F$ 3,6, DS

Quite as important as the formulas on each line of the proof are the justifications themselves, in this case those appearing on lines 5, 6, and 7. Each justification must include the number(s) of the previous line(s) used as well as the rule from which the present formula was derived. For example, line 5 can be read as saying that '$(G \rightarrow -T)$' was derived from lines 1 and 2 using the rule Hypothetical Syllogism. Line 6 is read as saying that '$-T$' was derived from lines 4 and 5 by the rule Modus Ponens. And line 7 may be read as saying that '$-F$' was derived from lines 3 and 6 by the rule Disjunctive Syllogism. It is important to remember that *a justification is required for each and every proof line.*

The method of constructing a proof in natural deduction involves at once a creative process and a mechanical process. It is mechanical, like the method of truth trees, insofar as there are a certain number of specific rules one uses. The *form* of each rule never changes, though the formulas to which the rules may be applied can be ever so much more complicated than the bare rules themselves. The creative aspect of the method of natural deduction has to do with one's ability to manipulate the symbols according to the rules in such a way as to derive the desired formula(s). It is the creative aspect that makes natural deduction a time consuming and sometimes difficult system with which to prove the validity of arguments in sentential logic.

Constructing a proof in natural deduction is, in a way, like playing a game of chess. You know that you have a number of options as to which chess pieces you can move, and from and to which squares. You think, "Well, if I move my knight here, then I'm in position to check my opponent's king. On the other hand, if I move my rook here, I can take my opponent's queen." These are both conditional statements. If one is really concentrating on a game, and if there are a great many options that look plausible, one keeps a notepad to remind one of the various possibilities. In constructing a proof in natural deduction, it is quite helpful to keep a notepad as well. This is how it works. Consider the following argument:

		Notepad

1.	-P	
2.	(S v R)	| (S → T)
3.	(S → P)	| (S → P)
4.	R → (P → T) ⊢ (S → T)	| (P → T)
		| R
		| -S
		| -P

Beginning from the top of the notepad, I see that what I'm looking for is the conclusion, which is '(S → T)'. I can derive the conclusion from the rule Hypothetical Syllogism if I could get the formulas '(S → P)' and '(P → T)' each on lines by themselves. The first of those formulas is on line 3 of the argument. So, it remains for me to find '(P → T)'. This formula can be derived by Modus Ponens from line 4, if 'R' can be derived on a line by itself. 'R' can be derived by Disjunctive Syllogism from line 2, if '-S' is derived on a line by itself. To get '-S', it suffices to get '-P' on a line by itself and to use that line with line 3 and the rule Modus Tollens. '-P' does appear on a line by itself, i.e., line 1. Below is the full proof, showing the validity of the argument above.

```
1.  -P                                 Notice that each of the justifications
2.  (S v R)                            cite 2 lines from which the line that
3.  (S → P)                            is justified is derived. This is
4.  R → (P → T) ⊢ (S → T)              critically important, for each of the
5.  -S              1,3, MT            rules used in this proof requires 2
6.  R               2,5, DS            fomulas to derive the third. Some of
7.  (P → T)         4,6, MP            the rules require only 1 line.
8.  (S → T)         3,7, HS
```

In the following example, the rule MP is used four times successively to derive the conclusion. See the notepad to the right of the proof.

```
1.  (F → G)                               Notepad
2.  (D → E)                           ---------------------
3.  (E → J)                           |       G
4.  (J → F)                           |       F
5.  D    ⊢   G                        |       J
6.  E    2,5, MP                      |       E
7.  J    3,6, MP                      |       D
8.  F    4,7, MP                      ---------------------
9.  G    1,8, MP
```

To see how MT, DS, Si, and CD are used to show the validity of more complicated arguments, the following may suffice.

```
        A
1.  [(X → Y) → (-L ↔ C)]
2.  -(-L ↔ C) • (L → X)    ⊢    -(X → Y)
3.  -(-L ↔ C)      2, Si
4.  -(X → Y)        1,3,  MT
```

In argument (A) above, in order to see how line 3 was derived from line 2 by Simplification, recall the rule Simplification and treat the formula '-(-L ↔ C)' as 'p' and treat '(L → X)' as 'q'. To see how line 4 was obtained from lines 1 and 3 by Modus Tollens, recall Modus Tollens and treat '(X → Y)' as 'p' and '(-L ↔ C)' as 'q'.

This is a good time to reiterate that 'p' and 'q' are variables and can stand for any symbolic sentence whatever. So, for example, 'p' may be a simple sentence on one line and a triple conjunction on another.

B
1. $[(B \cdot Q) \to U] \cdot (-I \to -Q)$
2. $(U \to A) \vee [(B \cdot Q) \vee -I]$
3. $-(U \to A)$ ⊢ $(U \vee -Q)$
4. $(B \cdot Q) \vee -I$ 2,3, DS
5. $(U \vee -Q)$ 1,4, CD

In argument (B), in order to see how line 4 was derived from lines 2 and 3 by Disjunctive Syllogism, recall the rule and treat the formula '(U → A)' as 'p' and treat '[(B • Q) v -I]' as 'q'. To see how line 5 was derived from lines 1 and 4 by Constructive Dilemma, recall the rule and treat '(B • Q)' as 'p', treat 'U' as 'q', treat '-I' as 'r', and treat '-Q' as 's'.

It is instructive to note early on that many arguments can be proven to be valid in more than one way, i.e., using either a different sequence or a different combination of the rules. Proof (A) below uses HS, Ad, CD, Si and Con, whereas proof (B) uses Si, MP, and Ad twice. Note also that since each proof shows the argument to be valid using correct applications of the rules of inference, both proofs are correct. Neither proof is "better" than the other except insofar as one counts it preferable to prove an argument valid in as few steps as possible. Proof (B) does, however, have a further point in its favor, i.e., it shows that premises 3 and 4 are, strictly, unnecessary for the validity of the argument. This can be seen by the fact that neither premise is noted in set of justifications in (B). These two considerations would lead logicians to call (B) "elegant" in comparison with (A).

A.		B.	
1. $(H \to R)$		1. $(H \to R)$	
2. $(H \cdot V)$		2. $(H \cdot V)$	
3. $(N \to O)$		3. $(N \to O)$	
4. $(V \to N) \vdash (R \vee O) \vee H$		4. $(V \to N)$ ⊢ $(R \vee O) \vee H$	
5. $(V \to O)$	3,4, HS	5. H	2, Si
6. $(H \to R) \cdot (V \to O)$	1,5, Con	6. R	1,5, MP
7. H	2, Si	7. $(R \vee O)$	6, Ad
8. $(H \vee V)$	7, Ad	8. $(R \vee O) \vee H$	7, Ad
9. $(R \vee O)$	6,8, CD		
10 $(R \vee O) \vee H$	9, Ad		

To get a clearer picture of how the rules were used in (A) above, it is useful to run through the lines and justifications of the proof. Line 5

MSU MOORHEAD BOOKSTORE
MOORHEAD, MN 56563
218-477-2111
MON-FRI 8:00-4:30

SALE   001 003 01431913
CASHIER SARA   01/14/05 8:58

01 JOURMANY/FIRST EDGE
      10680 USED/BK   1 N   1.00
         limited to trace
02
03
04
05
06

                    SUBTOTAL   3.95
                    Sales Tax   1.82

                    Total

VISA

was derived from lines 3 and 4 by Hypothetical Syllogism by (recall the rule) treating 'V' as 'p', 'N' as 'q', and 'O' as 'r'. Line 6 of the proof was derived from lines 1 and 5 by Con-junction by treating '(H → R)' as 'p' and by treating '(V → O)' as 'q'. Line 7 is a straightforward Simplification where 'H' is treated as 'p' and 'V' is treated as 'q'. Line 8 was derived from line 7 by Addition with the same treatment of 'H' and 'V' as was used to derive line 7. Line 9 was derived from lines 6 and 8 by Constructive Dilemma (recall the rule) by treating 'H' as 'p', 'R' as 'q', 'V' as 'r', and 'O' as 's'. Line 10 was derived from line 9 by Addition by treating '(R v O)' as 'p' and by treating 'H' as 'q'. Proof (B) above runs as follows. Line 5 was derived in precisely the same manner as line 7 was derived in proof (A). Line 6 is a straight Modus Ponens from lines 1 and 5, treating 'H' as 'p' and 'R' as 'q'. Line 7 is derived by the rule of Addition from line 6 by treating 'R' as 'p' and 'O' as 'q'. The rule of Addition is used, once again, to derive line 8 from line 7, this time by treating '(R v O)' as 'p' and 'H' as 'q', which is precisely the manner in which line 10 was obtained in proof (A).

Further examples of proofs are below.

1.	(P → E)			1.	[(R → S) • U]	
2.	(P • L)	⊢ E		2.	(S → U)	⊢ (R → U)
3.	P	2, Si		3.	(R → S)	1, Si
4.	E	1,3 MP		4.	(R → U)	2,3 HS

1.	D v (T → -E)			1.	(C → G)	
2.	-D • (-E → F)			2.	(S • C)	
3.	--E ⊢ (-K v L)			3.	(S → C)	⊢ J
4.	-D	2, Si		4.	(S → G)	1,3, HS
5.	(T → -E)	1,4, DS		5.	S	2, Si
6.	-T	3,5, MT		6.	G	4,5, MP
7.	(-T v E)	6, Ad				

1.	[(J → K) • L]	
2.	[(J → K) → (J → W)]	
3.	J ⊢ (K v W)	
4.	(J → K)	1, Si
5.	(J → W)	2,4, MP
6.	[(J → K) • (J → W)]	4,5, Com
7.	(J v J)	3, Ad
8.	(K v W)	6,7, CD

1. [-L → (M → A)]
2. (H v A) • (-L v -K)
3. [(H v A) → R]   ⊢   [R v (M → A)
4. [(H v A) → R] • [-L → (M → A)]   1,3,   Con
5. (H v A)   2, Si
6. [(H v A) v -L]   5, Ad
7. [R v (M → A)   4,6, CD

1. (S → L)
2. (D → S)
3. (L → G)
4. (A → D) ⊢ (A → G)
5. (A → S)   2,4, HS
6. (S → G)   1,3, HS
7. (A → G)   5,6, HS

1. (F → E)
2. [(A v N • (D v I)]
3. (N → F)
4. (A → K)   ⊢   (K v E)
5. (A v N)   2, Si
6. (N → E)   1,3, HS
7. (A → K) • (N → E)   4,6, Con
8. (K v E)   5,7, CD

1. -C → (W → U)
2. (--C → -R)
3. -(W → U) ⊢ (-R v R)
4. --C   1,3, MT
5. -R   2,4, MP
6. (-R v R)   5, Ad

1. [P → -(V → Y)
2. (V → H)
3. --(V → Y)
4. -P → (H → M) ⊢ (V → M)
5. -P   1,3, MT
6. (H → M)   4,5, MP
7. (V → M)   2,6, HS

Exercises 7.4

A. Fill in the blanks with the correct formula, as called for by the justification appearing to the right of the blank.

1. 1. (V → L)
    2. (V • U) ⊢ L
    3.   2, Si
    4.   1,3 MP

2. 1. (F v N) → P
    2. F   ⊢ P
    3.   2, Ad
    4.   1,3 MP

3. 1. (E • R)
    2. (T • D) ⊢ (T • E)
    3.   1, Si
    4.   2, Si
    5.   3,4 Con

4. 1. (B → S)
    2. (C → S) → L
    3. (C → B)   ⊢ L
    4.   1,3 HS
    5.   2,4 MP

5* 1. (F → J) → (-F v -D)
  2. -(-F v -D)
  3. (F → J) v F
  4. J • (F v -F)   ⊢ (F • J)
  5.   1,2, MT
  6.   3,5, DS
  7.   4, Si
  8.   6,7, Con

6. 1. (S v R) → (B → C)
  2. (R → S)
  3. (R • B) • S ⊢ (B → C)
  4.   3, Si
  5.   4, Si
  6.   2,5, MP
  7.   6, Ad
  8.   1,7, MP

7. 1. A → (A → E)
  2. I v (L → P)
  3. (-I • L)
  4. A   ⊢ (E v P)
  5.   1,4, MP
  6.   3, Si
  7.   2,6, DS
  8.   4, Ad
  9.   5,7, Con
  10   8,9, CD

8. 1.[H v (G ↔ L)] → (I → R)
  2. R v [H v (G ↔ L)]
  3. (-R • -H)
  4. (H → I)   ⊢ -I
  5.   3, Si
  6.   2,5, DS
  7.   1,6, MP
  8.   5,7, MT

9. 1. (-T • D) → (-T → -P)
  2. [(-T • D) • -P] • [(P → N) v T]
  3. (-N → N) ⊢ (-P v N)
  4.   2, Si
  5.   4, Si
  6.   1,5, MP
  7.   5, Si
  8.   3,6, Con
  9.   7, Ad
  10   8,9, CD

10*1. (Q v -I) → E
  2. (-H v G) → W
  3. Q   ⊢   (E v W) v -Q
  4.   3, Ad
  5.   4, Ad
  6.   1,2, Con
  7.   5,6, CD
  8.   7. Ad

B. Supply the correct justifications in the following proofs.

1. 1. [(V → G) • (L → O]
    2. V   ⊢ (G v O)
    3. (V v L)
    4. (G v O)

2. 1. (-F • G)
    2. (H → F)   ⊢ (-H v K)
    3. -F
    4. -H
    5. (-H v K)

3. 1. [(-V → V) • (L → O]
    2. -V   ⊢ (O v G)
    3. (-V v L)
    4. (V v O)
    5. O
    6. (O v G)

4. 1. [(-B v P) v S]
    2. [(S → O) • -(B v S)]
    3. -(-B v P)   ⊢   O
    4. S
    5. (S → O)
    6. O

5* 1. (A → W)
    2. (Y v A)
    3. (-Y • -Z) ⊢ W
    4. -Y
    5. A
    6. W

6. 1. (Q → D) • (J → U)
    2. (Q • D) • U ⊢ (D v U)
    3. (Q • D)
    4. Q
    5. (Q v J)
    6. (D v U)

7. 1. (R → F) • (I → D)
    2. R
    3. (F v -D) → (I → -L)
    4. F   ⊢   (F v -L)
    5. (R → F)
    6. (R v I)
    7. (F v -D)
    8.   (I → -L)
    9. (R → F) • (I → -L)
    10 (F v -L)

8. 1. (X • -T)
    2. (-Q • X) → Z
    3. (-Q • S)   ⊢ [(X • Z) v X]
    4. X
    5. -Q
    6. (-Q • X)
    7. Z
    8. (X • Z)
    9. [(X • Z) v X]

C. Show the following arguments to be valid using any of the first eight rules in the method of natural deduction.

1. 1. ((I • J) • L) ⊢ (I • (I • J))

2. 1. (F → H)
    2. (F → O)
    3. F   ⊢ (O • H)

3. 1. (R • A) ⊢ (R v (A v -A))

4. 1. (-Q v -J) → U
    2. -Q   ⊢ U

5* 1. (-L • J) • -{(S ↔ I) v [-I ↔ (S • S)]}
   2. [-L → --(S →I)]⊢   --(S →I)

6. 1. (S v D) → (T → I)
    2. (T → I) → (-E • L)
    3. (C v I) → S
    4. (C • I)   ⊢   -E

7. 1. (F → Y)
    2. (Y • S)
    3. Y → -(K → J)
    4. (K → J) v (Z → S)
    5. (J → Z) ⊢   (J → S)

8. 1. [(A → B) → (C → D)]
    2. [-(A → B) → -C]
    3. -(C → D)   ⊢   (-C v -B)

9. 1. (A → C)
    2. (B → A)
    3. (C → D)
    4. -D ⊢ [(-A • -B) • -C]

10*1. R → (S • T)
   2. S → (U • V)
   3. (R • S) ⊢ (S • T) • (U • V)

11 1. (M → I)
   2. -I
   3. (-M → W) ⊢ (W • -I)

12 1. [(-H v -Q) → -L]
   2. {[(Q v H) v -D] → (-H • -L)}
   3. (Q • -D)   ⊢   [-L • (Q • -D)]

13 1. (-X • U)
   2. (-X → S)
   3. (S → U)
   4. (U → --E)
   5. (-E v J) ⊢ J

14 1. T → (-A • W)
    2. O → (N v F)
    3. T
    4. (N v F) → A ⊢   -O

15*1. [(R → C) → (B → K)]
   2. [R v (R → C)]
   3. (R → C) ⊢ [C v (B → K)]

16 1. (C → L)
   2. C
   3. (L → N)
   4. (N → -S) ⊢ -S

17 1. (O → Q) • {(G ↔ O) → [(P → -R) v K]}
   2. {[(P → R) → (K → G)] → [(O → K) v -P]}
   3. {(O → Q) → [(P → R) → (K → G)]}   ⊢   [(O → K) v -P]

18 1. (-N → -M)
    2. (-M → -N)
    3. (-M v -M)   ⊢   (-N v -M)

19 1. (-M → N)
    2. (-M v N)
    3. (N → N)   ⊢   (N v N) v -M

20* 1. {[D → (G ↔ S)] • (G ↔ R)}
     2. (--D v S)
     3. -(G ↔ S)   ⊢   (S v R)

7.5 *The Principle of Replacement*

Many valid truth-functional arguments cannot be shown to be valid merely by using the rules of inference. Example:

$$-(N \lor W) \lor -S$$
$$-(S \to E) \quad \vdash \quad -N$$

To prove the validity of these sorts of arguments via natural deduction, an additional rule is necessary. The rule is called *The Principle of Replacement*, and is stated as follows: *Any sentence S, appearing on a line of a proof, may be replaced by any sentence logically equivalent to S.* For example, if '(F → G)' were to appear on a line of a proof, then '(-F v G)' could replace '(F → G)' on a further line because '(-F v G)' and '(F → G)' are logically equivalent. In fact, this particular replacement instance is an example of what is called Material Implication.

Each of the replacement instances (we will call them the *Axioms of Replacement*) are schematized directly below in the form of logical equivalences. The symbol '⇔' will function as denoting logical equivalence, and will be called the "hollow double arrow". Although this symbol is in itself truth functional, we will not make use of it when doing proofs in natural deduction. It will be employed here solely to indicate the logical equivalence of sentences in the axioms of replacement. The system of natural deduction we have adopted makes use of ten specific axioms of replacement. They are listed on the following page.

DE MORGAN'S THEOREMS (DM)
$$[-(p \vee q) \Leftrightarrow (-p \bullet -q)]$$
$$[-(p \bullet q) \Leftrightarrow (-p \vee -q)]$$

COMMUTATION (COM)
$$[(p \vee q) \Leftrightarrow (q \vee p)]$$
$$[(p \bullet q) \Leftrightarrow (q \bullet p)]$$

DISTRIBUTION
$$[p \bullet (q \vee r)] \Leftrightarrow [(p \bullet q) \vee (p \bullet r)]$$
$$[p \vee (q \bullet r)] \Leftrightarrow [(p \vee q) \bullet (p \vee r)]$$

ASSOCIATION (AS)
$$[p \bullet (q \bullet r)] \Leftrightarrow [(p \bullet q) \bullet r]$$
$$[p \vee (q \vee r)] \Leftrightarrow [(p \vee q) \vee r]$$

MATERIAL IMPLICATION (MI)
$$(p \rightarrow q) \Leftrightarrow (-p \vee q)$$

CONTRAPOSITION (CP)
$$(p \rightarrow q) \Leftrightarrow (-q \rightarrow -p)$$

MATERIAL EQUIVALENCE (ME)
$$(p \leftrightarrow q) \Leftrightarrow [(p \rightarrow q) \bullet (q \rightarrow p)]$$
$$(p \leftrightarrow q) \Leftrightarrow [(p \bullet q) \vee (-p \bullet -q)]$$

EXPORTATION (EXP)
$$[(p \bullet q) \rightarrow r] \Leftrightarrow [(p \rightarrow (q \rightarrow r)]$$

DOUBLE NEGATION (DN)
$$p \Leftrightarrow --p$$

REPLICATION (RE)
$$[(p \bullet p) \Leftrightarrow p]$$
$$[(p \vee p) \Leftrightarrow p]$$

It is possible to view the axioms of replacement outlined above as replacement *rules*, though in fact there is but one replacement rule as such. Viewing the *axioms* as *rules*, however, is only helpful as an activity-directed perspective. The activity referred to here is that of working proofs. In working proofs, then, when making use of the axioms, since the formula on one side of the hollow double arrow is logically equivalent to the formula on the other side of the hollow double arrow, one formula may replace the other formula whenever it occurs in a proof. For example, consider the proof below.

1.	(M v -T)		Here, a combination of the rules of
2.	(T • R)	⊢ P	inference **and** axioms have been used.
3.	T	2, Si	As you will notice, some proofs may be
4.	(-T v M)	1, Com	worked using only the rules of inference
5.	(T → P)	4, MI	and some using only axioms.
6.	M	3,5, MP	

Concentrating on lines 4 and 5 in the above argument, as the justifications for those lines each involve an axiom, we see that line 1 has been replaced by line 4 and line 4 by line 5. Recalling Commutation, to see how line 4 was obtained, treat 'M' in line 1 as 'p' and '-T' in 1 as 'q'. Similarly, recall Material Implication and see that line 5 was obtained from line 4 by treating '-T' in 4 as 'p' and 'M' in 4 as 'q'.

The following proof shows one important feature of axioms not shared by rules of inference. The axioms can be applied to parts of lines, whereas the rules of inference cannot. [Recall that it is an invalid inference to go from ['G → (M • E)]' to 'M' by Simplification, because '(M • E)' must appear on a line by itself to simplify to 'M'. The reasoning here is that '[G → (M • E)]' does not assert that the conjunction of 'M' and 'E' is true, but only that *if* 'G' is true, then '(M • E)' is true, whereas '(M • E)' on a separate line *does* assert that the conjunction is true and, hence, that 'M' is true. Therefore, where '(M • E)' is asserted as true, i.e., appears on a line by itself, 'M' follows by Simplification.]

1.	(-F → H) → C	⊢ (F → C)	
2.	(-H → --F) → C	1, Cp	It is interesting to note here
3.	(-H → F) → C	2. DN	that each line of the proof was
4.	-(-H → F) v C	3, MI	derived from the line directly
5.	-(--H v F) v C	4, MI	above it. Of course, this will
6.	(---H • -F) v C	5, DM	not always be the case, as in
7.	(-H • -F) v C	6, DN	the preceding example.

8. C v (-H • -F)   7, Com
9. (C v -H) • (C v -F) 8, Di
10 (C v -F) • (C v -H) 9, Com,
11 (C v -F)   10, Si
12 (-F v C)   11, Com
13 (F → C)   12, MI

The explication of the proof is as follows: Line 2 was obtained from line 1 and Contraposition by treating '-F' as 'p' and 'H' as 'q'. Accordingly, 'H' and '-F' have switched places and each has been negated. [Note that 'C', the consequent to the major conditional in line 1, is left untouched. This is as much as to say that the major conditional is not being treated at all in terms of applying Contraposition to line 1. Rather, the antecedent to the major conditional in line 1, which is '(-F → H)', is treated *as if* it appears on a separate line. This is legitimate insofar as we are replacing an occurrence of one formula with an occurrence of another, the result being a logically equivalent formula. When applying the rules of inference, however, one does not merely replace one formula with another; rather one actually draws an inference. Analogically, one might say inferences are one-way streets, whereas replacements are two-way streets.]

Line 3 replaces '--F' in line 2 with 'F', via Double Negation, leaving all other connectives and formulas in place. This is a perfect example how the axioms of replacement may be applied to parts of lines.

In line 4 we see that the second arrow has been changed into a wedge and that a negation sign has been inserted before the first disjunct. This has been done by treating '(-H → F)' as 'p' and 'C' as 'q', in accord with Material Implication.

Line 5 has also been obtained by MI, but this time '-H' in 4 is treated as 'p' and 'F' in 4 as 'q'.

In line 6, 'C' again remains untouched, as in lines 2, 3, and 5. ['C' was not untouched in line 4, since when MI was applied to line 3, 'C' went from being the consequent to the conditional in line 3 to being a disjunct in 4.] Line 6 replaces '-(--H v F)' in 5 with '(---H • -F)'. This is done (recall DM) by treating '--H' as 'p' and 'F' as 'q'. This version of De Morgan's changes a negated disjunction into a conjunction, negating each conjunct.

Line 7 is a straight Double Negation of '---H'. Again, not only is 'C' not affected by the replacement, neither are the other connectives, nor is '-F'.

Line 8 commutes line 7, treating '(-H • -F)' in 7 as 'p' and 'C' as 'q'.

Line 9 is an instance of Distribution, applied to line 8. Recall Di and treat 'C' in 8 as 'p', '-H' as 'q', and '-F' as 'r'. In effect, this version of Distribution changes a disjunction into a conjunction wherein each conjunct is itself a disjunction.

Line 10 commutes line 9, treating '(C v -H)' as 'p' and '(C v -F)' as 'q'.

Line 11 is a straight Simplification of '(C v -F)' from line 10.

Line 12 commutes 'C' and '-F' from line 10, treating the former as 'p' and the latter as 'q'.

Line 13 applies Material Implication to line 11, treating '-F' in 11 as 'p' and 'C' as 'q'.

Note that in line 4 Material Implication was applied to a conditional (arrow), changing it to a disjunction (wedge), with the first disjunct being negated. Line 13 is different in that it moves from a wedge in 13 (with the first disjunct negated) to an arrow in 13 (with the antecedent not being negated). Both are quite legitimate uses of MI. To make this point, though we can think of the axioms of replacement as replacement *rules*, some logicians schematize the axioms as biconditionals. Doing so makes it possible to talk about them as axioms of equivalence. To make this clearer, take Exportation; its truth table is:

```
{ [ (p  •  q)  →  r]     [p  →  (q  →  r) ] }
      t  t  t    t  t        t  t    t  t  t
      t  t  t    f  f        t  f    t  f  f
      t  f  f    t  t        t  t    f  t  t
      t  f  f    t  f        t  t    f  t  f
      f  f  t    t  t        f  t    t  t  t
      f  f  t    t  f        f  t    t  f  f
      f  f  f    t  t        f  t    f  t  t
      f  f  f    t  f        f  t    f  t  f
```

The fact that the truth values are identical under the primary connectives indicates that these sentences are logically equivalent, which means that the sentence forms have the same truth values in all possible worlds, or under every interpretation.

There is also a relation of implication from each of the statement forms to the other, as can be expressed by a biconditional. Consider the following formula:

$$\{[(p \cdot q) \to r] \to [p \to (q \to r)]\} \cdot \{[p \to (q \to r)] \to [(p \cdot q) \to r]\}$$

This is one version of Material Equivalence applied to Exportation. The same procedure can be applied to each of the axioms of replacement. Another way to show the equivalence of Exportation is to show that each side of the hollow double arrow follows from the other, derived by some of the other axioms of replacement. Below are two arguments, the first of which has one side of Exportation as the premise and the other side as the conclusion, the second of which has those formulas switched. Note also the symmetry of the justifications.

1. $(p \cdot q) \to r \vdash p \to (q \to r)$
2. $-(p \cdot q) \lor r$ 1, MI
3. $(-p \lor -q) \lor r$ 2, DM
4. $-p \lor (-q \lor r)$ 3, As
5. $p \to (-q \lor r)$ 4, MI
6. $p \to (q \to r)$ 5, MI

1. $p \to (q \to r) \vdash (p \cdot q) \to r$
2. $-p \lor (q \to r)$ 1, MI
3. $-p \lor (-q \lor r)$ 2, MI
4. $(-p \lor -q) \lor r$ 3, As
5. $-(p \cdot q) \lor r$ 4, DM
6. $(p \cdot q) \to r$ 5, MI

As one becomes more proficient at working proofs, one will naturally I think begin to see two or three or more moves ahead. There will be a tendency to use two rules/axioms at once. This is perfectly all right where it is clear what one is doing. In the following proof, Commutation and Simplification are used together in line 7. What this amounts to is simply bypassing making the Commutation explicit on a line by itself.

1. $(E \leftrightarrow G)$
2. $(-G \lor -E)$ $\vdash$ $-G$
3. $[(E \cdot G) \lor (-E \cdot -G)]$ 1, ME
4. $-(G \cdot E)$ 2, DM
5. $-(E \cdot G)$ 4, Com
6. $(-E \cdot -G)$ 3,5 DS
7. $-G$ 6, Com, Si

In the proofs that follow, only Double Negation, Commutation, Addition, and Simplification will be used in tandem. The reason for this is that these four rules are perhaps the simplest of all and one can save time by using them in conjunction. So, for example, one could use Double Negation twice, or Addition with Double Negation, or Commutation with Double Negation, and so on. Also, of course, it is not necessary for one to use them together. I do recommend these four rules only be used in tandem, but never three at once, as this becomes increasingly complicated.

At this point, it will be useful to show, by example, instances of how each of the various replacement instances is used in proofs. Uncommon uses will be noted and explained.

1.	-(-O v -I) v (O v F)	
2.	-F	⊢ O
3.	(--O • --I) v (O v F)	1, DM
4.	(O • I) v (O v F)	3, DN, DN
5.	[(O • I) v O] v F	4, As
6.	[O v (O • I)] v F	5, Com
7.	[(O v O) • (O v I)] v F	6, Di
8.	[O • (O v I)] v F	7, Re
9.	F v [O • (O v I)]	8, Com
10	O • (O v I)	2,9, DS
11	O	10, Si

It may be suspected that the use of Association in line 5 (from 4) is not a precise fit with the schematized axiom. However, one can see that it is a legitimate use of that axiom by treating (in line 4) '(O • I)' as 'p', 'O' as 'q', and 'F' as 'r'.

Another apparently uncommon use of a principle occurs in line 8 with the use of Replication from line 7. To obtain line 8, the first conjunct in the conjunction of line 7 was treated as '(p v p)' in the rule of Replication. It was replaced, in line 8, with 'O', which is there treated as 'p'. This is one more prime example of how a principle can be applied to a part of a line.

Consider the more complicated argument below.

1.	-(B v -C) v (-B v C)	
2.	-B → -(D v -B) ⊢	(C ↔ B)
3.	B v -(D v -B)	2, MI
4.	B v (-D • --B)	3, DM
5.	B v (-D • B)	4, DN
6.	B v (B • -D)	5, Com
7.	(B v B) • (B v -D)	6, Di
8.	(B v B)	7, Si
9.	B	8, Re
10	(B v -C)	9, Ad
11	(-C v B)	10, Com
12	(C → B)	11, MI
13	(B v -C) → (-B v C)	1, MI
14	(-C v B) → (-B v C)	13, Com
15	(C → B) → (-B v C)	14, MI
16	(-B v C)	12,15, MP
17	(B → C)	16, MI
18	(C → B) • (B → C)	12,17, Con
19	(C ↔ B)	18, ME

It occurs that this proof is, though long, not one in which any principle is used in a way that should give the student trouble.   The crucial insights here are 1) that the premises could be altered in such a way as to yield arrows, suggesting that the first version of ME may be used to obtain the conclusion, and 2) that 'B' could be obtained on a line by itself, and then '-C' Added to it to yield, ultimately, the first conjunct in line 18.

The further proofs below have some examples of various uses of the rules of inference and axioms of replacement.

1.	(P → -Q)		
2.	-(Q • P) → -M ⊢ -M		
3.	(--Q → -P)	1, Cp	
4.	(---Q v -P)	3, MI	
5.	(-Q v -P)	4, DN	
6.	-(Q • P)	5, DM	
7.	-M	2,6 MP	

1.	(L v T) ⊢ -(-T • -L) v L	
2.	(T v L)	1, Com
3.	(--T v L)	2, DN
4.	(--T v --L)	3, DN
5.	-(-T • -L)	4, DM
6.	-(-T • -L) v L	5, Ad

1.	-S → (G → W)		
2.	-(G → -H) ⊢ (S v W)		
3.	(-S • G) → W	1, Exp	
4.	-(-S • G) v W	3, MI	
5.	(--S v -G) v W	4, DM	
6.	(S v -G) v W	5, DN	
7.	(-G v S) v W	6, Com	
8.	-G v (S v W)	7, As	
9.	-(-G v -H)	2, MI	
10	(--G • --H)	9, DM	
11	--G	10, Si	
12	(S v W)	8,11, DS	

1.	(H v -G)		
2.	(G v -D)		
3.	-(G → H) ⊢ W		
4.	(-G v H)	1, Com	
5.	(-D v G)	2, Com	
6.	(G → H)	4, MI	
7.	(D → G)	5, MI	
8.	(D → H)	6,7 HS	
9.	-(-G v H)	3, MI	
10	(--G • -H)	9, DM	
11	G	10, Si, DN	
12	-H	10, Com, Si	
13	-G	6,12 MT	
14	(G v W)	11, Ad	
15	W	13,14 DS	

Something interesting is to be noted about the right-hand argument directly above. Note that lines 11 and 13 are contradictory. Line 13 directly denies what line 11 affirms. The last two lines of the proof show both that everything follows from a contradiction and also how this is accomplished in natural deduction. In the above proof, 'W' is derived; however, it could just as well have been 'R' or 'Q' or even '-(A → B)'. We will encounter more instances of premises generating contradictions as we go along, especially in the section on *Reductio ad Absurdum*.

1.	X → (U • W)	
2.	(-U → Z) → Y ⊢ (Y v -X)	
3.	-X v (U • W)	1, MI
4.	(-X v U) • (-X v W)	3, Di
5.	(-X v U)	4, Si
6.	(X → U)	5, MI
7.	-(-U → Z) v Y	2, MI
8.	-(--U v Z) v Y	7, MI
9.	-(U v Z) v Y	8, DN
10	(-U • -Z) v Y	9, DM
11	Y v (-U • -Z)	10, Com
12	(Y v -U) • (Y v -Z)	11, Di
13	(-U v Y)	12, Si, Com
14	(U → Y)	13, MI
15	(X → Y)	6,14, HS

16	(-Y → -X)	15, Cp
17	(--Y v -X)	16, MI
18	(Y v -X)	17, DN

1.	(N → -M)	
2.	(M ↔ N) ⊢ -(M v N)	
3.	(M • N) v (-M • -N)	2, ME
4.	(--M → -N)	1, Cp
5.	(M → -N)	4, DN
6.	(-M v -N)	5, MI
7.	-(M • N)	6, DM
8.	(-M • -N)	3,7, DS
9.	-(M v N)	8, DM

1.	-(-(E v Q) v -T) ⊢ E → (Q → T)	
2.	--(E v Q) • --T	1, DM
3.	--T • --(E v Q)	2, Com
4.	T • --(E v Q)	3, DN
5.	T	4, Si
6.	T v -(E • Q)	5, Ad
7.	-(E • Q) v T	6, Com
8.	(E • Q) → T	7, MI
9.	E → (Q → T)	8, Exp

1.	(P → Q) • (E → J)	
2.	(-Q v -J) ⊢ -(P • E)	
3.	(-Q → -P) • (E → J)	1, Cp
4.	(-Q → -P) • (-J → -E)	3, Cp
5.	(-P v -E)	2,4 CD
6.	-(P • E)	5, DM

Exercise 7.5

A. Show the following arguments to be valid using any combination of the rules of inference and the replacement instances.

1.
1. (R • G) → Q
2. -(S v -G)
3. (Q → S)   ⊢ -R

2.
1. L v -(B • N)
2. -(B → V) → -L
3. (-S • -Z)
4. -(B • N) → S   ⊢   V

3. 1. (P • Y)
    ⊢ P • (Y v T)

4. 1. [A v (-C v J)] → (J → -C)
    2. (C → A) v J ⊢ (-C v -J)

5* 1. -(N → -R)
    2. (R → W) ⊢ (W v N)

6. 1. -I → (-O v U)
    2. -(I v U)
    3. (-U v -O) ⊢ -O

7. 1. (X → Z) • (Z → V)
    2. (Z → D) • (V → T)
    3. (X v Z)
    ⊢ (D v V) v -(V • D)

8. 1. (E → A) → [T v (G • K)]
    2. (T → A)
    3. (G → -E)
    4. -(-T • -G) ⊢ -(-T • -K)

9. 1. [C → (F → G)]
    2. (C • -G)
    3. [(-R v Y) v A]
    4. [-F → (R • -Y)] ⊢ A

10* 1. -[N v (M v O)] → E
    2. -(S v E) ⊢ -N → (-O → M)

11 1. (F → -J) • (N → P)
    2. (P → T)
    3. (F v N)   ⊢   (N v -J) v T

12 1. (J → P) • [J → (J • O)]
    2. -(-J • -J)   ⊢   (P v O)

13 1. (I → J)
    2. (-F • S) v (D • -F)
    3. -(-Y v J) ⊢ (F ↔ I)

14 1. (N → M) → -P
    2. (L v O) → P
    3. -N   ⊢   -O

15* 1. (Aa ↔ Nn)   ⊢   (Aa → Aa) • (Nn → Nn)

16 1. (T → E)
    2. (-T → -I) • (P → G)
    3. -I → -(-I v G)   ⊢ I

17 1. -(-W → -X) → Y
    2. (-X → Z)
    3. (W v Y) → (-Z → A)
    4. -A   ⊢ Z

18 1. -[-R v (F → J)] → -R
    2. -R → (J • W)
    3. -[L v (J → R)] → --R
    4. -J ⊢ {-F • [L v (J → R)]}

19 1. (A • C) v [A • (C ↔ D)]
    2. -D → (A → E)
    3. -(B → C)   ⊢ (E v -A)

20* 1. (-R • T) v (Q v X)
    2. -(-R v L) ⊢ [T v (X v Q)]

21 1. (D • Q) → E
    2. (-R • D) ⊢ Q → (E v -D)

22 1. -[-(S v -O) v B]
    2. (B v O)
    3. (O v O) → S   ⊢ S

23 1. (P v Q) v (Q • R)
    2. -(-Q → P) ⊢ (Q v P) v Q

24 1. -(-K → L)
    2. (L • K) v (K • M)
       ⊢ (K v L) v M

25* 1. (E → S)
    2. -A   ⊢   [E → (A → S)]

26 1. (N v H) → (-H • -I)
    2. N v (H • J)
       ⊢   N v -(H v I)

27 1. (B v Y) → O
    2. Q → (Y • B)   ⊢ (-Q v O)

28 1. (D → -R) • (P → E)
    2. (-E v O)
    3. (-P → D)
           ⊢ R → (O • O)

29 1. (F → H)
    2. -(-H • F) → (J • -L)
    3. (-L v J) → (T v I)
    4. (T v C)   ⊢   [T v (C • I)]

30* 1. -(Z → A) → -Y
    2. Y → (-B v A)
    3. -A   ⊢   Y → -(B v Z)

7.6 Rule of Conditional Proof

There is a convenient method sometimes used in natural deduction to obtain conditional statements in proofs. It is employed in the main when the conclusion of the argument is a conditional, but it may be used to obtain a conditional statement at any point in a proof, such as when a conditional is necessary to obtain the conclusion, which may or may not itself be a conditional.

One part of this method is what is known as *The Rule of Conditional Proof* (RCP). The method proceeds as follows: 1) assume the antecedent to the desired conditional, 2) derive the consequent, using some finite sequence of the rules of inference and/or the axioms of replacement, 3) close the scope of the assumption, and 4) write the conditional on the line directly succeeding the closure of the assumption. RCP is explicated schematically below:

Premise | The number of premises is,
Premise | of course, variable, even

→ p   (A) Assumption

The number of premises is, of course, variable, even including the number 0, as will be made clear in the section on proving logical truths below.

```
→ ┌ p        (A)  Assumption
  │ •
  │ •
  │ •
  │ q
  └────────
    (p → q)
```

The scope of the assumption is designated by the arrow to the left of the assumed statement and the vertical and horizontal lines.

The following two proofs are examples of how RCP works. '(A)' is used in the justification line to indicate that the fomula written is an assumption.

A

1. (G → S)
2. G → (S → F) ⊢ (G → F)
→ 3. G   (A)   Assume the antecedent to the
   4. S   1,3, MP   desired conditional; derive the
   5. (S → F)   2,3, MP   consequent of the conditional;
   6. F   4,5, MP   write the conditional; justify it
   7. (G → F)   3-6, RCP   with *RCP*.

B

1. (E v H) → -E ⊢ (E → H)
→ 2. E   (A)
   3. (E v H)   2, Ad
   4. -E   1,3, MP
   5. (E → -E)   2-4, RCP
   6. (-E v -E)   5, MI
   7. -E   6, Re
   8. (-E v H)   7, Ad
   9. (E → H)   8, MI

In the first argument, the antecedent to the conclusion, 'G', is assumed and, through a series of applications of the rule of inference *modus ponens*, 'F' is derived on line 6, after which the scope of the assumption is closed. Line 7 is the conclusion, and says merely that *if* G is true, then F is true.

In the second argument, unlike the first, the conclusion does not appear on the line directly after the closure of the assumption. Rather, to derive the conclusion itself requires deriving a preliminary conditional. As mentioned, RCP may be used *whenever* a conditional is needed.

It is vital that every assumption be, at some juncture, closed, and that the next line of the proof be a conditional statement, consisting in the assumed statement as the antecedent and the final statement in the assumption as the consequent.

It is also essential to note that once an assumption is closed, one cannot use any formula in the assumption itself to obtain a further formula. The following proof contains two assumptions, and will make this point clear.

1.	$(T \vee P) \rightarrow (-T \vee K)$		
2.	$K \rightarrow (-T \rightarrow -K) \vdash (T \leftrightarrow K)$		
3.	T	(A)	Note that '(A)' and
4.	$(T \vee P)$	3, Ad	'RCP' can be used again
5.	$(-T \vee K)$	1,4, MP	and again in a proof, as
6.	$--T$	3, DN	can the principles of
7.	K	5,6, DS	replacement and the
8.	$(T \rightarrow K)$	3-7, RCP	rules of inference.
9.	K	(A)	
10	$(-T \rightarrow -K)$	2,9, MP	
11	$(K \rightarrow T)$	10, Cp	
12	T	9,11, MP	
13	$(K \rightarrow T)$	9-12, RCP	
14	$(T \rightarrow K) \cdot (K \rightarrow T)$	8,13, Con	
15	$(T \leftrightarrow K)$	14, ME	

Note that though 'K' appears on line 7 and is needed again to obtain the consequent ('$(-T \rightarrow -K)$') in line 2 on a further line (10), which is outside the first closed assumption, since line 7 is within the scope of a closed assumption, 'K' must be obtained by opening a further assumption.

The following proof shows how two assumptions can be open at the same time.

1. $-C \lor (-J \lor L)$
2. $-(A \to -J)$ ⊢ $C \to (U \to L)$
→ 3. C (A)
→ 4. U (A)
5. $-(-A \lor -J)$ 2, MI
6. $(--A \bullet --J)$ 5, DM
7. $C \to (-J \lor L)$ 1, MI
8. $(-J \lor L)$ 3,7, MP
9. $(--J \bullet --A)$ 6, Com
10. $--J$ 9, Si
11. L 8,10, DS
12. $(U \to L)$ 4-11, RCP
13. $C \to (U \to L)$ 3-12, RCP

We can justify the use of RCP in general by noting the following considerations. By treating the antecedent to the conditional in the conclusion as a further premise in the argument (and that is what is being done, in effect, when one assumes the antecedent), one claims that the revised set of premises is sufficient to derive the consequent to the conditional in the conclusion. However, since the assumption is not actually a member of the original set of premises, it would be illegitimate merely to write it on a further line without using some specified rule or other. Hence, it is put forth as a hypothetical, a *what if?*, which conditions all the inferences drawn after its introduction. Now, since it is treated strictly as a hypothetical, when the scope of the assumption is terminated, the original assumption becomes that which conditions the immediate further statement. It is as though one said, "Given the truth of these premises, let's pretend that the following statement is also true." Whatever follows *from* the pretense, then, is conditioned *by* the pretense. Hence the conditional statement required when the assumption is closed.

The Rule of Conditional Proof can also be a helpful method for deriving a conclusion which is not itself a conditional but is equivalent to a conditional (i.e., where one derives a sentence from which the conclusion can be derived through a finite number of applications of the rules and axioms). In these sorts of cases it is not always obvious that RCP will be helpful. Consider the following proof:

```
     1.  (B → E)
     2.  (Y ↔ B)   ⊢   (-Y v E)
→    3.  Y                          (A)
     4.  (Y → B) • (B → Y)          2, ME
     5.  (Y → B)                    4,  Si
     6.  B                          3,5, MP
     7.  E                          1,6, MP
     8.  (Y → E)                    3-7, RCP
     9.  (-Y v E)                   8, MI
```

The conclusion of the above argument can be changed into a conditional via Material Implication. So, also, the conditional could be changed into a disjunction. Recognizing this about a conclusion could suggest that RCP may be of assistance. This might in turn suggest that one examine the conclusion of the argument for which one is constructing a proof, to see whether RCP may be of some help.

Keep in mind, then, that RCP can be used *whenever* one is trying to find a conditional, even if the conclusion is not itself a conditional or derivable from a conditional. Examine once again the argument above with '(W ↔ D)' as the conclusion. In that instance, two conditionals were needed (lines 8 and 13).

Below are other examples of proofs using RCP.

```
     1.  (-Q → S)
     2.  -K v -(P v S)   ⊢   (K → Q)
→    3.  K                          (A)
     4.  --K                        3,   DN
     5.  -(P v S)                   2,4, DS
     6.  (-P • -S)                  5,   DM
     7.  (-S • -P)                  6,   Com
     8.  -S                         7,   Si
     9.  --Q                        1,8,  MT
    10   Q                          9, DN
    11   (K → Q)                    3-10,  RCP
```

1. (-R v W)
2. (-X v -R) → B
3. (-P → -X) ⊢ -B → (W v P)
4. -B   (A)
5. -(-X v -R)   2,4, MT
6. (--X • --R)   5, DM
7. (X → P)   3, Cp
8. (R → W)   1, MI
9. (X → P) • (R → W)   7,8, Con
10 X   6, Si,DN
11 (X v R)   10, Ad
12 (P v W)   9,11, CD
13 (W v P)   12, Com
14 -B → (W v P)   4-13, RCP

1. -(M v D) v (-M • I) ⊢   D → (F → I)
2. D   (A)
3. (-M • -D) v (-M • I)   1, DM
4. -M • (-D v I)   3, Di
5. (-D v I)   4, Com, Si
6. --D   2, DN
7. I   5,6, DS
8. (I v -F)   7, Ad
9. (-F v I)   8, Com
10 (F → I)   9, MI
11 D → (F → I)   2-10, RCP

1. -(-T • R) → [G v (Z • K)]
2.   -(-G → E)   ⊢   (R → T) → (K → Z)
3. (R → T)   (A)
4. K   (A)
5. (-R v T)   3, MI
6. --(-R v T)   5, DN
7. -(--R • -T)   6, DM
8. -(R • -T)   7, DN
9. -(-T • R)   8, Com
10 G v (Z • K)   2,9, MP
11 (G v Z) • (G v K)   10, Di
12 -(--G v E)   2, MI
13 -(G v E)   12, DN

```
    14  (-G • -E)              13, DM
    15  -G                     14, Si
    16  (G v Z)                11, Si
    17  Z                      15,16, DS
    18  (K → Z)                4-17, RCP
    19  (R → T) → (K → Z)      3-18, RCP
```

```
     1.  [M → (-N v O)]
     2.  [-(-O  v P) → -N]     ⊢   [-M v (N → P)]
 →   3.  M                     (A)
 →   4.  N                     (A)
     5.  (-N v O)              3,5, MP
     6.  --N                   4, DN
     7.  O                     5,6, DS
     8.  --(-O v P)            2,6, MT
     9.  (-O v P)              8, DN
    10.  --O                   7, DN
    11   P                     9,10, DS
    12  (N → P)                4-11, RCP
    13  [M → (N → P)]          3-12, RCP
    14  [-M v (N → P)]         13, MI
```

Exercise 7.6

Use RCP, and the rules of inference and axioms of replacement, to show that the following arguments are valid.

1. 1.   -(-I → S) v -V   ⊢ (V → -S)

2. 1.   (R v T)
    2.   (O → -Q)
    3.   (-O → -T) ⊢ (Q → R)

3. 1.   -S
    2.   -(-H v S) → U
    3.   (W → -U) ⊢ (H → -W)

4. 1. (-V • -V) → -E
   2. (-R v -V)
   3. (-R → Q) ⊢ (-E v Q)

5* 1. (A v -C)
   2. (-C v I)
   3. -(-N • A) ⊢ (N v -C)

6. 1. (G v -U) v -T
   2. (G → N) ⊢   -(T → J) → (U → N)

7. 1. [-(Q v -D) v P]
   2. {(-P v D) → (Q v -H)}
   3. [(P • P) → D]   ⊢ [H → (D ↔ Q)]

8. 1. [(J v L) v -C] → I
   2. (I v L) → E   ⊢ (C → J) → E

9. 1. -V → (S • G)
   2. (S v G) → L
   3. (L → -X) ⊢ (V v -X)

10*1. [(Z v -E) → T] • (E → Y)
    2. -(-T → S) ⊢ Z → (K → Y)

7.7 Reductio ad Absurdum

The truth tree method for showing arguments to be valid or invalid required that we deny the conclusion of the argument and work for contradictions on each branch of the tree. We saw that if it was possible to hold the premises true and the conclusion false without generating contradictions, then the argument was invalid.

A similar method in natural deduction, called *Reductio ad Absurdum*, uses RCP, the rules and axioms, and the denial of the conclusion as an assumption. The aim is to deny the conclusion, attempt to achieve statements that contradict one another, on separate lines, and proceed then to obtain the conclusion on a further line, *outside the scope of the assumption*. Essentially, what one does here is "reduce to an absurdity" (with 'p' and '-p' on separate lines), and from this absurdity, via Addition and Disjunctive Syllogism, derive the conclusion. The following lengthy proof will show the method.

```
    1.  (-F v H)
    2.  (F v S)
    3.  (S → T)   ⊢   (H v T)
→   4.  -(H v T)                    (A,DC)
    5.  (-H • -T)                   4, DM
    6.  (-T • -H)                   5, Com
    7.  -T                          6, Si
    8.  -S                          3,7, MT
    9.  (S v F)                     2, Com
    10  F                           8,9, DS
    11  --F                         10, DN
    12  H                           1,11, DS
    13  -H                          5, Si
    14  H v (H v T)                 12, Ad
    15  (H v T)                     13,14, DS
    16  -(H v T) → (H v T)          4-15, RCP
    17  --(H v T) v (H v T)         16, MI
    18  (H v T) v (H v T)           17, DN
    19  (H v T)                     18, Re
```

You will have noticed that there is something different about the line on which the assumption appears. It also contains 'DC'. This shows that the plan is to use *reductio ad absurdum* to derive the conclusion.

Some logicians use RAA differently from the way it is here used. The rule they cite is that "from a contradiction, the conclusion may be written on the line immediately following." In this way, one avoids the further steps of closing the assumption, applying the rules of Addition and Disjunctive, and using RCP. However, when these steps are deleted, one may know *that* anything at all can be obtained from contradictory statements without the least idea *how* to show it. We will employ *Reductio ad Absurdum* here as a method rather than as a rule.

When using the method *reductio ad absurdum*, after getting 'p' and '-p' on separate lines, there is a strict method for deriving the conclusion outside the scope of the assumption. The method is this: 1) Add the conclusion to 'p' (line 14 above), 2) derive the conclusion via Disjunctive Syllogism (15), 3) close the scope of the assumption, 4) apply RCP to the closure of the assumption, yielding a conditional statement (16) made up of the statement that was assumed (antecedent) and the conclusion (consequent), 5) use Material Implication to derive '(p v p)' (17), and 6) use Replication to derive the conclusion of the argument itself, outside the scope of any assumption. Two further examples of RAA follow:

1.	-(N v M) v (O • A)	
2.	-O ⊢ -N	
→ 3.	N	(A,DC)
4.	(N v M)	3, Ad
5.	(N v M) → (O • A)	1, MI
6.	(O • A)	4,5, MP
7.	O	6, Si
8.	(O v -N)	7, Ad
9.	-N	2,8, DS
10	(N → -N)	3-9, RCP
11	(-N v -N)	10, MI
12	-N	11, Re

1.	-X → (-R → -Z)	
2.	-(Z • -X) → -T ⊢ (T → R)	
→ 3.	-(T → R)	(A,DC)
4.	-(-T v R)	3, MI
5.	(--T • -R)	4, DM
6.	--T	5, SI
7.	--(Z • -X)	2,6, MT
8.	(Z • -X)	7, DN
9.	-X	8, Com,Si
10	(-R → -Z)	1,9, MP
11	-R	5, Com,Si
12	-Z	10,11, MP
13	Z	8, Si
14	Z v (T → R)	13, Ad
15	(T → R)	12,14, DS
16	-(T → R) → (T → R)	3-15, RCP
17	(T → R) v (T → R)	16, MI
18	(T → R)	17, Re

You will have noticed that lines 8-12 match with lines 14-18 in the two proofs above. That is, the rules cited in the justifications of these lines are precisely the same, and are in the same order. In fact, these are the rules and the order of the rules to be used as the last 5 lines of all proofs using the RAA method.

Many times it is the initiation of the denial of the conclusion that will greatly facilitate obtaining contradictory formulas in a proof. However, if one can obtain a contradiction without making any assumption, then one can get absolutely any formula at all, including the conclusion of the argument. Consider the following argument.

-(-E → K)
(E • R) v (E v K)   ⊢   H

If this argument appears odd to you, perhaps it is because you are wondering how 'H' could follow from premises that do not contain 'H' as a component. It *is* a valid argument since the premises are contradictory. Since they are contradictory, they cannot both be true at the same time. Hence, this argument cannot have all true premises as well as a false conclusion, which would prove invalidity. That the letter 'H' was chosen for the conclusion was completely arbitrary. It could just as well have been '-H' or '(H v Z)', or '(I → O)', or any other statement (atomic or molecular) you can conceive. The reason for this is that all statements follow from a contradiction, including their negatives. The proofs below bear this out, since in the first, 'H' is the conclusion, and in the second, it is '-H'.

1.   -(-E → K)
2.   (E • R) v (E v K)   ⊢   H
3.   -(--E v K)   1, MI
4.   -(E v K)   3, DN
5.   (-E • -K)   4, DM
6.   (E v K) v (E • R)   2, Com
7.   (E • R)   4,6, DS
8.   -E   5, Si
9.   E   7, Si
10 (E v H)   9, Ad
11 H   8,10, DS

1. -(-E → K)
2. (E • R) v (E v K)   ⊢   -H
3. -(--E v K)   1, MI
4. -(E v K)   3, DN
5. (-E • -K)   4, DM
6. (E v K) v (E • R)   2, Com
7. (E • R)   4,6, DS
8. -E   5, Si
9. E   7, Si
10 (E v -H)   9, Ad
11 -H   8,10, DS

Notice that these proofs are precisely alike except for the statements appearing on line 11 in each. In fact, even the justifications are the same, including lines cited.

The following is a further example of RCP which is a bit more complicated, but only in terms of the rules and principles used to derive line 18. Note the same method of working with RCP is employed here.

1. (Q • T) → D
2. (Q • -T) → -D   ⊢   {Q → [(T • D) v (-T • -D)]}
→ 3. Q   (A)
4. -(Q • T) v D   1, MI
5. (-Q v -T) v D   4, DM
6. -Q v (-T v D)   5, As
7. --Q   3, DN
8. (-T v D)   6,7, DS
9. -(Q • -T) v -D   2, MI
10 (-Q v T) v -D   9, DM, DN
11 -Q v (T v -D)   10, As
12 (T v -D)   7,11, DS
13 (-T v D) • (T v -D)   8,12, Con
14 (T → D) • (T v -D)   13, MI
15 (T → D) • (-D v T)   14, Con
16 (T → D) • (D → T)   15, MI
17 (T ↔ D)   16, ME
18 [(T • D) v (-T • -D)]   17, ME
19 Q → [(T • D) v (-T • -D)]   3-18, RCP

Exercise 7.7

Use RAA, and any combination of RCP, the rules and axioms to prove the following arguments to be valid.

1. 1. (T v -A) → B
    2. -(Q → B) ⊢ A

2. 1. S → (C v A)
    2. (-A • -C) ⊢ -S

3. 1. (W → K)
    2. (-I → -K) ⊢ (-I → -W)

4. 1. (-E → -V)
    2. (-X v T)
    3. (-T v -E) ⊢ -(V • X)

5* 1. (-N v -N) v U
    2. (N • U) → F   ⊢   (N • N) → F

6. 1. (Z v W) → A
    2. (-O • -W) → Z ⊢ O v (A v Z)

7. 1. H → (-S • -P)
    2. S → (H • -P)
    3. -(S → V) ⊢ (-H • -S)

8. 1. (M → -E)
    2. (K → -Q)
    3. (E v K) ⊢ (-M v -Q)

9. 1. -G
    2. (P v T) → (T → G)
    3. (G → T) • P ⊢ -T

10* 1. (I • J) v (-I • -J)
    2. -(-I → W) ⊢ -J

7.8 *Logical Truths*

Both Rule of Conditional Proof and *Reductio ad Absurdum* can be used to 'prove logical truths' (that is, show sentences to be logically true). The method here is simply to proceed as though the sentence in question is a conclusion to some argument which has no premises. In fact, recall that this was precisely the method of proving logical truths with truth trees. There, we indicated that there were 'zero premises' and we proceeded to treat the sentence in question as a conclusion by denying it. We can adopt the same schema here, as so:

1. Zero Premises ⊢ [Sentence to be proved]

Below is a proof showing the sentence '[P → (-P → P)]' to be L-true using RCP.

```
    1.  Zero Premises   ⊢   [P → (-P → P)]
→   2.  P                    (A)
    3.  (P v P)              2, Ad
    4.  (--P v P)            3, DN
    5.  (-P → P)             4, MI
    6.  [P → (-P → P)]       2-5 RCP
```

Here is a proof, with RAA, showing '[-(P • P) → -P]' L-true.

```
    1.  Zero Premises   ⊢   [-(P • P) → -P]
→   2.  -[-(P • P) → -P]                         (A, DC)
    3.  -[--(P • P) v -P]                         2 MI
    4.  [---(P • P) • --P]                        3 DM
    5.  ---(P • P)                                4 Si
    6.  --P                                       4 Com, Si
    7.  -(P • P)                                  5 DN
    8.  (-P v -P)                                 7 DM
    9.  -P                                        6,8 DS
   10   -P v [-(P • P) → -P]                      9 Ad
   11   [-(P • P) → -P]                           6,10 DS
   12   -[-(P • P) → -P] → [-(P • P) → -P]        2-11 RCP
   13   --[-(P • P) → -P] v [-(P • P) → -P]       12 MI
   14   [-(P • P) → -P] v [-(P • P) → -P]         13 DN
   15   [-(P • P) → -P]                           14 Re
```

Note that line 2 is an assumption. In proving logical truths, every 'line 2' will be an assumption. When using RCP, line 2 will be the assumption of the antecedent to the conditional one is trying to derive, as in the above proof. When using RAA, line 2 will simply be the negation of the sentence to be proved.

Exercise 7.8

Show that the sentences below are L-true.

1.   [F → (-T v F)]
2.   (T → F) ↔ (-F → -T)

3.   -(V • R) ↔ --(R → -V)
4.   [(H v -H) • (-H v H)]
5*   [(-N v D) v (N v -D)]
6.   -(E • R) → (-Q v -R)
7.   {[(I → Q) • I] → Q}
8.   -[(K → -L) ↔ (L • K)]
9.   -(F → G) v [-G → (F → -X)]
10*   [(-T → L) • -U] → (U → -L)
11   [-(C • D) • C] → -D
12   {-(B • W) v [B • (W v E)]}
13   -(A ↔ B) ↔ (-A ↔ B)
14   [Ee → (Ff → Gg)] → [(Ee → Ff) → (Ee → Gg)]
15*   [(R → S) ↔ -(R • -S]

8. Predicate Logic

8.1 Preliminaries

The present chapter is an extension of Chapters 5, 6, and 7. It deals again with translations and methods of proving various arguments to be valid or invalid. There are sections on both natural deduction and truth trees. But it goes beyond the simple sorts of sentences and arguments treated in those chapters. Adding a few symbols to our already existing set, we will be in a position to become extremely precise when translating sentences from natural language (in our case English) into symbolic notation.

Predicate logic will allow us to prove that many arguments which would be judged invalid in sentential logic are actually valid. For example:

(A)   All physical objects are extended in space.
(B)   Some physical objects are unobservable.
(C)   Hence, some unobservable objects are extended in space.

In sentential logic, we might translate this argument as

A
B ⊢ C

which is clearly invalid. But, since the original argument is valid, there should be a way of showing this. In Aristotelian logic, of course, this argument corresponds to the mood and figure of AII-2, and can be shown to be valid using Venn Diagrams. However, we seek a system of logic that can handle arguments that cannot be handled by the Aristotelian system and/or sentential logic. In short, we want a system that goes beyond both Aristotelian and sentential logics. Predicate logic is that system.

8.2   Translations

Let us begin with a sentence that might be uttered by any teacher of United States geography.

Baltimore is a city on the Chesapeake Bay.

To translate this sentence with precision, we need to introduce new notation. Since being a city on the Chesapeake Bay is what is being said, or predicated, of Baltimore, we will call the phrase 'is a city on the Chesapeake Bay' a **Predicate**. (Note here that the word "predicate" does not have the exact meaning the grammarian gives to it.) Predicates will be symbolized by the upper case letters of the alphabet, called **Predicate Letters**. Since 'Baltimore' is the name of the object that is being referred to, we will call 'Baltimore' a **Name**. To denote names of objects, things, or individuals we will use lower case letters of the alphabet from 'a' through 't', called **Name Letters**, also referred to as **Individual Constants**. Letting 'C' = 'is a city on the Chesapeake Bay' and letting 'b' = 'Baltimore', we symbolize the sentence above as: Cb.

Some further examples of this sort of notation are:

Toyon is a literary journal.	Lt
Charles Dickens was not a poet.	-Pd
Pink Floyd is a rock group.	Rp
Crazy Horse is a rock group.	Rc
Pink Floyd and Crazy Horse are rock groups.	(Rp • Rc)
If modern art is inexpensive, Sotheby's will go bankrupt.	(-Em → Bs)

The importance of a translation dictionary should be obvious with the above sentences and their symbolic translations. For example, in the fifth sentence, 'R' = 'is a rock group', 'p' = 'Pink Floyd', and 'c' = 'Crazy Horse'. The sentence written in symbolic notation literally says, "Pink Floyd is a rock group and Crazy Horse is a rock group", which has the exact meaning as "Pink Floyd and Crazy Horse are rock groups". In the last example, 'E' = 'is expensive', 'm' = 'modern art', 'B' = 'goes bankrupt', and 's' = 'Sotheby's'.

When we begin to translate more complex sorts of sentences, we find the need to introduce new symbolism. Take, for example, the sentence,

All human adults have rights.

Recall that this is a Universal Affirmative (**A**) sentence. What this sentence is saying is that if any being is a human adult, then it has a right. We might reword the sentence in the following ways:

> If anything is a human adult, then that thing has rights.
> If any object is a human adult, then that object has rights.

These sentences are about as precise as we can get, until we introduce the symbols of logic into the scheme. We begin as follows:

> Given any x, if x is a human adult, then x has rights.

The "x" you find occurring three times in the above sentence is called a *variable*. Variables may be thought of as place holders. The place they hold is for individual constants and name letters, such as 'k' in Lk, where 'L' = 'is lazy' and 'k' = 'Kathy'. (More will be said about variables as place holders in the section on proofs.) Variables are symbolized by lower case letters from the end of the alphabet: x,y,z. The phrase "Given any x", which in the original sentence is "All", corresponds to what we call the *Universal Quantifier*. (Other ways of referring to the Universal Quantifier in English are: "For any x" and "No matter what x is".) In predicate logic we express this quantifier as a single variable enclosed in parentheses: **(x)**. We can provide the following translation dictionary for the sentence: 'Ax' = 'x is a human adult'; 'Rx' = 'x has rights'. Note that only the conditional indicator ("if...then") is not covered by either the quantifier or the dictionary. That logical component will be translated with the arrow, our symbol for the conditional. The translated symbolized sentence, then, is:

> (x)(Ax → Rx)

It is very important to include the parentheses just as they are above. Each occurrence of a variable must be *bound* by a quantifier. A *free variable* is a variable that is not bound by, or within the scope of, any quantifier, as in **Ax**, which does not express any sentence in English. It is one thing for 'Ax' represent some phrase in a translation dictionary, quite another for it to *mean* and *refer* to something.

The scope of any given quantifier extends from the proximate grouper to its matching grouper. For example, in the sentence (x)[Rx v (Sx • Tx)] the scope of the quantifier extends from the left bracket to the right bracket. In (x)Rx → Ra, however, the scope of the quantifier extends only over 'Rx'.

All **A** sentences are translated in precisely the same way, though the content and hence the dictionary will change. There are a variety of ways in which **A** sentences can be expressed in English. Below are examples:

Every explorer is adventurous. $(x)(Ex \rightarrow Ax)$
Members of the Apache tribe are all Native Americans.
<Ax = x is a member of the Apache tribe> $(x)(Ax \rightarrow Nx)$
Each Hawaiian Island is beautiful. $(x)(Hx \rightarrow Bx)$
Dolphins are mammals. $(x)(Dx \rightarrow Mx)$
Only the Cubs play home games at Wrigley Field.
<Wx = x plays home games at Wrigley Field> $(x)(Wx \rightarrow Cx)$

We can also translate the other Universal categorical sentence, i.e., the Universal Negative (**E**). We use the universal quantifier and an appropriate translation dictionary. To translate 'No tigers are herbivorous', let 'Tx' = 'x is a tiger' and let 'Hx' = 'x is herbivorous'. The translated sentence is:

$$(x)(Tx \rightarrow -Hx)$$

which may be read as "Given any x, if x is a tiger, then x is not herbivorous. All **E** sentences are translated in the same way. One can express **E** sentences in a variety of ways in English. Below are a number of examples.

There aren't any bald hairdressers.
　　$(x)(Bx \rightarrow -Hx)$ or 　　　$(x)(Hx \rightarrow -Bx)$
Patient news reporters don't exist.
　　$(x)(Px \rightarrow -Rx)$ or 　　　$(x)(Rx \rightarrow -Px)$
Fish are not mammals.
　　$(x)(Fx \rightarrow -Mx)$ or 　　　$(x)(Mx \rightarrow -Fx)$
No person is both a rich and happy.
　　$(x)(Rx \rightarrow -Hx)$ or 　　　$(x)(Hx \rightarrow -Rx)$
The classes of reptiles and mammals are mutually exclusive.
　　$(x)(Rx \rightarrow -Mx)$ or 　　　$(x)(Mx \rightarrow -Rx)$

To translate Particular Affirmative sentences and Particular Negative sentences, we need a way of symbolizing the *Existential Quantifier* "some". The symbolic form of the existential quantifier is: $(\exists x)$. In predicate logic, we read '(∃x)' as 'There exists an x such that'. Consider the following sentence:

Some pets are loved by their owners.

What this sentence is saying is that there is a pet that is loved by its owner, or that there is a pet *and* this pet is loved by its owner. We can begin to translate the sentence by inserting the variable, like so:

There is an x such that x is a pet and x is loved by its owner.

Note that the above sentence is a conjunction. The translation dictionary is as follows: 'Px' = 'x is a pet'; 'Lx' = 'x is loved by its owner'. The original sentence can now be fully symbolized, as

(∃x)(Px • Lx)

All Particular Affirmative sentences are translated in the same way. Examples of ways of expressing Particular Affirmative sentences are:

There are conservative Democrats.	(∃x)(Cx • Dx)
A lot of German cars are overpriced.	(∃x)(Gx • Ox)
At least one head of state is a woman.	(∃x)(Hx • Wx)
Sometimes police sergeants are cranky.	(∃x)(Px • Cx)
Many war criminals escaped punishment.	(∃x)(Wx • Ex)

Particular Negative sentences are translated in the same way as Particular Affirmative sentences, i.e., as conjunctions, but with the second conjunct denied. 'Some pets are not loved by their owners' is translated as follows:

(∃x)(Px • -Lx)

The ways of expressing Particular Negative sentences in English are many. Some are:

Not all bees make honey.	(∃x)(Bx • -Mx)
Some calligraphers aren't graphic artists.	(∃x)(Cx • -Gx)
Many people are not afraid of snakes.	(∃x)(Px • -Ax)

There are talk show hosts who are not attractive.   ($\exists$x)(Tx • -Ax)
There is at least one airline pilot who doesn't have vertigo.

($\exists$x)(Ax • -Vx)

One can gain some insight into the translations of categorical sentences by seeing relationships that hold between them. For example, the following pairs of sentences are contradictories:

1.	2.
All surfers are athletic.	No surfers are athletic.
(x)(Sx $\rightarrow$ Ax)	(x)(Sx $\rightarrow$ -Ax)
Some surfers are not athletic.	Some surfers are athletic.
($\exists$x)(Sx • -Ax)	($\exists$x)(Sx • Ax)

Compare these translations with the Traditional Square of Opposition found in Chapter 2. Note especially the importance of Existential Import now that we've added the symbolic notation for quantifiers.

Further Translations

There are, of course, many things we can say that do not fit exactly into the form of the four categories of sentences treated above. Examples, and their translations follow. Keep in mind that the translation dictionary is vital for proper translation of any sentence in predicate logic. For instance, in the fourth sentence below, let Cx = x is a car, Wx = x is a work of art, Wp = Porsches are works of art.

The president of the confederacy wasn't a Virginian.
  -Vp
There aren't any ghosts.
  -($\exists$x)Gx
Anyone drunk enough to fight is too drunk to fight well.
  (x)(Fx $\rightarrow$ Wx)
If any cars are works of art, Porsches are.
  ($\exists$x)(Cx • Wx) $\rightarrow$ Wp
If all humans are persons, Willie Mays is a person.
  (x)(Hx $\rightarrow$ Px) $\rightarrow$ Pw
If ghosts exist, they're discontent but not evil.
  (x)[Gx $\rightarrow$ (-Cx • -Ex)]

Everything is observable.
   (x)Ox
Not everything in nature is physical.
   -(x)Px
Nothing is immaterial.
   -(∃x)-Mx
Everything is either observable or immaterial.
   (x)(Ox v -Mx)
All and only males are sons.
   (x)(Mx ↔ Sx)
No one is both a brother and a sister.
   -(∃x)(Bx • Sx)
Some daughters are not both mothers and grandmothers.
   (∃x)[Dx • -(Mx • Gx)]
Everyone is either a son or a daughter; and no one is both.
   [(x)(Sx v Dx) • -(∃x)(Sx • Dx)]
Some children, though certainly not all, are psychic.
   [(∃x)(Cx • Px) • (∃x)(Cx • -Px)]

Exercise 8.2

A. Use the following translation dictionary to translate the sentences below into symbolic notation. [Ax = x is a master composer; Bx = x is beautiful; Cx = x is music written by Buddy Holly; Dx = x was born in Denver; Hx = x is music written by Rimsky-Korsakov; Lx = x is worth listening to; Mx = x is music written by George Gershwin; Px = x helped write *Porgy & Bess*; Rx = x wrote *Rhapsody in Blue*; Sx = x wrote *Scheherazade*; Ux = x is music; Wx = x could have written *Scheherazade*; b = Buddy Holly; g = George Gershwin; h = *Rhapsody in Blue*; p = *Porgy & Bess*; r = Rimsky-Korsakov; s = *Scheherazade*]

1. George Gershwin was not born in Denver.
2. George Gershwin wrote *Rhapsody in Blue* and helped write *Porgy & Bess*.
3. Some of George Gershwin's music is not beautiful.
4. Not all of the music written by Buddy Holly is beautiful.
5* If any music written by George Gershwin was beautiful, *Rhapsody in Blue* certainly was.

6. *Scheherazade* is beautiful music that was written by Rimsky-Korsakov, though not all music written by Rimsky-Korsakov is beautiful or worth listening to.
7. Only a master composer could have written *Scheherazade*.
8. If Buddy Holly helped write *Porgy & Bess*, then some of Buddy Holly's music is beautiful.
9. Buddy Holly didn't write *Scheherazade* and neither did George Gershwin, but it's beautiful.
10* All of George Gershwin's music is beautiful only if some of Buddy Holly's music is beautiful.

B. Translate the following symbolic sentences into normal English using the dictionary for exercise 8b. A.

1. -(x)Bx
2. -(∃x)Bx
3. (∃x)Bx → Bp
4. (x)Bx → (x)(Cx → Bx)
5* (x)[Ux → (Bx v -Lx)]

6. (Wb → Bs)
7. (∃x)(Rx • Sx)
8. (∃x)-(Rx v Sx)
9. (x){[(Hx v Cx) v Mx] → Lx}
10* (x)[-(Px → Wx) • (Rx → Wx)]

C. Create dictionaries for the following sentences and translate them into the symbolic notation of predicate logic.

1. Some day-care providers are both beautiful and intelligent.
2. Not all paper-boys are honest as well as efficient.
3. There are people who neither vote nor care who runs for president.
4. If Socrates taught anyone, then he taught Plato.
5* Each scientist uses the scientific method.
6. Some people claim to be both scientists and creationists.
7. Affirmative Action advocates all commit *Argumentum ad Misericordiam*.
8. Any computer has intelligence only if Rodney Dangerfield has.
9. Some children don't know the value of a buck.
10* Nothing has absolute and intrinsic value.
11 Not all people in Florida grow oranges.
12 One French Impressionist was either mentally ill or a nonconformist.
13 Every visitor to Tenerife misunderstood the guide's instructions.
14 It is false that all criminals are unhappy and genetic mutants.

15* Children are innocent only if they have no moral awareness.
16 There are children who are neither innocent nor morally blameworthy.
17 Puerto Rico will become a state just in case its economy improves.
18 If all people are good, then some of my enemies are good.
19 Research on the genetic basis of criminal behavior is unscientific.
20* It is false that no intelligent logicians write poetry.

8.3 Proofs in Natural Deduction

To work proofs in predicate logic, we retain all of the Rules of Inference and Principles of Replacement found in Chapter 7.

Our method of proof will be *Reductio ad Absurdum*, but we will approach it in a somewhat different manner from the way we did in Chapter 7. We will use RAA as a rule now, rather than as a method. The rule for RAA will be: *Whenever a contradiction is explicitly found on a line of a proof, write the conclusion on the next line of the proof, which will then be the last line.* The starting point of a Reductio proof is always the same, i.e., one assumes the denial or negation of the conclusion. In schematic form:

-Ca	\<Assumption: denial of conclusion\>
•	\<A further line in the proof\>
•	\<A further line in the proof\>
•	\<A further line in the proof\>
(Da • -Da)	\<An explicit contradiction\>
Ca	\<The conclusion\>

Using RAA as a rule is strictly a logician's short-cut. Using RAA as a rule, we are freed from having to make explicit use of the Rule of Conditional Proof. We know we *could*, in every case, go from contradictory sentences to any further sentence, using Addition, Disjunctive Syllogism, then closing the scope of the assumption and using RCP, Material Implication, Double Negation [sometimes], and Replication. (Recall the method as outlined at the end of Chapter 7.) Those seven steps are avoided by simply making the contradiction explicit in the proof, and then drawing the conclusion itself. Let's try it out.

1. $(Jp \rightarrow Hp)$
2. $-[Jp \lor (Fp \lor -Jp)]$ ⊦ $(Fp \rightarrow Hp)$
3. $-(Fp \rightarrow Hp)$ (A,DC)
4. $-(-Fp \lor Hp)$ 3, MI
5. $(--Fp \bullet -Hp)$ 4, DM
6. $-Hp$ 5, Com, Si
7. $-Jp$ 1,6, MT
8. $[-Jp \bullet -(Fp \lor -Jp)]$ 2, DM
9. $-(Fp \lor -Jp)$ 8, Com, Si
10 $(-Fp \bullet --Jp)$ 9, DM
11 $--Jp$ 10, Com, Si
12 Jp 11, DN
13 $(Jp \bullet -Jp)$ 7,12, Con
14 $(Fp \rightarrow Hp)$ 3-13, RAA

Note that the scope of the assumption is not formally expressed, except in the justification of line #3 where 'A' indicates an assumed sentence. Line #13 expresses the contradiction outright. From there, we don't formally close the assumption, but rather simply write the conclusion on the next line (#14), indicating that we have used lines 3-13 and RAA.

8.3.1 Universal Instantiation

To work proofs in predicate logic using quantifiers requires a few further rules. We need a way of going from quantified sentences to unquantified sentences. We can begin with the universal quantifier. Take the following sentence and its translation, where 'Fx' = 'x is an FBI agent' and 'Cx' = 'x is cleared for viewing top secret papers'.

Only FBI agents are cleared for viewing top secret papers.
    $(x)(Cx \rightarrow Fx)$

Obviously, none of our existing rules of inference or replacement would apply to this sentence. It is only when it is unquantified that our rules will apply. To render this sentence unquantified, we simply pick out an individual, say, Perry, (where 'p' = 'Perry') and replace the occurrences of the bound variable with the individual constant. We derive the sentence $(Cp \rightarrow Fp)$, which says "If Perry is cleared for viewing top secret papers, then Perry is an FBI agent." What we've done here is pick out an individual instance to replace the variable, dropping the quantifier because the sentence no longer refers to just any individual, but only to Perry. Dropping the quantifier and substituting an individual instance for every bound variable (every variable over which the quantifier ranges) is called *Universal Instantiation*. One is actually deriving one instance of the universal quantification. In other words, to instantiate is to replace a variable with an individual constant. The same variable is always to be replaced with the same individual constant in any given instantiation. The rule is called Universal Instantiation and is abbreviated as **UI**. Note that from the sentence above we can derive any individual instantiation. For example, letting 'j' = 'Mick Jagger', we derive "If Mick Jagger is cleared for viewing top secret papers, then Mick Jagger is an FBI agent". The sentence would then be instantiated with respect to 'j' and would appear as follows: (Cj → Fj). [It is standard practice to pick 'a', 'b' and 'c' as individual constants when no translation dictionary is provided.]

Let's work a proof with the rules we have so far.

1.	(x)(Fx → -Jx)	
2.	(x)(Jx v -Gx)	
3.	(x)Fx ⊢ -(x)Gx	
4.	--(x)Gx	(A,DC)
5.	(x)Gx	4, DN
6.	Ga	5, UI
7.	(Fa → -Ja)	1, UI
8.	(Ja v -Ga)	2, UI
9.	Fa	3, UI
10	-Ja	7,9, MP
11	-Ga	8,10, DS
12	(Ga • -Ga)	6,11, Con
13	-(x)Gx	3-12, RAA

To be able to work with the sentences appearing in lines 1, 2, 3, and 5, it required that the rule for Universal Instantiation be applied in each of those cases. The individual 'a' is not named, of course, since there is no translation dictionary. However, since each of those sentences applies universally, then each of those sentences can have 'a' as an instance, no matter who or what 'a' refers to. We *could* have picked 'b', or 'c', or 'd', or *any* other individual constant. But, if we had instantiated with respect to 'a' in line #5, but with respect to 'b' in lines 1, 2, or 3, then we would not have derived the desired contradiction in line #12. Instead, we would have derived the sentence "(Ga • -Gb)".

8.3.2 Quantifier Exchange

Before proceeding to the instantiation of the existential quantifier, let us introduce four essential rules of predicate logic. They are commonly known as the *Quantifier Exchange Rules*. They are:

$$(x)Rx \leftrightarrow -(\exists x)-Rx$$
$$-(x)Rx \leftrightarrow (\exists x)-Rx$$
$$(\exists x)Rx \leftrightarrow -(x)-Rx$$
$$-(\exists x)Rx \leftrightarrow (x)-Rx$$

Each of these rules expresses a legitimate logical equivalence, and each is abbreviated as **QE**. The formula on the left side of the double arrow is equivalent to the formula on the right side of the double arrow. The one may be "exchanged" for the other whenever either occurs in a proof or a tree. To see the need for these rules, consider the formula -(x)(Rx v Sx). There is no rule of inference or principle of replacement that applies to this formula. In fact, UI doesn't apply either, since that formula is not a universal quantification, but rather a negated universal quantification. By turning the formula into an existential quantification, that is, '(∃x)-(Rx v Sx)', we can now use an instantiation rule.

To better understand the quantifier exchange rules as equivalence rules, it may be helpful to offer examples in English. Let 'Rx' = 'x is movable'. Each of the following pairs of sentences corresponds to one of the QE rules.

(x)Rx	Everything is movable.
-(∃x)-Rx	It is false that there exists a thing that is immovable.
-(x)Rx	Not all things are movable.
(∃x)-Rx	There is something that is immovable.
(∃x)Rx	Something is movable.
-(x)-Rx	Not all things are immovable.

-(∃x)Rx   Nothing is movable.
(x)-Rx   Everything is immovable.

8.3.3 Existential Instantiation

The second instantiation rule (there are only two since there are only two quantifiers) makes use of the existential quantifier '(∃x)' and is called *Existential Instantiation*. It is abbreviated as **EI** and allows us to pick an instance of an existential quantification. As a universal quantification is a formula beginning with a universal quantifier, so an existential quantification is a formula beginning with an existential quantifier. There is one very important restriction to the use of EI: When using the rule EI, one must *not* instantiate with respect to any individual constant that appears in a line of the proof (including the premises) prior to the existential instantiation itself. For example, if one is working a proof in which '(x)Rx v Ra' appears as one of the premises, then if some existential quantification, say '(∃x)(Gx v Hx)', appears in one of the lines of the proof, it would be illegitimate to use EI to derive '(Ga v Ha)' as a further line, since 'a' appears prior to the instantiation of '(∃x)(Gx v Hx)'.

As a way of noting in the proof that some individual constant has been chosen by way of EI, we will adopt the practice of "flagging" the letter used in the instantiation. We will write an asterisk followed by the letter as part of the justification of the instantiation. So, if 'c' has been used as part of an existential instantiation, we will write "*c" to the far right. In this way we will indicate that 'c' has not appeared previously in the proof. There is, of course, no reason to flag any letter used as part of a universal instantiation, since there is no restriction on the use of individual constants in UI. An example of flagging follows.

1. (∃x)(Gx v Lx)
2. (x)-Lx   ⊦   Ga
3. (Ga v La)   1, EI   *a
4. -Ga   (A,DC)
5. -La   2, UI
6. La   3,4 DS
7. (La • -La)   5,6 Con
8. Ga   4-7 RAA

Note that in the proof above, while 'a' appears in the conclusion (stated in line 2), it is used in the instantiation in line 3. This is legitimate since the statement of the conclusion in line 2 is not part of the proof itself. Hence, the rule that a constant which appears in a line of a proof prior to an existential instantiation cannot be used in the instantiation is not violated.

Consider the following proof.

1.	$(x)(Ax \rightarrow Bx)$		
2.	$(x)-(Cx \vee Bx)$	⊢	$(x)-Ax$
3.	$-(x)-Ax$	(A,DC)	
4.	$(\exists x)--Ax$	3, QE	
5.	$--Aa$	4, EI *a	
6.	$(Aa \rightarrow Ba)$	1, UI	
7.	$-(Ca \vee Ba)$	2, UI	
8.	$(-Ca \bullet -Ba)$	7, DM	
9.	Aa	5, Si	
10	Ba	6,9, MP	
11	$-Ba$	8, Com, Si	
12	$(Ba \bullet -Ba)$	10,11, Con	
13	$(x)-Ax$	3-12, RAA	

If one were to have used UI before EI in this case, it would not have been possible to show that the argument is valid. This is so because using UI first would have put the occurrence of 'a' prior to the use of EI, in which case when EI was used one would have had to instantiate with respect to another individual constant besides 'a', such as 'b' or 'c'. It would have been impossible to derive the explicit contradiction in such a case.

A prudent rule to adopt is this: **EI before UI.**

The examples below use the rules introduced in this chapter. Note again that the system of predicate logic retains each of the rules of inference and the principles of replacement. Note also, again, that we are using Reductio ad Absurdum as a rule now, not as a method.

No being without a brain can think. Amoebae have no brains. Thus, amoebae cannot think. [Ax = x is an ameoba; Bx = x has a brain; Tx = x can think]

1.	(x)(-Bx → -Tx)		
2.	(x)(Ax → -Bx)	⊢	(x)(Ax → -Tx)
3.	-(x)(Ax → -Tx)		(A,DC)
4.	(∃x)-(Ax → -Tx)		3, QE
5.	-(Ar → -Tr)		4, EI *r
6.	-(-Ar v -Tr)		5, MI
7.	(--Ar • --Tr)		6, DM
8.	Ar		7, Si, DN
9.	--Tr		7, Com, Si
10	(Ar → -Br)		2, UI
11	-Br		8,10, MP
12	(-Br → -Tr)		1, UI
13	-Tr		11,12, MP
14	(-Tr • --Tr)		9,13, Con
15	(x)(Ax → -Tx)		3-14, RAA

Nothing is both uncaused and finite. Hence, everything finite has a cause. [Fx = x is finite; Gx = x has a cause]

1.	-(∃x)(-Gx • Fx)	⊢	(x)(Fx → Gx)
2.	-(x)(Fx → Gx)		(A,DC)
3.	(∃x)-(Fx → Gx)		2, QE
4.	-(Fa → Ga)		3, EI *a
5.	(x)-(-Gx • Fx)		1, QE
6.	-(-Ga • Fa)		5, UI
7.	(--Ga v -Fa)		6, DM
8.	(-Fa v Ga)		7, Com, DN
9.	(Fa → Ga)		8, MI
10	[(Fa → Ga) • -(Fa → Ga)]		4,9, Con
11	(x)(Fx → Gx)		3-10, RAA

For the next argument, two ways are shown of proving validity, the first using RAA, the second not using RAA.

There is no logic teacher who does not use à book in class. Dale and Hannah are both logic teachers. So, both Dale and Hannah use books in class. [Bx = x uses a book in class; Tx = x teaches logic; d = Dale; h = Hannah] Translation: 1. -(∃x)(Tx • -Bx); 2. (Td • Th); ⊢ (Bd • Bh)

1. -(∃x)(Tx • -Bx)
2. (Td • Th)   ⊢   (Bd • Bh)
3. -(Bd • Bh)   (A,DC)
4. (x)-(Tx • -Bx)   1, QE
5. -(Th • -Bh)   4, UI
6. (-Th v --Bh)   5, DM
7. Th   2, Com, Si
8. --Th   7, DN
9. --Bh   6,8, DS
10 Bh   9, DN
11 (-Bd v -Bh)   3, DM
12 -(Td • -Bd)   4, UI
13 (-Td v --Bd)   12, DM
14 --Td   2, Si, DN
15 --Bd   13,14, DS
16 -Bh   11,15, DS
17 (Bh • -Bh)   10,16, Con
18 (Bd • Bh)   3-17, RAA

1. -(∃x)(Tx • -Bx)
2. (Td • Th)   ⊢   (Bd • Bh)
3. (x)-(Tx • -Bx)   1, QE
4. -(Td • -Bd)   3, UI
5. -(Th • -Bh)   3, UI
6. (-Td v --Bd)   4, DM
7. (-Th v --Bh)   5, DM
8. --Td   2, Si, DN
9. Th   2, Com, Si
10 --Th   9, DN
11 Bd   6,8, DS, DN
12 Bh   7,10, DS, DN
13 (Bd • Bh)   11,12, Con

Although the number of steps is large in each of the proofs above, neither is very complicated. The key is to see why universal instantiation must be used twice in each proof. In the first proof, in line 4, the universal quantifier ranges over both 'Tx' and '-Bx'. It is improper to carry out more than one instantiation at a time, yielding '-(Td • -Bh)' from '(x)-(Tx • -Bx)'.

It's all right to kill nonhumans. If fetuses have no moral values, then they're not human. Fetuses don't have moral values. Hence, it's all right to kill fetuses. (Student's argument) [Fx = x is a fetus; Hx = x is human; Kx = it's all right to kill x; Mx = x has moral values]

1. (x)(-Hx → Kx)
2. (x)[(Fx • -Mx) → -Hx]
3. (x)(Fx → -Mx)   ⊦   (x)(Fx → Kx)
4. -(x)(Fx → Kx)   (A,DC)
5. (∃x)-(Fx → Kx)   4, QE
6. -(Fs → Ks)   5, EI *s
7. (Fs • -Ms) → -Hs   2, UI
8. (Fs → -Ms)   3, UI
9. -(-Fs v Ks)   6, MI
10 (--Fs • -Ks)   9, DM
11 Fs   10, Si, DN
12 -Ms   8,11, MP
13 (Fs • -Ms)   11,12, Con
14 -Hs   7,13, MP
15 (-Hs → Ks)   1, UI
16 Ks   14,15, MP
17 -Ks   10, Com, Si
18 (Ks • -Ks)   16,17, Con
19 (x)(Fx → Kx)   4-18, RAA

This is a good place to note that while 's' was used above in the existential instantiation, 's' is an arbitrary choice here. Any other constant could have been chosen. There is no restriction here.

Consider another translation and proof:

Some ethical dilemmas are avoidable. If there is any ethical dilemma that is avoidable, then either the dilemma is not a "life or death dilemma" or it is of minor importance. There is no such thing as a minor ethical dilemma. It follows that there is at least one ethical dilemma that is neither of minor importance nor is a life or death dilemma. [Ax = x is avoidable; Ex = x is an ethical dilemma; Lx = x is a life or death dilemma; Mx = x is of minor importance]

1. (∃x)(Ex • Ax)
2. (x)[(Ex • Ax) → (-Lx v Mx)]
3. -(∃x)(Ex • Mx)   ⊢   (∃x)[Ex • (-Mx v -Lx)]
4. -(∃x)[Ex • (-Mx v -Lx)]   (A,DC)
5. (x)-[Ex • (-Mx v -Lx)]   4, QE
6. (En • An)   1, EI *n
7. -[En • (-Mn v -Ln)]   5, UI
8. [(En • An) → (-Ln v Mn)]   2, UI
9. (-Ln v Mn)   6,8, MP
10 En   6, Si
11 --En   10, DN
12 (Mn v -Ln)   9, Com
13 [-En v -(Mn v -Ln)]   7, DM
14 -(Mn v -Ln)   11,13, DS
15 [(Mn v -Ln) • -(Mn v -Ln)]   12,14, Con
16 (∃x)[Ex • (Mx v -Lx)]   4-15, RAA

Note here that the third premise is not used in the proof of the validity of the argument. What this means is that the third premise is does not lend any support to the argument. It may be a persuasive premise and hence get the listener to lean toward accepting the argument, but it does no logical work here.

There are many arguments that are easier to prove valid without using RAA. One such argument, along with a proof, is:

No event is uncaused. Making the decision to have an abortion is an event. Rhoda made the decision to have an abortion. Hence Rhoda's decision was caused. [Cx = x is caused; Dx = x made the decision to have an abortion; Ex = x is an event; r = Rhoda]

1. (x)(Ex → Cx)
2. (x)(Dx → Ex)
3. Dr   ⊢   Cr
4. (Dr → Er)   2, UI
5. (Er → Cr)   1, UI
6. (Dr → Cr)   4,5, HS
7. Cr   3,6, MP

Exercise 8.3

A. Fill in the blank spaces with either the appropriate proof line or the appropriate justification for the proof line.

1.
1. (x)(Fx → Gx)
2. (x)-(Hx v Gx) ⊢ -Fe
3.   (A,DC)
4.   1, UI
5. -(He v Ge)
6.   5, DM
7. -Ge
8.   4,7, MT
9.   3,8, Con
10 -Fe

2.
1. (x)[Px • (Qx • Rx)]
2. (x)[(Qx v Rx) → Sx] ⊢ Sf
3. -Sf
4.   1, UI
5.   2, UI
6. (Qf • Rf)
7.   6, Si
8. (Qf v Rf)
9.   8,5, MP
10   3,9, Con
11 Sf

3.
1. (x)Lx ⊢ (-Ld → Hs)
2.   (A,DC)
3. -(--Ld v Hs)
4.   3, DM
5. Ld
6.   4, DN
7.   6, Si
8.   5,7, Con
9. (-Ld → Hs)

4*
1. (x)[(Tx v Yx) • (-Ux v Yx)]
2. (x)-(-Yx → -Ux)   ⊢   Tn
3. -Tn
4.   1, UI
5. -(-Yn → -Un)
6.   5, MI
7. (---Yn • --Un)
8. [(Yn v Tn) • (Yn v -Un)]
9.   8, Di
10 -Yn
11   9,10, DS
12 Tn
13   3,12, Con
14 Tn

B. Show that the following arguments are valid using natural deduction.

1.
1. (x)(Bx → Dx)
2. (x)(Bx v Bx) ⊢ Dr

4.
1. (x)[Fx → (Sx → Mx)]
2. (x)Sx   ⊢   (Mo v -Fo)

2.
1. (x)(Rx → Cx)
2. -(-La → Ca) ⊢ -Ra

5*
1. (x)(Ox • Wx)
2. (x)(Ox ↔ -Wx) ⊢ -(x)Wx

3. 1. (x)[Kx ∨ (Ax • Ix)]
    2. (x)-(Ix ∨ -Ax) ⊢ -(x)-Kx

6. 1. (x)[Gx → (Px → Nx)]
    2. (x)(-Nx • Px) ⊢ -Gc

C. Fill in the missing lines and justifications in each proof.

1. 1. (x)(Dx ∨ -Sx) ⊢ (x)-(Sx • -Dx)
    2.   (A,DC)
    3.   2, QE
    4.   3, EI *p
    5.   4, DN
    6.   1, UI
    7.   5, Si, DN
    8.   6, Com
    9.   7,8, DS
    10   5, Com, Si
    11   9,10, Con
    12   2-11, RAA

2. 1. (x)[(-Ix → Rx) ∨ -Lx]
    2. (x)Rx → Ra
    3. (x)-(Lx → Ix) ⊢ (x)Rx
    4.   (A,DC)
    5.   4, QE
    6.   5, EI *k
    7.   1, UI
    8.   3, UI
    9.   7, MI
    10   9, DN, Com
    11   10, As
    12   6,11, DS
    13   8, MI
    14   13, DM
    15   14, Si
    16   12, Com
    17   15,16, DS
    18   14, Com, Si
    19   17,18, Con
    20   4-19, RAA

3.   1.   (x)(Lx → Tx)
     2.   (x)(Lx → Wx) ⊢ (x)[Lx → (Tx • Wx)]
     3.   (A,DC)
     4.   (∃x)-[Lx → (Tx • Wx)]
     5.   4, EI *u
     6.   2, UI
     7.   (Lu → Tu)
     8.   5, MI
     9.   [--Lu • -(Tu • Wu)]
     10   9, Si
     11 Tu
     12   6,10, MP
     13   11,12, Con
     14   9, Com, Si
     15   13,14, Con
     16 (x)[Lx → (Tx • Wx)]

4.   1.   (x)[-(Ax → Bx) → -Cx]
     2.   (∃x)-Bx ⊢ (∃x)(-Cx v -Ax)
     3.   (A,DC)
     4.   3, QE
     5.   -Ba
     6.   4, UI
     7.   1, UI
     8.   [Ca → (Aa → Ba)]
     9.   8, Ex
     10 -(Ca • Aa)
     11 (--Ca • --Aa)
     12 (Ca • Aa)
     13   10,12, Con
     14 (∃x)(-Cx v -Ax)

5* 1. (x)Fx → (x)Gx
   2. (∃x)-Gx
   3. (x)(Hx → Fx)   ⊢   (∃x)-Hx
   4. -(∃x)-Hx
   5. -(x)Gx
   6. -(x)Fx
   7. (∃x)-Fx
   8. -Fa
   9. (Ha → Fa)
   10 -Ha
   11 (x)--Hx
   12 --Ha
   13 Ha
   14 (Ha • -Ha)
   15 (∃x)-Hx

6. 1. (x)(Lx → Rx) → (y)(Ty → -Ly)
   2. (∃x)-(Lx → Rx) → [(x)Cx • ((y)Ry • (z)Lz)]
   3. (∃y)-(Ty → Ly)   ⊢   (y)Ry
   4. -(y)Ry   (A,DC)
   5.   3, QE
   6. -(x)(Lx → Rx)
   7.   6, QE
   8.   7,3, MP
   9. [((y)Ry • (z)Lz)) • (x)Cx]
   10   9, As
   11 (y)Ry
   12 (y)Ry • -(y)Ry
   13 (y)Ry   4-12, RAA

D. Prove the following arguments to be valid.

1. 1. (∃x)(Cx • Fx)
   2. (x)(Kx v -Cx)   ⊢   (∃x)(Kx • Fx)

2. 1. (∃x)-Ix
   2. (x)(Gx → Ix) ⊢ (∃x)(-Gx v Hx)

3. 1. (Jc → Pc)   4. 1. (x)(Rx v Qx)
   2. -(∃x)Px ⊢ (∃x)-Jx   2. (x)[Px v (-Qx • -Rx)] ⊢ (x)Px

5* 1. (∃x)(Fx → Hx)   6. 1. (x)-(Sx • -Lx)
     ⊢ (∃x)[(Hx v Lx) v -Fx]   2. (x)(Rx • Sx)
                                      3.(x)[Lx → (Fx → -Rx)] ⊢ (x)-Fx

7. 1. -(∃x)-(-Ex v -Ax)   8. 1. (x)[(Kx v Jx) v -Lx]
  2. (∃x)-(Mx → -Ex)   2. (x)[-Mx → -(Nx v Kx)]
    ⊢   (∃x)-(Ax v -Mx)   ⊢ (x)[(-Lx v --Jx) v Mx]

9. 1. (x)[-(Bx → Cx) → -Ax]
  2. (x)[(Ax • Bx) v -(Bx v Ax)]
  3. (x)-(-Cx → -Dx) ⊢ (x)-Ax

10* 1. (x)(Zx v -Tx)
    2. (x)(Tx → Wx) ⊢ (x)[-(Wx • Zx) → -Tx]

E. Rewrite the following sentences using the quantifier exchange rules.

    1. Nothing is unexplainable.
    2. There is something that is precious.
    3. Each thing is corporeal.
    4. It is true that there are angels.
    5* Not everything is art.
    6. It is false that everything is audible.
    7. It is false that nothing is caused.
    8. Not all things are humorous.
    9. It is false that something is sacred.
    10* Everything is natural.

F. Translate the following arguments into symbolic notation and prove them to be valid using the method of natural deduction. A dictionary is provided.

    1. If anyone gives a speech on animal rights at the rally, then someone will speak out in favor of experimentation on animals in medical research. If someone speaks in favor of animal experimentation in medical research, then either Abe will write to the editor of the newspaper, or Bonny will research the subject for her term paper. But Bonny is researching the habitat of wolves in the Yukon Territory for her term paper and not animal experimentation. So, if anyone speaks on

animal rights, Abe will write to the editor. [Ax = x gives a speech on animal rights at the rally; a = Abe; b = Bonny; Ex = x speaks in favor of experimentation...; Tx = x researches the topic of experimentation on animals in medical research for a term paper; Wx = x writes to the newspaper editor; Yx = x is researching wolve's habitats in the Yukon]

2. Anybody who believes in the death penalty is guilty of a contradiction, from which it follows that if everybody believed in the death penalty, then everybody would be guilty of a contradiction. [Bx = x believes in the death penalty; Gx = x is guilty of a contradiction]

3. Combinations of atoms exist. Either everything is a combination of atoms or everything is a combination of monads. No combinations of atoms are combinations of monads. Therefore, everything is a combination of atoms. [Ax = x is a combination of atoms; Mx = x is a combination of monads]

4. Everything is genetically controlled if and only if nothing is affected by its environment. So, either something is affected by its environment or everything is genetically controlled. [Ex = x is affected by its environment; Gx = x is genetically controlled]

5.* If Cory successfully evades paying his taxes this year, he will have enough money to buy the sailboat he's been wanting. If he gets that much money, he will surely contribute to the March of Dimes. Hence, if Cory successfully evades his taxes, then someone will contribute to the March of Dimes. [c = Cory; Ex = x successfully evades paying taxes; Mx = x contributes to the March of Dimes; Sx = x has enough money to buy the sailboat]

6. Some people aren't very good at handling money matters, but all Certified Public Accountants (CPA) are good at handling money matters. If any person isn't very good at handling money matters, then that person should hire a CPA. And whoever is good at handling money matters should offer her/his services to welfare recipients. So, some CPA's should offer their services to welfare recipients. [Cx = x is a CPA; Gx = x is good at handling money matters; Hx = x should hire a CPA; Ox = x should offer her/his services to welfare recipients; Px = x is a person]

7. Anyone who is thought of as dull either listens only to classical music or drinks nothing but sherry. Anyone who is thought of as hip either enjoys the Grateful Dead or drinks beer. Since everyone is thought of as either dull or hip, it follows that everyone either listens only to classical music or drinks sherry or enjoys the Grateful Dead or drinks beer. [Bx = x drinks beer; Dx = x is thought of as dull; Gx = x enjoys the Grateful Dead; Lx = x listens only to classical music; Sx = x drinks nothing but sherry]

8. Every rapist is mentally ill and every sexist is ignorant, from which it follows that if everyone who is mentally ill is sexist, then every rapist is ignorant. [Ix = x is ignorant; Mx = x is mentally ill; Rx = x is a rapist; Sx = x is sexist]

9. Some people have been killed by bears. A bear will only kill a person if the bear feels threatened or is hungry. Bears never feel threatened, but they're always hungry. We can conclude that there are hungry bears.[Bx = x is a bear; Hx = x is hungry; Kx = x was killed by a bear; Px = x is a person; Tx = x feels threatened]

10.* The location of the lowest point in the continental United States is in Death Valley. The location of the highest point in the continental United States is on Mt. Whitney. Neither Death Valley nor Mt. Whitney is at sea level. Hence, neither the lowest nor the highest points is at sea level. [Dx = x is in Death Valley; Hx = x is the location of the highest point in the continental United States; Lx = x is the location of the lowest point in the continental United States; Mx = x is on Mt. Whitney; Sx = x is at sea level]

8.4 Truth Trees

Just as proofs in natural deduction can be worked in predicate logic, so truth tree proofs are also possible. Recall that one of the favorable aspects of truth trees in sentential logic is that one can show valid arguments to be valid *and* invalid arguments to be invalid whereas with natural deduction one cannot show invalid arguments to be invalid. This feature is retained in predicate logic as well, except that now we will see that some invalid arguments yield *infinite trees*. An infinite tree is a tree that will never close, no matter how many different instantiations one performs.

The other aspect that was favored in trees over natural deduction is that the former are said to be mechanical. This, largely, is also retained, though there will be times when imaginative creativity will serve one very well when doing trees in predicate logic. This imaginative creativity will be needed when selecting individual constants in instantiations. More on this later.

The method of truth trees is the same in predicate logic as in sentential logic. That is, one sets up the argument in the same fashion, including the denial of the conclusion.   The difference in procedure comes when there are quantified sentences in the argument. Then, at some point, one must instantiate with respect to the variables. Let's take a simple argument:

$(x)(Px \to Qx)$
$-Qi \quad \vdash \quad (Pi \to Ri)$

Now the first premise in this argument is not a conditional. Rather, it is a universal quantification. Hence, the only rule that could be applied to it is Universal Instantiation (UI in natural deduction). The truth tree rule for UI, in schematic form, is:

$$(f)Af$$
$$------$$
$$A\alpha$$

where 'f' is any variable and 'α' is any individual constant. In English, we express this as follows: If a universal quantification falls on a branch of a tree, choose an individual constant, replace each occurrence of the variable with that constant and write the sentence on the same branch. In this way, we can derive the following instantiations (among others):

$(x)Cx$	$(x)-Cx$	$(x)(Cx \lor Dx)$	$(x)[Cx \bullet (-Dx \leftrightarrow Ex)]$
$----$	$-----$	$--------$	$------------$
Ca	$-Cf$	$(Cg \lor Dg)$	$[Cs \bullet (-Ds \leftrightarrow Es)]$

It is important to understand that, even though there is no justification line in truth trees, each sentence that can be checked must be checked and numbered. This rule applies to universal quantifications as much as to any other formula, whether it be a conditional, a disjunction, or whatever. So, all instantiations are to be checked and numbered. Regarding the argument above, the following tree shows it to be valid.

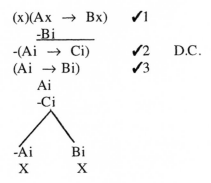

The first premise in this argument is known as a universal quantification. The rule for universal instantiation is applied to it directly after the denial of the conclusion. It would be well to understand why 'i' was chosen. If any other constant were chosen, say 'a', the requisite contradictions would not be found. Note that the first premise has been checked and numbered. Each sentence that to which a rule is applied must always be checked and numbered. All branches close, showing the original argument to be valid.

This is our first clue that truth trees in predicate logic are not wholly mechanical. That choosing 'i' was necessary to show the argument to be valid indicates that one cannot simply appeal to knowledge of the truth tree rules when constructing a tree. One must also use a certain amount of forward-looking creativity in judging how to construct the tree.

Consider the following more complicated tree:

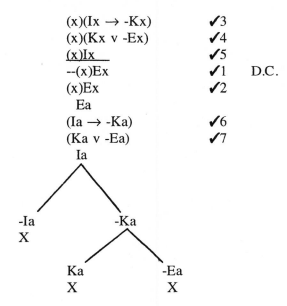

Since the denied conclusion is a doubly negated universal quantification, the only truth tree rule that can be applied to it is the rule for double negation. When "double negation" has been applied, *then* the truth tree rule for universal instantiation can be applied, as was done and indicated by "✓2".

The instantiation rules carry over from natural deduction to truth trees; quantifier exchange rules also carry over. Every quantifier exchange is checked and numbered in a truth tree.

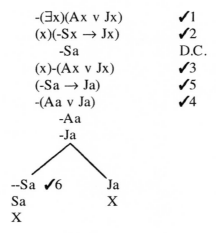

-(∃x)(Ax v Jx)	✓1
(x)(-Sx → Jx)	✓2
-Sa	D.C.
(x)-(Ax v Jx)	✓3
(-Sa → Ja)	✓5
-(Aa v Ja)	✓4
-Aa	
-Ja	

--Sa ✓6   Ja
Sa   X
X

The first rule applied to a sentence in the above tree is a quantifier exchange, where '-(∃x)(Ax v Jx)' becomes '(x)-(Ax v Jx)'. Though it is not necessary that this be the first step in the tree, it is a necessary step, as no rule other than quantifier exchange can be applied to the first premise.

The truth tree rule for existential instantiation can be presented in a schematic form as follows:

$$(\exists f)Af$$
$$- - - - - - -$$
$$A\beta$$

where 'f' is any variable and where 'β' is any individual constant not appearing in any sentence prior to the instantiation. The schematic form of the rule is deceptive because it fails to take into account the proviso that the individual constant one chooses cannot have appeared in any line of the tree prior to the existential instantiation itself. It is very important to keep this in mind and, hence, as in natural deduction, we adopt the practice of "flagging" with an asterisk each and every existential instantiation, indicating the constant one has chosen. To prevent infinite trees, we will adopt the rule that an existential quantification be checked and numbered at most once. The following six examples will suffice to demonstrate these features.

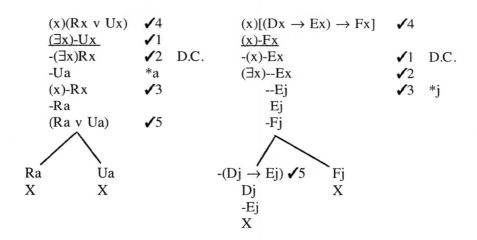

$(x)(Rx \lor Ux)$ ✓4
$(\exists x)-Ux$ ✓1
$-(\exists x)Rx$ ✓2   D.C.
$-Ua$ *a
$(x)-Rx$ ✓3
$-Ra$
$(Ra \lor Ua)$ ✓5

Ra   Ua
X   X

$(x)[(Dx \to Ex) \to Fx]$ ✓4
$(x)-Fx$ ✓4
$-(x)-Ex$ ✓1   D.C.
$(\exists x)--Ex$ ✓2
$--Ej$ ✓3 *j
Ej
$-Fj$

$-(Dj \to Ej)$ ✓5   Fj
Dj   X
-Ej
X

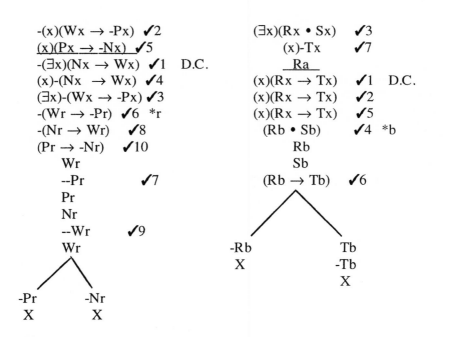

$-(x)(Wx \to -Px)$ ✓2
$(x)(Px \to -Nx)$ ✓5
$-(\exists x)(Nx \to Wx)$ ✓1   D.C.
$(x)-(Nx \to Wx)$ ✓4
$(\exists x)-(Wx \to -Px)$ ✓3
$-(Wr \to -Pr)$ ✓6 *r
$-(Nr \to Wr)$ ✓8
$(Pr \to -Nr)$ ✓10
Wr
$--Pr$ ✓7
Pr
Nr
$--Wr$ ✓9
Wr

-Pr   -Nr
X   X

$(\exists x)(Rx \cdot Sx)$ ✓3
$(x)-Tx$ ✓7
$\underline{Ra}$
$(x)(Rx \to Tx)$ ✓1   D.C.
$(x)(Rx \to Tx)$ ✓2
$(x)(Rx \to Tx)$ ✓5
$(Rb \cdot Sb)$ ✓4 *b
Rb
Sb
$(Rb \to Tb)$ ✓6

-Rb   Tb
X   -Tb
                   X

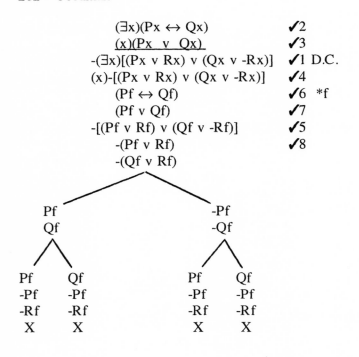

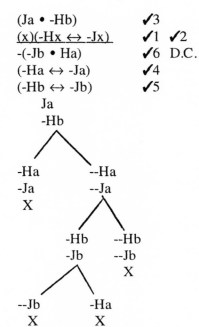

At this point we can introduce rather more complicated argu-ments. Consider the following argument, and especially the third premise which is a conditional in which both antecedent and consequent are existential quantifications.

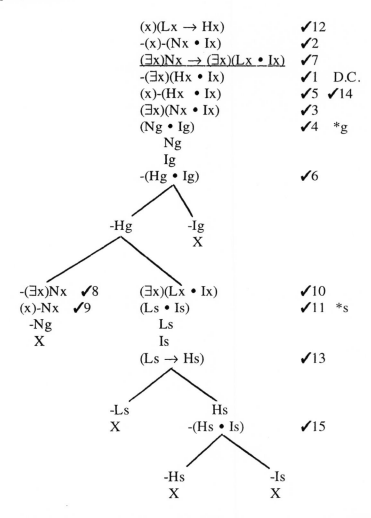

$(x)(Lx \rightarrow Hx)$ ✓12
$-(x)-(Nx \cdot Ix)$ ✓2
$\underline{(\exists x)Nx \rightarrow (\exists x)(Lx \cdot Ix)}$ ✓7
$-(\exists x)(Hx \cdot Ix)$ ✓1   D.C.
$(x)-(Hx \cdot Ix)$ ✓5 ✓14
$(\exists x)(Nx \cdot Ix)$ ✓3
$(Ng \cdot Ig)$ ✓4   *g
Ng
Ig
$-(Hg \cdot Ig)$ ✓6

-Hg   -Ig
    X

$-(\exists x)Nx$ ✓8 $(\exists x)(Lx \cdot Ix)$ ✓10
$(x)-Nx$ ✓9 $(Ls \cdot Is)$ ✓11   *s
-Ng   Ls
X   Is
    $(Ls \rightarrow Hs)$ ✓13

-Ls   Hs
X $-(Hs \cdot Is)$ ✓15

-Hs   -Is
X   X

Notice again that the third premise is a conditional and hence that only the rule for the conditional can apply to it. When the rule is applied to it, the antecedent, $(\exists x)Nx$, is negated while the consequent is not. This is just as it should be on the truth tree rule for conditionals. When the rule has been applied to the third premise, the result is the appearance of two quantified sentences on two different branches. The quantified sentences are then treated as quantifications and only the rules for quantified sentences apply to them.

Second, you will see that one sentence has been checked twice. This is a major departure from truth trees in sentential logic where it was never necessary to check a sentence more than once. Strictly speaking, it was not necessary to check the sentence twice, but it serves as a good example for it being legitimate to do so. Recall that this is not allowed for existential quantifications.

Third, one must take special care to indicate, for every existential instantiation, which individual constant one has chosen. The two asterisks in the tree above show which constants were chosen at which junctures. Also note that the "flagging" of the constants takes place on the sentence that is being instantiated, not on the sentence that is derived from the instantiation. This is merely a convention, and one we shall adopt here. Further examples of trees are below.

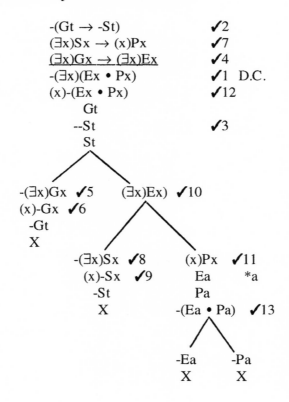

(∃x)Cx → (x)Hx   ✔6
(∃x)(Cx → -Hx)   ✔2
-(∃x)-Cx   ✔1 D.C.
(x)--Cx   ✔3
(Cm → -Hm)   ✔5 *m
--Cm   ✔4
Cm

```
        /\
       /  \
   -Cm    -Hm
    X      /\
          /  \
         /    \
   -(∃x)Cx ✔7   (x)Hx ✔9
   (x)-Cx  ✔8   Hm
    -Cm          X
     X
```

(x)(-Gx ↔ Fx)   ✔5
(∃x)(Hx • Gx)   ✔2
-(∃x)(-Fx • Hx)   ✔1
(x)-(-Fx • Hx)   ✔4
(Ho • Go)   ✔3 *o
Ho
Go
-(-Fx • Hx)   ✔7
(-Gx ↔ Fx)   ✔6

```
        /\
       /  \
    -Go    --Go
    Fo     -Fo
    X       /\
           /  \
          /    \
        --Fo   -Ho
         X      X
```

(∃x)(Ix • Nx) → (y)(Ly → Dy) ✔7
(∃x)(Lx • -Dx)   ✔5
-(x)(Ix → -Nx)   ✔1
(∃x)-(Ix → -Nx)   ✔2
-(Ig → -Ng)   ✔3 *g
Ig
--Ng   ✔4
Ng
(Le • -De)   ✔6 *e
Le
-De

```
              /\
             /  \
            /    \
  -(∃x)(Ix • Nx) ✔8      (y)(Ly → Dy) ✔11
  (x)-(Ix • Nx   ✔9      (Le → De)    ✔12
  -(Ig • Ng)     ✔10        /\
      /\                   /  \
     /  \                -Le   De
   -Ig   -Ng              X    X
    X     X
```

So far we have dealt only with valid arguments. It is time to consider the other side of the validity coin, i.e., invalid arguments. As an example, we can use what knowledge we have of inferences to see that '(x)(-Rx v -Bx)' does not follow from '(x)(Rx • Bx)'. Letting 'Rx' = 'x is a raven' and 'Bx' = 'x is black', we would have the following argument: "All ravens are black. Therefore everything is either a non-raven or is not black." In the tree directly below, we see that the branch does not close after each of the sentences that can be checked has been checked. The problem is that it is always possible to instantiate with respect to another letter, say, 'b'. Though it is logically possible to use existential instantiation more than once on any existential quantification, if we were to do so, there would be no end to the tree we could construct; that is, we would have an infinite tree. To make the method of truth trees in predicate logic more mechanical, we adopt the convention of checking existential quantifications at most once. This violates no logical principle and gives more ease of proof.

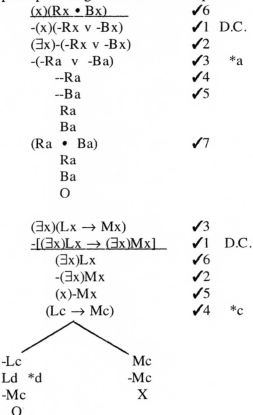

(x)(Rx • Bx)	✓6
-(x)(-Rx v -Bx)	✓1 D.C.
(∃x)-(-Rx v -Bx)	✓2
-(-Ra v -Ba)	✓3 *a
--Ra	✓4
--Ba	✓5
Ra	
Ba	
(Ra • Ba)	✓7
Ra	
Ba	
O	

(∃x)(Lx → Mx)	✓3
-[(∃x)Lx → (∃x)Mx]	✓1 D.C.
(∃x)Lx	✓6
-(∃x)Mx	✓2
(x)-Mx	✓5
(Lc → Mc)	✓4 *c

```
        -Lc              Mc
        Ld *d            -Mc
        -Mc              X
         O
```

Note here that since 'c' has been used to instantiate the premise, 'c' cannot again be used for the instantiation on '(∃x)Lx'. Hence, some other constant must be chosen. But in that case, one will be unable to close at least one of the branches. Precisely this occurs when 'd' is chosen at '✓6' leading to the left-hand branch remaining open. It should be clear that no matter which individual constant one chooses here, other than 'c', the branch will remain open. Hence, the argument is invalid.

As with truth trees in sentential logic, the following rule applies to trees in predicate logic. Before any argument can be designated invalid, each and every formula that can be checked must be checked. This is precisely the reason '(∃x)Lx' was checked in the tree above. Checking that sentence did not produce a contradiction, but it was necessary to *show* that it wouldn't.

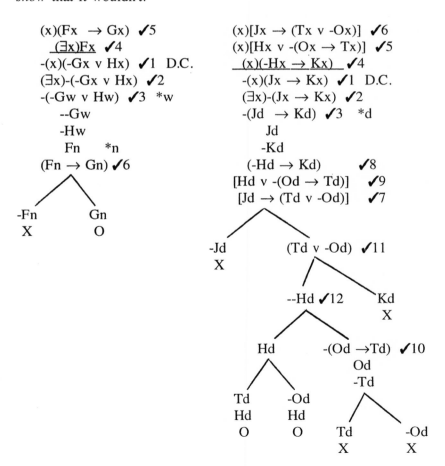

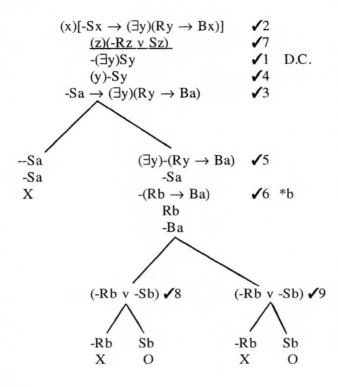

$(x)[-Sx \rightarrow (\exists y)(Ry \rightarrow Bx)]$ ✓2
$(z)(-Rz \lor Sz)$ ✓7
$-(\exists y)Sy$ ✓1 D.C.
$(y)-Sy$ ✓4
$-Sa \rightarrow (\exists y)(Ry \rightarrow Ba)$ ✓3

$--Sa$ $(\exists y)-(Ry \rightarrow Ba)$ ✓5
$-Sa$ $-Sa$
X $-(Rb \rightarrow Ba)$ ✓6 *b
     Rb
     $-Ba$

$(-Rb \lor -Sb)$ ✓8 $(-Rb \lor -Sb)$ ✓9

$-Rb$ Sb $-Rb$ Sb
X   O   X   O

Exercise 8.4

A. Determine which of the following arguments are valid and which are invalid using the method of truth trees.

1. $(\exists x)Cx \rightarrow (y)Cy$
$(\exists x)(Cx \lor Hx)$
$(\exists x)Hx$

2. $(x)(Ax \rightarrow Bx)$
$(x)(-Cx \rightarrow -Bx)$
$(x)(Cx \lor -Ax)$

3. $(x)[Rx \rightarrow (Sx \bullet Tx)]$
$(x)(Rx \leftrightarrow Tx)$
$(x)Sx$

4. $(x)Fx \lor (x)-Dx$
$(Ds \rightarrow Ls)$
$(x)(Lx \rightarrow -Fx)$

5* $(\exists x)Wx \leftrightarrow (\exists x)Px$
$(\exists x)(Wx \rightarrow Px)$

6. $-[(\exists x)Hx \bullet (x)Jx]$
$-(x)Jx \rightarrow Cg$
$(x)(Cx \rightarrow -Hx)$
$(\exists x)-Hx$

7. (x)[(Dx → Fx) v (Lx • -Fx)]   8. (x)(Mx • Kx) → (∃y)Zy
   (x)(-Fx → Lx)   (x)-(-Kx v Zx)
   (x)(Dx • -Fx)   (∃x)(-Zx → -Mx)
   -(x)(Lx • Ox)

9. (x)[Ax ↔ (Sx ↔ Ix)]   10* (∃x)Kx ↔ -(∃y)-Ky
   (x)[(Sx ↔ Qx) ↔ -Vx]   (x)Kx → (∃y)Ky
   (∃x)Ax v (∃x)-Sx   (x)(Ax → -Kx)
                                       -(x)Kx

B.   Translate the following arguments into symbolic notation. Then, determine whether each is valid using a truth tree.

1.   If all theories are falsifiable, then Newton's theory is. If the correct theory is falsifiable, then Einstein's theory is. All theories are either correct or not falsifiable. Hence, either Newton's or Einstein's theory is falsifiable. [Cx = x is correct; Fx = x is falsifiable; Tx = x is a theory; e = Einstein's theory; n = Newton's theory]

2.   Most, but not all, things are carbon based. Whatever is carbon based has a genetic code. There is nothing with a genetic code that is immortal. It follows that most things are not immortal. [Cx = x is carbon based; Gx = x has a genetic code; Mx = x is mortal]

3.   Nothing is both a vampire and a saint, though there are saints who were killed by fire. It follows from these points that there existed a being who was not a vampire but was killed by fire. [Fx = x was killed by fire; Sx = x is a saint; Vx = x is a vampire]

4.   If anybody has knowledge, then skepticism is false. Skepticism is false if, and only if, inductive inferences are acceptable. Inductive inferences being acceptable implies that somebody's having knowledge implies, and is implied by, skepticism being false. So, everyone has knowledge. [Ax = x is acceptable; Fx = x is false; Kx = x has knowledge; i = inductive inferences; s = skepticism]

5* No sentence is both logically true as well as logically false. Any sentence that is logically true is also actually true. There are no actually true sentences that are meaningless. Hence, logically false sentences that are meaningful don't exist. [Ax = x is actually true; Lx = x is logically true; Mx = x is meaningful; Sx = x is a sentence]

C. Any argument appearing in the section on natural deduction may be treated with truth trees. You know that the arguments in that section are all valid, but it would still be excellent practice to construct trees using those arguments. Another way to practice is to create original arguments yourself, translate them into symbolic notation, and construct trees.

8.5 Relations

Up to this point we have considered only one-place predicates, represented with one predicate and one individual constant, such as 'Aa'. At this point we will introduce two-place predicates, represented with one predicate and two individual constants, e.g., 'Aab'. A two-place predicate represents a relation between two individuals and is called a *Binary Relation*. An example of this is: "Galileo lived after Aristotle". (A *Ternary Relation* involves a three-place predicate, such as "Roger borrowed a pen from Jessie".) Consider the relation "admires". If we want to say that Byron admires Clarice, we might stipulate the following dictionary: 'Axy' = 'x admires y'; 'b' = 'Byron'; 'c' = 'Clarice'. We would then represent the sentence "Byron admires Clarice" as "Abc". Simple enough. But if we want to represent the sentence "Everybody admires somebody", we need to add quantifiers to represent "everybody" and "somebody". We can reword the sentence to say, "No matter what x is, there is a y such that x admires y." The translation is $(x)(\exists y)Axy$. "Everybody admires everybody" would be translated as $(x)(y)Axy$. Below are some of the many binary relations that can be represented in predicate logic:

loves	respects	cares for
sympathizes with	is the mother of	is greater than
is next to	is to the left of	is between
has the same color eyes as	is as tall as	is shorter than
wants to go out with	batted against	is angry at
took a class from	is a sister of	admires

The translation dictionary will again prove essential to the adequate representation of sentences in symbolic notation. Take, for example, the sentence "All logicians are feared by their students", where 'Lx' = 'x is a logician'; 'Sxy' = 'x is a student of y'; 'Fxy' = 'x fears y'. We can translate the sentence as follows: $(x)(y)[(Lx \cdot Syx) \rightarrow Fyx]$.

Another important concept to understand is that of a *Domain* (Universe of Discourse). A domain is a class of things or objects over which quantifiers and variables range. Another way to put it is to say that a domain is the class of things one is talking about in any given sentence. Up to this point, our domain has been everything. Sometimes, however, we will want to specify a domain smaller than the class of everything. Take the sentence "All Protestant Republicans fear God" [Fxy = x fears y; Px = x is a Protestant; Rx = x is a Republican; g = God]. If our domain is everything, the translation would be:

$$(x)[(Px \bullet Rx) \rightarrow Fxg]$$

If, on the other hand, our domain is Republicans, the translation would be cut down to (x)(Px → Fxg); if our domain is Protestant Republicans, we get (x)Fxg. In what follows, unless otherwise specified, our domain will be everything. It is proper to express a domain within braces, as follows: {People}, which can be read as "the class of people". We will henceforth abbreviate 'domain' with 'Dom' and 'dictionary' with 'Dict'. Examples of translations with relations follow.

[Dom: {People}; Dict: m = Mary; s = Sam; Wxy = x wrote a letter to y]

Sam wrote a letter to Karen.	Wsk
Sam wrote letters to Karen and Mary.	(Wsk • Wsm)
Someone wrote Karen a letter.	(∃x)Wxk
Karen wrote a letter to somebody.	(∃x)Wkx
Mary wrote a letter to herself.	Wmm

[Dom: {People}; Dict: m = Mary; Lx - x looks tall; Rxy = x looks taller than y; Sxy = x stands next to y; Txy = x is taller than y]

Everyone is taller than Mary.	(x)Txm
Nothing is taller than itself.	-(∃x)Txx
No one is taller than everyone.	-(∃x)(y)Txy
Anyone who stands next to Mary looks tall.	(x)(Sxm → Lx)
Whoever looks taller than Mary is taller than Mary.	(x)(Rxm → Txm)

[Dom: {People}; Dict: Fxy = x is a friend to y; Dx = x is drunk; Exy = x envies y; Lxy = x lets y drive; Oxy = x is y's lover; Uxy = x understands y]

Everybody is somebody's friend.	$(x)(\exists y)Fxy$
Friendship implies respect.	$(x)(y)(Fxy \rightarrow Rxy)$
Friendship does not imply envy.	$(x)(y)-(Fxy \rightarrow Exy)$
Some friends are lovers.	$(\exists x)(\exists y)(Fxy \bullet Oxy)$
Friends don't let friends drive drunk.	$(x)(y)[Fxy \rightarrow (Dy \rightarrow -Lxy)]$
Only a drunk understands a drunk.	$(x)(y)[Dx \rightarrow (Uyx \rightarrow Dy)]$

[Dom: {Numbers}; Dict: a = two; b = ten; Ex = x is even; Dxy = x is divisible by y; Ixy = x is identical to y; Ox = x is odd; Px = x is prime]

Two is prime but ten is not.	$(Pa \bullet -Pb)$
Every even number is divisible by two.	$(x)(Ex \rightarrow Dxa)$
No odd number is even.	$-(\exists x)(Ox \bullet Ex)$
All even numbers are self-identical.	$(x)(Ex \rightarrow Ixx)$
No number is both prime and non-prime.	$-(\exists x)(Px \bullet -Px)$
Two is the only even prime.	$\{(Ea \bullet Pa) \bullet (x)[(Ex \bullet Px) \rightarrow Ixa]\}$
There is just one even prime.	$(\exists x)\{(Ex \bullet Px) \bullet (y)[(Ey \bullet Py) \rightarrow Iyx]\}$

[Dom: {People}; Dict: Ax = x is an argument; a = Aristotle; Ex = x is acceptable; f = Frege; g = Gödel; Lx = x is a logician; q = Quine; Rxy = x respects y; r = Russell]

All logicians respect acceptable arguments.
$$(x)[Lx \rightarrow (y)(Ay \bullet Ey) \rightarrow Rxy)]$$

Only logicians respect logicians.	$(x)(y)[(Lx \bullet Ryx) \rightarrow Ly]$
Some logicians don't respect anyone.	$(\exists x)(y)(Lx \bullet -Rxy)$

Every logician respects either Aristotle and Gödel or Russell,
Frege and Quine. $(x)\{Lx \rightarrow (Rxa \bullet Rxg) \lor [Rxr \bullet (Rxf \bullet Rxq)]\}$

[Dom: {Sentences}; Dict: Ax = x is an argument; Cx = x is a conditional; c(xy) = the conjunction of x and y; Dx = x is a disjunction; d(xy) = the disjunction of x and y; Ex = x is acceptable; Ixy = x implies y; Sx = x is consistent; Tx = x is true]

An inconsistent sentence implies every sentence.	$(x)(-Sx \rightarrow (y)Ixy)$
True sentences imply only true sentences.	$(x)[Tx \rightarrow (y)(Ixy \rightarrow Ty)]$
Each conditional implies some disjunction.	$(x)[Cx \rightarrow (\exists y)(Dy \bullet Ixy)]$

The conjunction of any two true sentences is itself a true sentence.
$$(x)(y)[(Tx \bullet Ty) \rightarrow Tc(xy)]$$
Sentences that imply one another imply exactly the same sentences.
$$(x)(y)[(Ixy \bullet Iyx) \rightarrow (z)(Ixz \leftrightarrow Iyz)]$$

Disjunctions are true only if one or both disjuncts are true.

$$(x)(y)\{Td(xy) \to [(Tx \text{ v } Ty) \text{ v } (Tx \bullet Ty)]\}$$

No false sentence implies, nor is implied by, any true sentence.

$$(x)(y)[(-Tx \bullet Ty) \to (-Ixy \bullet -Iyx)]$$

8.5.1 Relations: Natural Deduction

The methods of truth trees and natural deduction may be applied to relational arguments in predicate logic. All of the rules previously in force for those two systems remain in force here. Some examples will help.

Consider the following argument and proof:

1.	(x)-Hxa		
2.	(x)(Fx → (∃y)Gyx)		
3.	(x)(-Gxa v Hxa)	⊢	-Fa
4.	Fa	(A,DC)	
5.	(Fa → (∃y)Gya)	2, UI	
6.	(∃y)Gya	4,5, MP	
7.	Gba	6, EI *b	
8.	(-Gba v Hba)	2, UI	
9.	(Gba → Hba)	8, MI	
10	Hba	7,9, MP	
11	-Hba	1, UI	
12	(Hba • -Hba)	10,11, Con	
13	-Fa	4-12, RAA	

This is a fairly straight forward proof. Note that instead of writing '--Fa' as the denial of the conclusion, 'Fa' was written. Also note the flagging of 'b' in line 7. Since 'a' appears prior to the EI in 7, some letter besides 'a' had to be chosen. The following example is a bit more complicated.

1.	(x)-Axx		
2.	(x)(y)(z)[(Axy • Ayz) → Axz]	⊢	(x)(y)(Axy → -Ayx)
3.	-(x)(y)(Axy → -Ayx)	(A,DC)	
4.	(∃x)-(y)(Axy → -Ayx)	3, QE	
5.	-(y)(Aay → -Aya)	4, EI *a	
6.	(∃y)-(Aay → -Aya)	5, QE	
7.	-(Aab → -Aba)	6, EI *b	

```
 8.  -(-Aab v -Aba)          7, MI
 9.  (--Aab • --Aba)         8, DM
10   (Aab • Aba)             9, DN,DN
11   (y)(z)[(Aay • Ayz) → Aaz]   2, UI
12   (z)[(Aab • Abz) → Aaz]      11, UI
13   [(Aab • Aba) → Aaa]         12, UI
14   Aaa                     10,13, MP
15   -Aaa                    1, UI
16   (Aaa • -Aaa)            14,15, Con
17   (x)(y)(Axy → -Ayx)      3-16, RAA
```

Some crucial points in the above proof are the following: (A) the existential instantiations in lines 5 and 7 are flagged, it being impossible to existentially instantiate with respect to 'a' in line 7 since 'a' appears in a prior line in the proof; (B) the quantifier exchanges in lines 3 and 5 were necessary before the existential instantiations in 5 and 7, because 3 and 5 are negative quantifications rather than quantifications, whereas 5 and 7 are quantifica-tions; (C) the universal instantiations in lines 11, 12, and 13 are as they are to be able to apply *modus ponens* in line 14 and then the conjunction in line 16.

```
 1.  (x)(y)(Lxy → Axy)
 2.  (x)(y)[Axy → (Lxy → Cxy)]
 3.  (x)(y)Lxy ⊢ (x)(y)Cxy
 4.  -(x)(y)Cxy                   (A,DC)
 5.  (∃x)-(y)Cxy                  4, QE
 6.  -(y)Cfy                      5, EI *f
 7.  (∃y)-Cfy                     6, QE
 8.  -Cfk                         7, EI *k
 9.  (y)(Lfy → Afy)               1, UI
10   (Lfk → Afk)                  9, UI
11   (y)[Afy → (Lfy → Cfy)]       2, UI
12   [Afk → (Lfk → Cfk)]          11, UI
13    [(Afk • Lfk) → Cfk]         12, Ex
14   -(Afk • Lfk)                 8,13, MT
15   (-Afk v -Lfk)                14, DM
16   (-Lfk v -Afk)                15, Com
17   (y)Lfy                       3, UI
18   Lfk                          17, UI
19   --Lfk                        18, DN
```

Instead of simply using a series of *modus ponens* in this proof, I chose to use Exportation and a few other rules. It makes it a bit more interesting and it is good practice. You might try doing this proof using a third set of rules. Does it turn out shorter?

20	-Afk	16,19, DS
21	Afk	10,18, MP
22	(Afk • -Afk)	20,21, Con
23	(x)(y)Cxy	4-22, RAA

1.	(∃x)[(y)(Cy → Wxy) • Mx]	⊢ (∃x)[(-Cn v Wxn) • Mx]
2.	-(∃x)[(-Cn v Wxn) • Mx]	(A,DC)
3.	(x)-[(-Cn v Wxn) • Mx]	2, QE
4.	[(y)(Cy → Wry) • Mr]	1, EI *r
5.	-[(-Cn v Wm) • Mr]	3, UI
6.	[-(-Cn v Wm) v -Mr]	5, DM
7.	(--Cn • -Wm) v -Mr]	6, DM
8.	[(Cn → Wm) • Mr]	4, UI
9.	Mr	8, Com,Si
10	--Mr	9, DN
11	[-Mr v (--Cn • -Wm)]	7, Com
12	(--Cn • -Wm)	10,11, DS
13	Cn	12, Si,DN
14	(Cn → Wm)	8, Si
15	Wm	13,14, MP
16	-Wm	12, Com,Si
17	(Wm • -Wm)	15,16, Con
18	(∃x)[(Cn → Wxn) • Mx]	2-17, RAA

Exercise 8.5.1

A. Translate the following sentences into symbolic notation, constructing your own domains and dictionaries.
1. Not everybody is afraid of the snakes, but Jeremy sure is.
2. Everyone admired Socrates, and Plato revered him.
3. If Strawson thought Russell was wrong, he didn't admire him.
4. Moore admired Russell only if both Wittgenstein and Ryle did.
5* Somebody admires everybody; however, nobody is admired by everybody.
6. If any psychologist admired and respected Freud, then somebody thought Freud wasn't a madman.
7. All of Freud's patients feared, but loved, him.
8. If any judge had believed Degas, he wouldn't have gone to Devil's Island.

9. If the skeptic is right, then no one is certain of anything.

10* The tallest person in the world can see further than anybody.

B. Show the following arguments to be valid using the method of natural deduction.

1.   1.   -(x)(y)-(-Rx → -Axy)
      2.   (x)(y)Axy ⊢ (∃x)Rx

2.   1.   -(x)(∃y)(Dxy v Fxy) ⊢ (∃x)-Fxx

3.   1.   (x)(y)(∃z)-(-Myx → Mxz)
      2.   (∃x)(y)(Mxy ↔ Myx) ⊢ (∃x)-(y)Mxy

4.   1.   (x)(y)Jxy → (x)(∃y)Pxy
      2.   (x)Px • (∃x)(y)-Pxy   ⊢ -(x)(y)Jxy

5* 1.   (∃x)(∃y)Fxy ⊢ (∃x)(∃y)Fyx

6.   1.   (x)(y)(z)[(Bxy • Byz) → Bxz]
      2.   -(∃x)Bxx ⊢ (x)(y)(-Bxy v -Byx)

7.   1.   (x)(Txx → L)   ⊢   (-L → -(∃x)Txx)

8.   1.   (x)Pxx → (∃y)Eyy
      2.   (x)Pxx → -(∃y)Eyy   ⊢   (x)-Pxx

9.   1.   (x)(-Rrx v Sxs)
      2.   -(∃x)Sxs v (∃y)Ssy ⊢ -(∃x)Rrx v (∃y)Ssy

10* 1.   (x)-Hxx
    2.   (x)(y)(Hxy → Hyx)
    3.   (x)(y)(z)[(Hxy → -Hyz) → Hxz]
      ⊢   (x)(y)-[Hxy → (z)(Hzx → Hzy)]

C. Translate the following arguments into symbolic notation and prove them to be valid using the method of natural deduction.

1. Every mountaineer is either crazy or unafraid. If a mountaineer is crazy, then that person shouldn't handle sharp objects. On the other

hand, if a mountaineer is simply unafraid, that person shouldn't use ropes. It follows that every mountaineer either shouldn't handle sharp objects or shouldn't use ropes. [Ax = x is afraid; Cx = x is crazy; Mx = x is a mountaineer; Oxy = x should use/handle y; r = rope; s = sharp object] [Dom: {Mountaineers}]

2. Some, though not all, psychologists are Jung scholars. No Jung scholars are interested in the writings of either Mary Hesse or Judith Jarvis Thomson; Whoever is not a Jung scholar is interested in the writings of Freud. Hence, someone is interested in the writings of freud. [Ixy = x is interested in the writings of y; Jx = x is a Jung scholar; f = Freud; j = Judith Jarvis Thomson = Mary Hesse] [Dom: {Psychologists}]

3. Anyone who interviews an I.R.A. soldier and runs for Parliament in Northern Ireland will be elected, since, anyone who inter-views an I.R.A. soldier will be breaking British law, and anyone who breaks British law and runs for Parliament in Northern Ireland will be elected. [Bx = x breaks British law; Ex = x is elected; Ixy = x interviews y; Rx = x runs for Parliament in Northern Ireland; s = I.R.A. soldier]

4. Some team wants each athlete who is both strong and dedicated, and since every athlete is strong and dedicated, any athlete who is strong is wanted by some team. [Ax = x is an athlete; Dx = x is dedicated; Sx = x is strong; Wxy = x wants y]

5* No honest person lies to somebody. But, everybody either admires or lies to everybody. So, all honest people admire somebody. [Axy = x admires y; Hx = x is honest; Lxy = x lies to y]

8.5.2 Relations: Truth Trees

Truth trees on relational arguments are not very different from trees on nonrelational arguments. The method and the procedure are the same. The main point to keep in mind has to do with universal and existential instantiations. As in natural deduction, one must not instantiate with respect to more than one individual constant in any given instantiation. One must also take care to flag all existential instantiations, proceeding with the restriction on that rule in mind. A few examples will help.

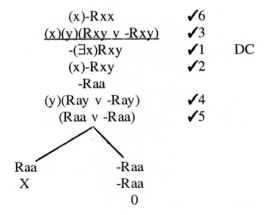

$$(x)-Rxx \qquad \checkmark 6$$
$$\underline{(x)(y)(Rxy \vee -Rxy)} \qquad \checkmark 3$$
$$-(\exists x)Rxy \qquad \checkmark 1 \qquad DC$$
$$(x)-Rxy \qquad \checkmark 2$$
$$-Raa$$
$$(y)(Ray \vee -Ray) \qquad \checkmark 4$$
$$(Raa \vee -Raa) \qquad \checkmark 5$$

```
          Raa              -Raa
           X               -Raa
                            0
```

The first thing to notice here is that the argument is invalid. This is shown by the ring below the last occurrence of '-Raa'. There are no contradictions on that branch and every fomula that can be checked has been checked. The branch remains open. Second, there is no existential instantiation in this proof. Hence, no flags. Third, if one had chosen different letters to instantiate on, yielding, say 'Rab' and '-Rab', still the tree wouldn't close.

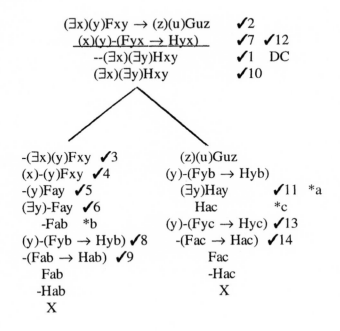

$$(\exists x)(y)Fxy \rightarrow (z)(u)Guz \qquad \checkmark 2$$
$$\underline{(x)(y)-(Fyx \rightarrow Hyx)} \qquad \checkmark 7 \quad \checkmark 12$$
$$--(\exists x)(\exists y)Hxy \qquad \checkmark 1 \qquad DC$$
$$(\exists x)(\exists y)Hxy \qquad \checkmark 10$$

```
         -(∃x)(y)Fxy  ✓3            (z)(u)Guz
         (x)-(y)Fxy   ✓4            (y)-(Fyb → Hyb)
         -(y)Fay      ✓5            (∃y)Hay        ✓11  *a
         (∃y)-Fay     ✓6            Hac            *c
          -Fab  *b                 (y)-(Fyc → Hyc) ✓13
         (y)-(Fyb → Hyb) ✓8        -(Fac → Hac)   ✓14
         -(Fab → Hab)  ✓9           Fac
          Fab                       -Hac
          -Hab                       X
           X
```

There are at least three interesting points to be made about this tree. First, on the right branch neither '(z)(u)Guz' nor '(y)-(Fyb → Hyb)' is checked. That's all right, since the branch on which those formulas occur closes without checking them. If the branch had remained open when all other formulas had been checked, then those formulas would also have had to be checked.

Second, note that 'a' is flagged on the right branch even though it occurs on the left branch. This is legitimate because we treat each branch as a separate entity, or, as in the rows of truth tables, as different interpretations. In short, the occurrences of 'a' on the left branch are not considered *prior* to the occurrences of 'a' on the right branch. Otherwise, the restriction which goes with the rule for existential instantiation would be violated.

Third, you will see that the second premise is checked twice. There is no restriction on universal instantiation. The second instantiation on the second premise was necessary for the closing of the right branch. The reason we couldn't use '(y)-(Fyb → Hyb)' is because we needed to use '(∃x)(∃y)Hxy' to close the branch and since 'b' occurs prior to '(∃x)(∃y)Hxy' on that branch, i.e., in '(y)-(Fyb → Hyb)', we couldn't use 'b' on '(∃x)(∃y)Hxy'. Hence, we had to use some other individual constant; 'c' was chosen.

This third point brings up a matter regarding "double checking". You can double check both universal as well as existential quantifications. The restriction would be on the latter of these two, where you would have to instantiate with respect to a different constant on the second instantiation. For example, from '(∃x)(Rx v Bx)' you could derive both '(Ra v Ba)' as well as '(Rb v Bb)'. The only restriction here would be that when you instantiate using 'a', 'a' must not have appeared previously in the tree (or proof). The same is true for 'b'. This can be shown in schematic form as follows:

$$(\exists x)(Rx \lor Bx) \quad \checkmark1 \ \checkmark2$$
$$(Ra \lor Ba) \quad *a$$
$$(Rb \lor Bb) \quad *b$$

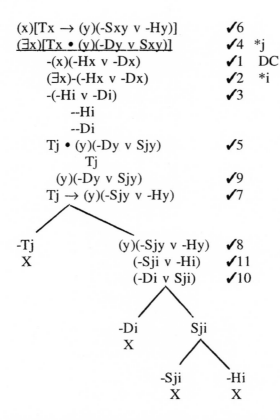

(x)[Tx → (y)(-Sxy v -Hy)]	✓6
(∃x)[Tx • (y)(-Dy v Sxy)]	✓4 *j
-(x)(-Hx v -Dx)	✓1 DC
(∃x)-(-Hx v -Dx)	✓2 *i
-(-Hi v -Di)	✓3
--Hi	
--Di	
Tj • (y)(-Dy v Sjy)	✓5
Tj	
(y)(-Dy v Sjy)	✓9
Tj → (y)(-Sjy v -Hy)	✓7

The crucial moves in this tree are the instantiations. Once 'i' is used, it cannot be used again on the second premise; so, 'j' was used. Then, it was possible to instantiate with both 'i' and 'j' when the universals were instantiated. It is important to remember that one cannot apply a truth tree rule to any quantified formula. For example, the first premise is a universal quantification, not a conditional. Hence, the tree rule for conditional does not apply to that formula. One needs to instantiate the first premise before it becomes a conditional.

Exercises 8.5.2

A. Determine whether the following arguments are valid or invalid using the method of truth trees.

1. (x)Dxx
    (x)Dxx → (y)Hyy
    (∃x)-Hxx

2. (x)(y)(Fxy v Gxy)
    (x)(∃y)-Gyx
    (∃x)(∃y)Fyx

3. [Srj ↔ (x)(y)Cxy]
    [Crj v (x)(y)-Eyx]
    [(x)(y)Cxy → -Erj]

4. (x)(y)(z)[(Rxy • Ryz) → Rxz]
    (x)-Rxx
    (x)(y)(Rxy → Ryx)

5* -(x)-(y)Jxy → (z)Jzz
    (x)Jxx • (y)(z)-Jyz
    (y)Lyy

6. (x)(y)[Pxy → (z)Hzy]
    (x)(y)-(Pxy v -Hyx)
    (∃x)(y)-Hxy

7. -(x)(∃y)(Txy • -Wxy)
    (x)(y)(Wxx → Myy)
    (∃x)[(Txx ↔ Mxx) → -Wxx]

8. (x)(y)Dxy ↔ (∃x)-Ox
    (x)[Ox → (∃y)Ixy]
    (x)-Ox v (∃y)Oy

9. (x)(y)[Axy • (Gyx → Lyy)]
    (x)(y)-(-Lxy → Nxy)
    (x)(y)(Ayx → Nyy)
    (∃x)(∃y)(Gyx → Nxx)

10* (x)(∃y)Kxy • (x)(y)Cyx
    (x)(y)-(Kxy • Jxy)
    (x)(y)[Cxy → (Jxy → Zxy)]
    (∃x)(∃y)(Zxy v Sxy)

B. Translate the following arguments into symbolic notation and determine the validity of each using truth trees.

1. All things bear some relation to each other. Whatever bears some relation to something else has something in common with that thing. Whatever has something in common with another thing is analogous to that thing. Hence, Jesus is analogous to Hitler. [Axy = x is analogous to y; Bxy = x bears some relation to y; Cxy = x has something in common with y; h = Hitler; j = Jesus]
2. So long as a person exists, he has not yet died, and once he has died, he no longer exists; so there seems to be no time when death, if it is a misfortune, can be ascribed to its unfortunate subject. (Thomas Nagel, "Death") [Do: Everything; Dict: Dx = x has died; d = death; Ex = x exists; Mx = x is a misfortune; Mxy = x is a misfortune for y]
3. Some, but not all, scientists are inductivists. No inductivist ever won a Nobel Prize. Some inductivists think their the greatest. Hence, some scientists who have never won a Nobel prize think they are the greatest.

[Do: Scientists; Dict: Gxy = x thinks y is the greatest; Ix = x is an inductivist; Wxy = x won y; p = the Nobel Prize]

4. If any professional thief can open any bank safe, then since every metropolitan city has at least one professional thief, no bank is impenetrable. But, not every bank is penetrable. Therefore, not every thief can open every bank safe. [Bx = x is a bank; Cx = x is a metropolitan city; Hxy = x has y; Oxy = x can open y; Px = x is penetrable; Sx = x is a bank safe; Tx = x is a professional thief]

5* If Folk Psychology can explain desires, then anything can. Every dualist system can explain desire and Folk Psychology is a dualist system. Now, Sociobiology is a materialist system. It follows that some materialist systems can explain desires. [Dx = x is dualist system; d = desires; Exy = x can explain y; f = Folk Psychology; Mx = x is a materialist system; s = Sociobiology]

C. Which of the following sentences are true and which are false?

1. 'Alice resembles Linda.' expresses a binary relation.
2. 'Alice walked up the hill with Everett.' expresses a ternary relation.
3. Translations can be made simpler, in some cases, by specifying a domain.
4. In predicate logic with relations it is always necessary to work a quantifier exchange prior to either an existential or universal instantiation.
5* A domain is a set of objects over which quantifiers and variables range.
6. It is never proper to specify "everything" as the domain.
7. '-(x)(y)Rxy' is a negated universal quantification.
8. '(x)-(y)Ryx' is a negated universal quantification.
9. If 'Fxy' = 'x fears y', then '(x)(y)Fxy' and '(x)(y)Fyx' express the same sentence.
10* Both (a) and (b) below follow from '(∃x)(y)Rxy':
    a. (Rcc v Rcd)
    b. [(Rcc v Rcd) • (Rdc v Rdd)]

8.6 Identity

Consider the following argument:

John and Nicole both have blue eyes.
John and Nicole are the only people in the cave.
Hence, everyone in the cave has blue eyes.

Translating this argument into symbolic notation using the symbols we have now, we can see that the symbolic argument would be invalid. On our present system, where 'Bx' = 'x has blue eyes', 'Cx' = 'x is in the cave', 'Ixy' = 'x is identical with y', 'j' = 'John', 'n' = 'Nicole', with {People} as the domain, we would translate the argument thus:

(Bj • Bn)
(x)[Cx → (Ixj v Ixn)]   ⊢   (x)(Cx → Bx)

The following counterexample will show that the symbolized argument is invalid. Domain: {0,1,2,...}; Dictionary: 'j' = '0'; 'n' = '0'; 'Bx' = 'x is even'; 'Cx' = 'x is odd'; 'Ixy' = 'x is greater than y'. However, since we know the original argument is valid, our translation must be inadequate. We can show the argument to be valid by adding one further symbol to our list, viz., the identity symbol (=).

We need to be clear about what function the identity symbol is to have in our system. To that end, note that the verb "to be" is ambiguous. In the sentence "Julie is shy", 'is' is the "is of predication". That is, shyness is being predicated of Julie and the proper translation would be "Sj". However, in the sentence "Michael Caine is Maurice Micklewhite", "is" is the "is of identity" since it *identifies* Michael Cain with Maurice Micklewhite. The proper translation of that sentence is "c = m".

Consider now the following argument and translation, letting 'a' = 'Woody Allen'; 'Dxy' = 'x directed y'; 's' = '*Sleeper*''; 'k' = 'Allen Konigsberg'.

Woody Allen directed *Sleeper*	Das
Woody Allen is Allen Konigsberg.	a = k
Hence, Allen Konigsberg directed *Sleeper*.	Dkh

To show this argument to be valid, we only need to stipulate the appropriate rules for dealing with formulas/sentences such as "a = k". One such rule we will call the **Rule of Identity (ID)**, the schematic form of which is:

(...x...)
x = y   ⊢   (...y...)

Another rule to be adopted now, the **Rule of Self-Identity (SID)**, says that the formula "(x)(x = x)" may be introduced as a new line of a proof in natural deduction, or may be introduced on a branch of a tree, at *any* time.

The third rule we include here is the **Rule of Identity Symmetry (IS)**. This rule can be schematized with the following formula:

$$(x)(y)(x = y \rightarrow y = x).$$

As with the Rule of Self-Identity, the formula for Identity Symmetry can be introduced as a new line of a proof, or on a branch of a tree, at any time.

We can now translate the argument about John and Nicole more precisely and hence show it to be valid, the proof of which follows.

1.	(Bj • Bn)	
2.	(x)[Cx → (x = j v x = n)] ⊢ (x)(Cx → Bx)	
3.	-(x)(Cx → Bx)	(A,DC)
4.	(∃x)-(Cx → Bx)	3, QE
5.	-(Ca → Ba)	4, EI *a
6.	[Ca → (a = j v a = n)]	2, UI
7.	-(-Ca v Ba)	5, MI
8.	(--Ca • -Ba)	7, DM
9.	Ca	8, Si, DN
10	(a = j v a = n)	6,9, MP
11	-Ba	8, Com, Si
12	(-Bj v -Bn)	10,11, ID
13	--Bj	1, Si, DN
14	-Bn	12,13, DS
15	Bn	1, Com, Si
16	(Bn • -Bn)	14,15, Con
17	(x)(Cx → Bx)	3-16, RAA

The Rule of Identity applied in line 12 is the crucial step allowing us to derive the contradiction. The tree on the following page shows how the rule applies in truth trees.

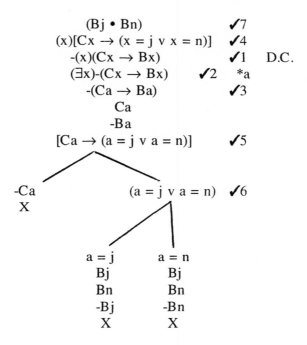

The sentences '-Bj' and '-Bn' at the very bottom of the branches of the tree are the result of applying the Rule of Identity using '-Ba', which resulted from '✓3', and 'a = j' on the left-hand branch, and 'a = n' on the right-hand branch. Note that neither 'a = j' nor 'a = n' are checked.

8.6.1 Translations With Identity

With the inclusion of the identity sign, we can translate many sentences that were closed to us before. Examples are below. A note is in order on the symbolization of *nonidentity*. There are two acceptable ways of indicating nonidentity symbolically: $(x \neq y)$ and $-(x = y)$. I prefer the latter of these and will use it throughout the rest of the chapter.

Dictionary: Ax = x is/was an astronomer; Axy = x admired y; a = Aristotle; Bx = x is a biologist in this class; Cx = x is a chemist in this class; e = Einstein; g = Galileo; Lxy = x liked y; Nx = x is a novelist in this class; Px = x is/was a philosopher; p = Plato; Sxy = x was a student of y; s = Socrates.

There were at least two philosophers Aristotle admired.

$$(\exists x)(\exists y)[(Aax \bullet Aay) \bullet -(x = y)]$$

There are at least three biologists in this class.

$$(\exists x)(\exists y)(\exists z)\{[(Bx \bullet By) \bullet Bz] \bullet \{[-(x = y) \bullet -(x = z)] \bullet -(y = z)\}\}$$

There is at most one chemist in this class. $(\exists x)[Cx \bullet (y)(Cy \rightarrow x = y)]$

There are at most two novelists in this class.

$$(\exists x)(\exists y)\{(Nx \bullet Ny) \bullet (z)[Nz \rightarrow (z = x \vee z = y)]\}$$

There was exactly one philosopher that Einstein admired.

$$(\exists x)[(Px \bullet Aex) \bullet (y)(Aey \rightarrow x = y)]$$

Galileo admired exactly two astronomers.

$$(\exists x)(\exists y)\{[Ax \bullet Agx) \bullet (Ay \bullet Agy)] \bullet (z)[(Az \bullet Agz) \rightarrow$$
$$(z = x \vee z = y)]\}$$

Every philosopher except Plato admired Aristotle.

$$\{(Pp \bullet -Apa) \bullet (x)\{[Px \bullet -(x = p)] \rightarrow Axa\}\}$$

Domain: {natural numbers}; Dictionary: Dxy = x is divisible by y; Ex = x is even; Gxy = x is greater than y; Ixy = x implies y; Lxy = x is less than y; Ox = x is odd; o = one; Px = x is prime; s = seven; t = two; z = zero.

All numbers are self-identical. $(x)x = x$

No two numbers are identical. $-(\exists x)-(\exists y)[-(x = y) \bullet x = y]$

There is exactly one even prime.

$$(\exists x)\{(Ex \bullet Px) \bullet (y)[(Ey \bullet Py) \rightarrow x = y]\}$$

Two is less than every other prime. $(x)\{[Px \bullet -(x = t)] \rightarrow Ltx\}$

 Two is the only even prime. $\{(Et \bullet Pt) \bullet (x)[(Ex \bullet Px) \rightarrow x = t]\}$

Every number except zero is greater than zero. $(x)[-(x = z) \rightarrow Gxz]$

One is divisible only by itself. $\{Doo \bullet (x)[-(x = o) \rightarrow -Dox]\}$

Zero, one, and two are different numbers.

$$\{[-(z = o) \bullet -(z = t)] \bullet -(o = t)\}$$

Two numbers are identical only if they imply one another.

$$(x)(y)[x = y \rightarrow (Ixy \bullet Iyx)]$$

If two is odd and seven is even, there are two numbers that are not identical. $(Ot \bullet Es) \rightarrow (\exists x)(\exists y)-(x = y)$

Numbers divisible by the same numbers are themselves the same.

$$(x)(y)[(z)(Dxz \leftrightarrow Dyz) \rightarrow x = y]$$

A number is prime if, and only if, it is divisible only by one and itself.

$$(x)\{Px \leftrightarrow (y)[Dxy \rightarrow (y = x \vee y = o)]\}$$

Domain: {Human Beings}; Dict: Axy = x admires y; Cx = x is clever; Dxy = x is more admired than y; Ex = x is an elf; Fxy = x fears y; Hxy = x hates y; Jxy = x is more jolly than y; Mxy = x is more famous than y; Nx = x was born in North Carolina; Px = x was the eleventh U.S. President; p = Plato; Rxy = x is more ruthless than y; Sxy = x was the student of y; Txy = x was the teacher of y;

The eleventh U.S. President was born in North Carolina.
$$(\exists x)\{[Px \bullet (y)(Py \rightarrow (x = y))] \bullet Nx\}$$
Everybody fears the most ruthless person in the world.
$$(\exists x)\{(y)[-(x = y) \rightarrow Rxy] \bullet (z)Fzx\}$$
The most ruthless person fears every clever person.
$$(\exists x)\{(y)[-(x = y) \rightarrow Rxy] \bullet (z)(Cz \rightarrow Fxz)\}$$
If the most ruthless person is clever, that person fears her/himself.
$$(\exists x)\{[(y)(-(x = y) \rightarrow Rxy) \bullet Cx] \rightarrow Fxx\}$$
No one hates the jolliest elf.
$$-(\exists x)\{(y)\{(z)[((Ey \bullet Ez) \bullet -(y = z)) \rightarrow Jyz] \bullet Hxy\}\}$$
Plato's most famous student did not admire Plato's teacher.
$$(\exists x)\{(y)[[(Sxp \bullet Syp) \bullet -(x = y)] \rightarrow Mxy)] \bullet (\exists z)[(u)(Tzp \bullet$$
$$(u = z)] \rightarrow -Axz)\}$$
The most famous of Plato's students is also the most admired.
$$(\exists x)(\exists y)\{(z)[(Sxp \bullet Szp) \bullet (-(x = z) \rightarrow Mxz)] \bullet (u)[-(y = u) \rightarrow$$
$$Dyu] \bullet (x = y)\}$$

Exercise 8.6

A. Show that the following arguments are valid using natural deduction.

1.　1. (x)(Dx → Rx)　　　　2.　1. (x)Fxj • -(∃y)Fyg
　　2. (x)(y)(Rx → x = y)　　　2. (x)(Fjx → x = g)　⊢　(y)Fyg
　　3. (∃x)(∃y)-(x = y)　⊢　(∃x)-Dx

3.　1. (∃x)(y)(y = x ↔ Ny)　　4.　1. (x)(∃y)(x = y)
　　⊢　(x)Nx → (y)(∃z)y = z　　　⊢　(x)(∃y)[(Jxy v Jxx) → Jyy]

5*　1. (x)(∃y)(Sxy v Syx)　⊢　(x)(∃y)(x = y → Sxy)

6. 1. (x)(y)(z)[(Rxy v Ryz) → Rxz]
    2. (∃x)(y)Ryx   ⊢   (x)(y)[Rxy v -(x = y)]

7. 1. (x)(y)(Fxy → Lxy)
    2. (x)(y)[x = x → (-Gxy • -Lxy)]   ⊢   (x)(∃y)[Fxy → (∃z)Gzy]

8. 1. (∃x)(y){[-(x = y) → Hxy] • Wx}
        ⊢   (x){Wx v (∃y)[Hyx • -(x = y)]}}

9. 1. (∃x)(y)(y = x ↔ Ky)   ⊢   (x)Kx → (y)(z)y = z

10* 1. (x)(y)[(Axy • Ayx) → x = y]
    2. (x)(y)-(-Ayx • Axy)   ⊢   (x)[(∃y)(Ayx v Axy) → Axx]

B. Determine the validity of the following arguments via truth trees.

1. (∃x)(∃y)-(x = y)
    (x)[-(x = f) → -Mx]
    (∃x)-Mx

2. (x)(y)(z)[(Qxy • Qyz) → Qxz]
    (∃x)(∃y)x = y
    (∃x)Qxx

3. (x)(y)(Exy v -Exy)
    (x)(y)[-(x = y) • -Eyx]
    (y)-Eyy

4. (x)Pxx • (y)(z)Pyz
    (x)(∃y)[-(x = y) → -Pyy]
    (∃x)(y)(Pxy → Kyx)

5* (x)(∃y)(∃z)(x = y v x = z)
    (x)(y)(Sxy → -Gxy)
    (∃x)(∃y)(-Gyx → Sxy)

6. r = j
    (x)(y)(Ixy → Iyx)
    -(Ije • -Iej)

7. (x)[-Gx v -(y)-(Fxy • Ey)]
    (Gs • s = t)
    (x)(y)(Fxy → Fyx)
    (∃x)(Ex • Fxt)

8. (x)(y)(z)(Nyx → Nxz)
    (∃x)x = d
    (∃x)Nxx

9. a = b v a = c
    (x)(y)[Cy → (-Pxa → Kc)]
    (x)(y)(-Kx v -Pay)
    (∃x)Pxx

10* (x)(y)[(-Rx • x = y) → Ry]
    (∃x)(∃y)x = y
    (∃x)(∃y)(Lxy → Rx)

Solutions to Exercises in Chapter 1

1.A   5 False;   10 False;   15 True.

1.B

5   *Premise:* I have not said anything that would rule out the possibility of somone's treating considerations as authoritative that would ordinarily be regarded as amoral, or morally eccentric, or even immoral.

Conclusion: A complementary objection would be that I have exaggerated the degree to which a fine-grained naturalistic view can accommodate traditional ideas about the authority of morality and it might be said that I have not given any reason to think that the considerations that are authoritative for an individual will always be moral considerations, in any plausible sense of that term.

10   *Premise #1:* Individuals of the same variety or subvariaty of our older cultivated plants and animals differ more from each other than do the individuals of any species or variety of the same nature.

Premise #2: There is a vast diversity of the plants and animals which have been cultivated, and which have varied during all ages under the most different climates and treatment.

Conclusion: This great variability is due to our domestic productions having been raised under condtions of life so uniform as, and somewhat different from, those which parent species had been exposed under nature.

1.C

5   There are two arguments in this passage:
   A. *Premise #1:* There are no pictures or conversations in the book.
      Premise #2: There is no use to a book without pictures or conversations.
      Conclusion: There is no use to the book.
   B. *Premise #1:* There are no pictures or conversations in the book.
      Premise #2: A book without pictures or conversations is boring.
      Conclusion: Alice is bored.

10   There are two arguments in this passage.
   A. *Premise #1:* The self presents itself as an organized whole, and integrated structure.
      Premise #2: Experiences are related to one another not through but within the whole.
      Conclusion: When the structure is modified the nature of the experiences and relationships between them are also modified.

B. *Premise:* The different experiential groups of the self are interdependent.
Conclusion: The self is a structure which is organized and "makes sense" and that each member occupies its proper place within the universe.

1.D

5   Sting is either a singer or a bass guitarist.
Sting is a singer.
So, he isn't a bass guitarist..

10 No goats are Venusians.
No mammals are Venusians.
So, no goats are mammals.

Solutions to Exercises in Chapter 2

2.1 A

5   Subject term: toreadors who have bloodies the suit of lights
Predicate: toreadors who are fearless in the ring

10 Subject term: physicians
Predicate term: people who are not confident in placebos

2.1 B

5   All things identical with Coke are things that are it.

10 Some U.S. Presidents are people who are guilty of treason.

2.1 C

5   Subject term: articles by psychologists who graduated between 1934 and 1964 from Harvard University.
Predicate term: things read by Harvard's Society of Fellows.

10 Subject term: conservatives
Predicate term: socialists

2.2

5   Particular Affirmative; 10 Particular Negative

2.3 A

5   Both terms are distributed.

10 Neither term is distributed.

2.3 B

5   All unions are forced to accept some compromises.
Subject: unions
Predicate: things forced to accept some compromises.
This is an A sentence.
Subject term distributed.

10 Some people are people who desire a reduction in teaching hours per tem.
Subject: people
Predicate: people who desire a reduction in teaching hours per tem
This is an I sentence.
Neither term distributed.

15 All things identical with the Hope Diamond are blue stones.
Subject: things identical with the Hope diamond.
Predicate: blue stones
This is an A sentence.
Subject term distributed.

20 Some dogs are not things with tails.
Subject: dogs
Predicate: things with tails
This is an O sentence.
Predicate term distributed.

2.3 C   5 is True; 10 is false; 15 is true.

2.4 B   4: b and d are undetermined, c is false.

2.4 C   4: b is false.

2.5 A
5   Some very intelligent people are extremely attractive models.
Equivalent.

10   Some wealthy tax evaders are marijuana growers.
Equivalent.

2.5 B
5   No corporate executives are non-owners of yachts.

10   No creatures with hearts are creatures without kidneys.

*Note:The truth value of each of these sentences is equivalent to the truth value of the original sentences.

2.5 C
5   Some people unopposed to mandatory AIDS testing are non-AIDS victims.   Not equivalent.

10   Some sister-helping-sisters are not non-sisters.
Equivalent.

2.6 A

5

10

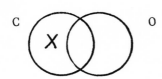

15.

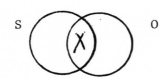

2.6 B

In each case, the diagrams are the same as the originals.

2.6 C

5. No actors are as shy as Martin Short.
No things as shy as Martin Short are actors. (Conversion)
Some things as shy as Martin Short are not actors.
(Subalternation)

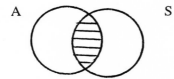

Solutions to Exercises in Chapter 3

3.2 A

5   IAA-2   10   AAA-2   15   EIO-3

3.2 B

5	No m are p.	10	No p are m.	15	All m are p.
	No s are m.		No s are m.		No m are s.
	Some s are p.		No s are p.		Some s are p.
20	Some p are m.	25	Some m are not p.		
	No m are s.		Some s are m.		
	No s are p.		Some s are not p.		

3.2 C

5 Some Arctic Wolves are animals that lower their heads when playful.

All Arctic Wolves are animals that raise their hackles when they are about to attack.

Hence, some animals that raise their hackles when about to attack are animals that lower their heads when playful.

IAI-3

3.3 A Valid: 25; Invalid: 5, 10, 15, 20.

3.3 B 5 AAI-4 Invalid; 10 IEA-3 Invalid

3.3 C True: 5, 10

3.4 A

5 Undistributed Middle

10 Undistributed Middle; Illicit Major

15 Affirmative Conclusion from Negative Premise

20 Existential Fallacy

25 Valid

3.4 B True: 10; False: 5, 15

Solutions to Exercises in Chapter 4

4.1

5 Implied ad Baculum

10 ad Populum

15 ad Hominem Circumstantial

20 ad Hominem *Tu Quoque*

25 No Fallacy

30 Deontic Fallacy

Solutions to Chapter 5

5.2 A

5   [(S • -E) → O]

     <E = England sees a threat to its own economy; O = The Orkney Islands will become an independent state; S = Scotland is willing to grant independence to the Orkney Islands>

10   [-J • (A • -B)]

     <A = Janet apologizes profusely to Carla; B = Janet will borrow Carla's notes again; J = Janet will remember to return Carla's notes>

15   [R → (H v L)]

     <H = a high pressure front moves in with the jet stream tonight; L = a low pressure front moves in with the jet streasm tonight; R = It will rain tomorrow>

20   {(P → E) v [(B → P) • -(B → E)]}

     <B = one understands Bohr; E = one understands Einstein; P = one obtains a Ph.D. in physics>

5.2 B

5   Brahe rejected the Copernican theory only if he (Brahe) was not admired by Kepler.

10   If Copernicus was the father of astronomy, then if he held a heliocentric theory, then neither was Ptolemy the father of astronomy nor did Kepler admire Brahe.

15   If Brahe's rejecting the Copernican theory implies that Copernicus held a heliocentric theory, then Copernicus didn't contradict Ptolemy.

5.2 C

Dictionary: C = the leaders are creative; I = production is increased; L = there are good students; R = there is such a thing as good teaching; W = the workers are satisfied.

5   If good teaching implies and is implied by the existence of good students, then there is such a thing as good teaching.

10   If creative leadership implies increased production, then that implication itself implies and is implied by satisfied workers.

5.2 D   5 True;   10 False;   15 True.

Solutions to Chapter 6

6.2 A

5 Disjunction;   10 Biconditional;

15 Conditional;   20 Negated Biconditional.

6.2 B   True: 10 & 20 True; 5 & 15 False

6.3 A   5 & 15 L-true; 10 L-false; 20 L-Indeterminate

6.3 B   5, 10 & 20 Incompatible; 15 Contradictory

6.3 C   5 & 10 are True.

6.4 A   5, 10 & 15 are True

6.4 B   5, 10, 15 & 20 are Valid

6.4 C

   5   Invalid

      $[-O \rightarrow (G \bullet C)]$ $[O \bullet H) \rightarrow P]$ $(O \bullet J)$ $\vdash$ S

      <C = we should concentrate on more down to earth matters than searching for truth; G = we should give up the search for truth; H = securing the truth would help us solve many "down to earth" matters; J = it is the job of the philosopher to seek the truth; O = it is possible to obtain/secure the truth; P = we should pay people to search for the truth; S = we should pay philosophers to search for the truth>

   10 Invalid

      $[(-C \bullet B) \rightarrow O]$ $[-O \rightarrow (C \rightarrow E)]$ $(-E \text{ v } H)$ $-H \vdash$ O

      <B = the Britrail pass is good for eleven days; C = the cost of the London hotel is too expensive; E = we will stay in Edinburgh; H = we will visit Hume's birthplace; O = we will take our vacation in October>

   15 Valid

      $(S \text{ v } -T)$ $(-P \bullet --T)$ $\vdash$ S

      <P = no reputable publisher of a logic book would let the truth table for the conditional be correct; S = a conditional sentence is true when the consequent is true; T = the truth table is correct>

6.5   5 & 20 Valid; 10 & 15 Invalid

6.6 A   5, 10 & 15 Valid; 20 Invalid

   B   5 L-true; 10 L-false; 15, 20, 25, 30 L-indeterminate

   C   5 $\{[P \bullet (Lo \bullet Lr) \text{ v } (-T \bullet -L)\}$

           $[T \rightarrow (C \bullet P)]$

           $[(-Rp \bullet -Rl) \rightarrow (-T \bullet -L)]$

           Rp $\vdash$ M   Invalid

        10 $[(R \text{ v } L) \rightarrow (F \rightarrow B)]$

            $\{-(F \text{ v } S) \rightarrow [R \rightarrow (M \text{ v } C)]\}$

            $(F \text{ v } R)$

            -F $\vdash$ $[L \bullet (M \text{ v } C)]$ Invalid

15 [(-D • B) v W]
   [W → (B → R)]
   [-C → (D • B)]
   -C   ⊢ R   Valid
20 [R → (Ra • F)]
   [(-R → -P) → -M] ⊢ (-M → -R)   Invalid

Solutions to Exercises in Chapter 7

7.4 A

5   5   -(F → J)
    6   F
    7   J
    8   (F • J)
10 4   (Q v -I)
    5   [(Q v -I) v (-H v G)]
    6   {[(Q v -I) → E] • [(-H v G) → W]}
    7   (E v W)
    8   [(E v W) v -Q]

7.4 B

5   4   3, Si
    5   2,4 DS
    6   1,5 MP

7.4 C

5   3   (-L • J)   1, Si
    4   -L   3, Si
    5   --(S → I)   2,4 MT
10 4   R   3, Si
    5   (S • T)   1,4 MP
    6   S   5, Si
    7   (U • V)   2,6 MP
    8   [(S • T) • (U • V)]   5,7 Con
15 4   {(R → C) • [(R → C) → (B → K)]},3 Con
    5   [C v (B → K)]   2,4 CD
20 4   [D → (G ↔ S)]   1, Si
    5   -D   3,4 MT
    6   S   2,5 DS
    7   (S v R)   6, Ad

7.5 A

5	3	-(-N v -R)	1, MI
	4	(--N • --R)	3, DM
	5	--R	4, Com, Si
	6	R	5, DN
	7	W	2,6 MP
	8	(W v N)	7, Ad
10	3	(-S • -E)	2, DM
	4	-E	3, Com, Si
	5	--[N v (M v O)]	1,4 MT
	6	[N v (M v O)]	5, DN
	7	[N v (O v M)]	6, Com
	8	[--N v (--O v M)]	7, DN, DN
	9	[-N → (--O v M)]	8, MI
	10	[-N → (-O → M)]	9, MI
15	2	[(Aa → Nn) • (Nn → Aa)]	1 MI
	3	(Aa → Nn)	2, Si
	4	(Nn → Aa)	2, Com, Si
	5	(Nn → Nn)	3,4 HS
	6	(Aa → Aa)	3,4 HS
	7	[(Aa → Aa) • (Nn → Nn)]	5,6 Con
20	3	(--R v -L)	2, DM
	4	-(-R • L)	3, DM
	5	(Q v X)	1,4 DS
	6	[(Q v X) v T]	5, Ad
	7	[T v (X v O)]	6, Com, Com
25	3	(-E v S)	1, MI
	4	[(-E v S) v -A]	3, Ad
	5	[-A v (-E v S)]	4, Com
	6	[(-A v -E) v S]	5, As
	7	[(-E v -A) v S]	6, Com
	8	[-E v (-A v S)]	7, As
	9	[E → (-A v S)]	8, MI
	10	[E → (A → S)]	9, MI

30 4	$--Y \rightarrow --(Z \rightarrow A)$	1, Cp
5	$Y \rightarrow --(Z \rightarrow A)$	4, DN
6	$Y \rightarrow (Z \rightarrow A)$	5, DN
7	$-Y \lor (-B \lor A)$	2, MI
8	$-Y \lor (Z \rightarrow A)$	6, MI
9	$-Y \lor (-Z \lor A)$	8, MI
10	$(-Y \lor -Z) \lor A$	9, As
11	$(-Y \lor -B) \lor A$	7, As
12	$A \lor (-Y \lor -Z)$	10, Com
13	$A \lor (-Y \lor -B)$	11, Com
14	$[A \lor (-Y \lor -B)] \bullet [A \lor (-Y \lor -Z)]$	12,13 Con
15	$A \lor [(-Y \lor -B) \bullet (-Y \lor -Z)]$	14, Di
16	$(-Y \lor -B) \bullet (-Y \lor -Z)$	3,15 DS
17	$-Y \lor (-B \bullet -Z)$	16, Di
18	$Y \rightarrow (-B \bullet -Z)$	17, MI
19	$Y \rightarrow -(B \lor Z)$	18, DM

7.6

5

	4	$-N$	(A)
	5	$(--N \lor -A)$	3, DM
	6	$-A$	4,5 DS
	7	$-C$	1,6 DS
	8	$(-N \rightarrow -C)$	4-7 RCP
	9	$(--N \lor -C)$	8, MI
	10	$(N \lor -C)$	9, DN

10

	3	Z	(A)
	4	K	(A)
	5	$(Z \lor -E) \rightarrow T$	1, Si
	6	$(E \rightarrow Y)$	1, Com, Si
	7	$-(--T \lor S)$	2, MI
	8	$(---T \bullet -S)$	7, DM
	9	$-T$	8, Si, DN
	10	$-(Z \lor -E)$	5,9 MT
	11	$(-Z \bullet --E)$	10, DM
	12	$--E$	11, Com, Si
	13	E	12, DN

14 Y	6,13 MP
15 (K → Y)	4-14, RCP
16 Z → (K → Y)	3-15, RCP

7.7

5.

3.	-[(N • N) → U]	(A,DC)
4.	-[-(N • N) v U]	3, MI
5.	--(N • N) • -U	4, DM
6.	(N • N) • -U	5, DN
7.	-U • (N • N)	6, Com
8.	-U	7, Si
9.	-(N • F)	2,8, MT
10	(-N v -F)	9, DM
11	(N • N)	6, Si
12	N	11, Re
13	--N	12, DN
14	-F	9,13, DS
15	F v (-N v -N)	1, Com
16	(-N v -N)	14,15, DS
17	-N	16, Re
18	N v [(N • N) → U]	12, Ad
19	(N • N) → U	17,18, DS
20	-[(N • N) → U] → [(N • N) → U]	3-19, RCP
21	--[(N • N) → U] v [(N • N) → U]	20, MI
22	[(N • N) → U] v [(N • N) → U]	21, DN
23	(N • N) → U	22, Re

10

3.	J	(A,DC)
4.	(I ↔ J)	1, ME
5.	(I → J) • (J → I)	4, ME
6.	(J → I) • (I → J)	5, Com
7.	(J → I)	6, Si
8.	-(--I v W)	2, MI
9.	-(I v W)	8, DN
10	(-I • -W)	9, DM
11	-I	10, Si

12 I	3,7, MP
13 (I v -J)	12, Ad
14 -J	11,13, DS
15 (J → -J)	3-14, RCP
16 (-J v -J)	15, MI
17 -J	16, Re

7.8

5 1 Zero Premises ⊢ (-N v D) v (N v -D)

2	-[(-N v D) v (N v -D)]	(A,DC)
3	-(-N v D) • -(N v -D)	2, DM
4	-(-N v D)	3, Si
5	(--N • -D)	4, DM
6	-(N v -D)	3, Com, Si
7	(-N • --D)	6, DM
8	-N	7, Si
9	N	5, Si, DN
10	N v (-N v D) v (N v -D)	9, Ad
11	(-N v D) v (N v -D)	8,10 DS

12 -(-N v D) v (N v -D) → (-N v D) v (N v -D)	2-11 RCP
13 --(-N v D) v (N v -D) v (-N v D) v (N v -D)	12, MI
14 (-N v D) v (N v -D) v (-N v D) v (N v -D)	13, DN
15 (-N v D) v (N v -D)	14, Re

10 1 Zero P's ⊢ [(-T → L) • -U] → (U → -L)

2	-{[(-T → L) • -U] → (U → -L)}	(A,DC)
3	-{-[(-T → L) • -U] v (U → -L)}	2, MI
4	--[(-T → L) • -U] • -(U → -L)	3, DM
5	[(-T → L) • -U] • -(U → -L)	4, DN
6	(-T → L) • -U	5, Si
7	-(U → -L)	5, Com, Si
8	-(-U v -L)	7, MI
9	(--U • --L)	8, DM
10	U	9, Si, DN
11	-U	6, Com, Si
12	U v [(-T → L) • -U] → (U → -L)	10, Ad
13	[(-T → L) • -U] → (U → -L)	11,12 DS

14 -{[(-T → L) • -U] → (U → -L)} →
      {[(-T → L) • -U] → (U → -L)} 2-13 RCP

15 --{[(-T → L) • -U] → (U → -L)} v
      {[(-T → L) • -U] → (U → -L)}   14, MI

16 {[(-T → L) • -U] → (U → -L)} v
      -{[(-T → L) • -U] → (U → -L)}15, DN

17 [(-T → L) • -U] → (U → -L)   16, Re

15 1   Zero Premises   ⊢   [(R → S) ↔ -(R • -S]

    → 2   (R → S)   (A)

      3   (-R v S)   2, MI

      4   (-R v --S)   3, DN

      5   -(R • -S)   4, DM

      6   (R → S) → -(R • -S)   2-5 RCP

    → 7   -(R • -S)   (A)

      8   (-R v --S)   7, DM

      9   (R → --S)   8, MI

      10 (R → S)   9, DN

      11 [(R → S) → -(R • -S]   7-10 RCP

      12 [(R → S) → -(R • -S)] • [(R → S) ↔ -(R • -S]   6,11 Con

      13 [(R → S) ↔ -(R • -S]   12, ME

Solutions to Chapter 8

8.2 A

5 (∃x)(Mx • Bx) → Bh

10 (x)(Mx → Bx) → (∃x)(Cx • Bx)

8.2 B

5. Music is either beautiful or not worth listening to.

10 It is false that whoever helped write *Porgy & Bess* could have written *Scheherazade*, but whoever wrote *Rhapsody in Blue* could have written *Scheherazade*.

8.2 C

5. (x)(Mx → Sx)   15 (x)[(Cx • Ix) → -Mx]

10 -(∃x)(Ax • Ix)   20 -(x)(Ix → -Wx)

8.3 A

4. 1. $(x)][(Tx \lor Yx) \bullet (-Ux \lor Yx)]$
   2. $(x)-(-Yx \rightarrow Ux)$ ⊢ Tn
   3. -Tn (A,DC)
   4. $(Tn \lor Yn) \bullet (-Un \lor Yn)$ 1, UI
   5. $-(-Yn \rightarrow -Un)$ 2, UI
   6. $-(--Yn \lor -Un)$ 5, MI
   7. $(---Yn \bullet --Un)$ 6, DM
   8. $(Yn \lor Tn) \bullet (Yn \lor -Un)$ 4, Com,Com
   9. $[Yn \lor (Tn \bullet -Un)]$ 8, Di
   10 -Yn 7, Si,DN
   11 $(Tn \bullet -Un)$ 9,10, DS
   12 Tn 11, Si
   13 $(-Tn \bullet Tn)$ 3,12, Con
   14 Tn 3-13, RAA

8.3 B

5. 1. $(x)-(Ox \bullet Wx)$
   2. $(x)(Ox \leftrightarrow -Wx)$ ⊢ $-(x)Wx$
   3. $--(x)Wx$ (A,DC)
   4. $(x)Wx$ 3, DN
   5. Wp 4, UI
   6. $(Op \leftrightarrow -Wp)$ 2, UI
   7. $(Op \lor -Wp) \bullet (-Op \lor --Wp)$ 6, ME
   8. $(-Wp \lor Op)$ 7, Si,Com
   9. $--Wp$ 5, DN
   10 Op 8,9, DS
   11 $-(Op \bullet Wp)$ 1, UI
   12 $(-Op \lor -Wp)$ 11, DM
   13 $--Op$ 12, DN
   14 -Wp 12, 13, DS
   15 $(Wp \bullet -Wp)$ 5,14, Con
   16 $-(x)Wx$ 3-15, RAA

8.3 C

5.
1. (x)Fx → (x)Gx
2. (∃x)-Gx
3. (x)(Hx → Fx) ⊢ (∃x)-Hx
4. -(∃x)-Hx   (A,DC)
5. -(x)Gx   2, QE
6. -(x)Fx   1,5, MT
7. (∃x)-Fx   6, QE
8. -Fa   7, EI *a
9. (Ha → Fa)   3, UI
10 -Ha   8,9, MT
11 (x)--Hx   4, QE
12 --Ha   11, UI
13 Ha   12, DN
14 (Ha • -Ha)   10,12, Con
15 (∃x)-Hx   4-14, RAA

8.3 D

5
1. (∃x)(Fx → Hx) ⊢ (∃x)[(Hx v Lx) v -Fx]
2. -(∃x)[(Hx v Lx) v -Fx] (A,DC)
3. (x)-[(Hx v Lx) v -Fx]   2, QE
4. (Fc → Hc)   1, EI *c
5. -[(Hc v Lc) v -Fc]   3, UI
6. -(Hc v Lc) • --Fc   5, DM
7. --Fc   6, Com,Si
8. -(Hc v Lc)   6, Si
9. (-Hc • -Lc)   8, DM
10 -Hc   9, Di
11 -Fc   4,10, MT
12 (-Fc • --Fc)   7,11, Con
13 (∃x)[(Hx v Lx) v -Fx]   2-12, RAA

10 1. (x)(Zx v -Tx)
   2. (x)(Tx → Wx) ⊢   (x)[-(Wx • Zx) → -Tx]
   3. -(x)[-(Wx • Zx) → -Tx]   (A,DC)
   4. (∃x)-[-(Wx • Zx) → -Tx]   3, QE
   5. -[-(Wj • Zj) → -Tj]   4, EI *j
   6. (Zj v -Tj)   1, UI
   7. (Tj → Wj)   2, UI
   8. -[--(Wj • Zj) v -Tj]   5, MI
   9. [---(Wj • Zj) • --Tj]   8, DM
   10 [-(Wj • Zj) • Tj]   9, DN,DN
   11 Tj   10, Com,Si
   12 Wj   7,11, MP
   13 (-Wj v -Zj) • Tj   10, DM
   14 --Tj   11, DN
   15 (-Tj v Zj)   6, Com
   16 Zj   14,15, DS
   17 (-Wj v -Zj)   13, Si
   18 --Wj   12, DN
   19 -Zj   17,18, DS
   20 (Zj • -Zj)   16,19, Con
   21 (x)[-(Wx • Zx) → -Tx]   3-20, RAA

8.3 E
  5 Something is not art.
  10 Nothing is non-natural.

8.3 F
  5 1. (Ec → Sc)
   2. (Sc → Mc) ⊢ Ec → (∃x)Mx
   3. -[Ec → (∃x)Mx]   (A,DC)
   4. -[-Ec v (∃x)Mx]   3, MI
   5. [--Ec • -(∃x)Mx]   4, DM
   6. -(∃x)Mx   5, Com,Si
   7. (x)-Mx   6, QE
   8. (Ec → Mc)   1,2, HS
   9. -Mc   7, UI
   10 -Ec   8,9, MT
   11 Ec   5, Si,DN
   12 (Ec • -Ec)   10,11, Con
   13 Ec → (∃x)Mx   3-13, RAA

10 1. (x)(Lx → Dx)
    2. (x)(Hx → Mx)
    3. (x)[Sx → (-Dx • -Mx)] ⊢ (x)[Sx → (-Lx • -Hx)]
    4. -(x)[Sx → (-Lx • -Hx)]   (A,DC)
    5. (∃x)-[Sx → (-Lx • -Hx)]   4, QE
    6. -[Sa → (-La • -Ha)]   5, EI   *a
    7. -[-Sa v (-La • -Ha)]   6, MI
    8. --Sa • -(-La • -Ha)   7, DM
    10 Sa   8, Si,DN
    11 Sa → (-Da • -Ma)   3, UI
    12 (-Da • -Ma)   10,11, MP
    13 (La → Da)   1, UI
    14 (Ha → Ma)   2, UI
    15 (La → Da) • (Ha → Ma)   13,14, Con
    16 -(-La • -Ha)   8, Com,Si
    17 (--La v --Ha)   16, DM
    18 (La v Ha)   17, DN,DN
    19 (Da v Ma)   15,18, CD
    20 -(Da v Ma)   12, DM
    21 (Da v Ma) • -(Da v Ma)   19,20, Con
    22 (x)[Sx → (-Lx • -Hx)]   4-21, RAA

8.4 A
5 Valid; 10 Invalid

8.4 B
5 Invalid
   (x)[Sx → -(Lx • -Lx)]
   (x)[(Sx • Lx) → Ax]
   -(∃x)[(Sx • Ax) • -Mx]

   -(∃x)[(Sx • -Lx) • Mx]

8.5.1 A
5   (∃x)(y)Axy • -(∃x)(y)Ayx
10 (x)(y){[(Px • Py) • Txy] → (z)Sxz}

8.5.1 B

5
1. (∃x)(∃y)Fxy   ⊢   (∃x)(∃y)Fyx
2. -(∃x)(∃y)Fyx   (A,DC)
3. (∃y)Fmy   1, EI *m
4. Fmp   3, EI *p
5. (x)-(∃y)Fyx   2, QE
6. -(∃y)Fyp   5, UI
7. (y)-Fyp   6, QE
8. -Fmp   7, UI
9. (Fmp • -Fmp)   4,8, Con
10 (∃x)(∃y)Fyx   2-9, RAA

10
1. (x)-Hxx
2. (x)(y)(Hxy → Hyx)
3. (x)(y)(z)[(Hxy → -Hyz) → Hxz]
    ⊢   (x)(y)-[Hxy → (z)(Hzx → Hzy)]
4. -(x)(y)-[Hxy → (z)(Hzx → Hzy)]   (A,DC)
5. (∃x)-(y)-[Hxy → (z)(Hzx → Hzy)] 4, QE
6. -(y)-[Hay → (z)(Hza → Hzy)] 5, EI *a
7. (∃y)--[Hay → (z)(Hza → Hzy)] 6, QE
8. --[Hab → (z)(Hza → Hzb)] 7, EI *b
9. [Hab → (z)(Hza → Hzb)] 8, DN
10 (y)(z)[(Hay → -Hyz) → Haz] 3, UI
11 (z)[(Hab → -Hbz) → Haz] 10, UI
12 (Hab → -Hba) → Haa 11, UI
13 -Haa 1, UI
14 -(Hab → -Hba) 12,13, MT
15 -(-Hab v -Hba) 14, MI
16 (--Hab • --Hba) 15, DM
17 Hab 16, Si,DN
18 (z)(Hza → Hzb) 9,17, MP
19 (Hba → Hbb) 18, UI
20 --Hba 16, Com,Si
21 Hba 20, DN
22 Hbb 19,21, MP
23 -Hbb 1, UI
24 (Hbb • -Hbb) 22,23, Con
25 (x)(y)-[Hxy → (z)(Hzx → Hzy)] 4-24, RAA

8.5.1 C

5   1. (x)(∃y)(Hx → -Lxy)
      2. (x)(y)(Axy v Lxy)   ⊢   (x)(∃y)(Hx → Axy)
      3. -(x)(∃y)(Hx → Axy)   (A,DC)
      4. (∃x)-(∃y)(Hx → Axy)   3, QE
      5. -(∃y)(Hg → Agy)   4, EI   *g
      6. (y)-(Hg → Agy)   5, QE
      7. (∃y)(Hg → -Lgy)   1, UI
      8. (Hg → -Lgt)   7, EI   *t
      9. -(Hg → Agt)   6, UI
     10 -(-Hg v Agt)   9, MI
     11 (--Hg • -Agt)   10, DM
     12 Hg   11, Si,DN
     13 -Agt   11, Com,Si
     14 -Lgt   8,12, MP
     15 (y)(Agy v Lgy)   2, UI
     16 (Agt v Lgt)   15, UI
     17 Lgt   13,16, DS
     18 (Lgt • -Lgt)   14,17, Con
     19 (x)(∃y)(Hx → Axy)   3-18, RAA

8.5.2 A

5 & 10:   Valid

8.5.2 B

5   Efd → (x)Exd
     (x)(Dx → Exd) • Df   Valid
     <u>Ms   </u>
     (∃x)(Mx • Exd)

8.5.2 C

5 & 10: True

8.6 A

5   1. (x)(∃y)(Sxy v Syx) ⊢ (x)(∃y)(x = y → Sxy)
     2. -(x)(∃y)(x = y → Sxy)   (A,DC)
     3. (∃x)-(∃y)(x = y → Sxy)   2, QE
     4. -(∃y)(r = y → Sry)   3, EI *r
     5. (y)-(r = y → Sry)   4, QE
     6. (∃y)(Sry v Syr)   1, UI
     7. (Src v Scr)   6, EI *c
     8. -(r = c → Src)   5, UI
     9. -[-(r = c) v Src]   8, MI
   10 --(r = c) • -Src   9, DM
   11 r = c   10, Si,DN
   12 -Src   10, Com,Si
   13 Scr   7,12, DS
   14 Scc   11,13, ID
   15 Src   11,14, ID
   16 (Src • -Src)   12,15, Con
   17 (x)(∃y)(x = y → Sxy)   2-16, RAA

10 1. (x)(y)[(Axy • Ayx) → x = y]
     2. (x)(y)-(-Ayx • Axy) ⊢ (x)[(∃y)(Ayx v Axy) → Axx]
     3. -(x)[(∃y)(Ayx v Axy) → Axx]   (A,DC)
     4. (∃x)-[(∃y)(Ayx v Axy) → Axx]   3, QE
     5. -[(∃y)(Ayc v Acy) → Acc]   4, EI *c
     6. -[-(∃y)(Ayc v Acy) v Acc]   5, MI
     7. --(∃y)(Ayc v Acy) • -Acc   6, DM
     8. (∃y)(Ayc v Acy)   7, Si,DN
     9. -Acc   7, Com,Si
   10 (Awc v Acw)   8, EI *w
   11 (y)[(Awy • Ayw) → w = y]   1, UI
   12 (Awc • Acw) → w = c   11, UI
   13 (y)-(-Ayw • Awy)   2, UI
   14 -(-Acw • Awc)   13, UI
   15 (--Acw v -Awc)   14, DM
   16 (-Acw → -Awc)   15, MI
   17 (--Awc v Acw)   10, DN

18 (-Awc → Acw)   17, MI
19 (-Acw → Acw)   16,18, HS
20 (--Acw v Acw)   19, MI
21 (Acw v Acw)   20, DN
22 Acw   21, Re
23 (y)-(-Ayc • Acy)   2, UI
24 -(-Awc • Acw)   23, UI
25 (--Awc v -Acw)   24, DM
26 (-Acw v Awc)   25, Com,DN
27 --Acw   22, DN
28 Awc   26,27, DS
29 (Awc • Acw)   22,28, Con
30 w = c   12,29, MP
31 Acc   28,30, ID
32 (Acc • -Acc)   9,31, Con
33 (x)[(∃y)(Ayx v Axy) → Axx]   3-33, RAA

8.6 B   5 Invalid; 10 Valid

GLOSSARY

This glossary is designed to give the reader partial understanding of how certain terms are used throughout the text. It is not designed to give either very detailed or complete information. For that, it is requisite that the reader consult the appropriate chapter(s), designated by the numbers in parentheses.

Acceptable argument: An argument that is taken to have true premises which lead to a conclusion either conclusively or with a high degree of probably. An argument that could lead one to action. (1)

Accident: An informal fallacy occurring when one applies a general rule incorrectly to a specific case or in a specific situation. (4)

Antecedent: The component in conditional sentences that implied the consequent. Example: 'A' is the antecedent in '(A → B)'. (7)

Argument: A series of sentences, one of which (the conclusion) is intended to follow from the other(s) (premises) either conclusively or with a high degree of probability. (1)

Argumentum ad Baculum: An informal fallacy occurring when one person threatens another person in order to persuade the second person to accept some conclusion. (4)

Argumentum ad Hominem/Abusive: An argument directed toward a person in which the arguer attacks the character of the person in an abusive manner. An informal fallacy. (4)

Argumentum ad Hominem/Circumstantial: An argument directed toward a person in which the arguer attacks the person by pointing out the special situation the person is in. An informal fallacy. (4)

Argumentum ad Hominem/Tu Quoque: An argument directed toward a person in which the arguer accuses the person of having said or done something similar to what the arguer allegedly said or did. An informal fallacy. (4)

Argumentum ad Ignorantiam: An informal fallacy occurring when one states that nothing is or can be known about some object and then states something that is known about the object. (4)

Argumentum ad Misericordiam: An informal fallacy occurring when one appeals to a listener's feeling of pity for some person(s) in order to get the listener to accept some conclusion or other. (4)

Argumentum ad Populum: An informal fallacy occurring when one appeals to a listener's desire or need to be 'one of the group' to get the listener to accept some conclusion or other. (4)

Argumentum ad Vericundiam: An informal fallacy occurring when one appeals exclusively to the authority of a person to get some conclusion or other accepted. (4)

Arrow: Logical symbol used to designate conditional sentences. Example: $(A \rightarrow B)$ (5,6,7,8)

Bar: Logical symbol used to designate negative sentences. Examples: -A, -(A v B). (5,6,7,8)

Begging the question: See Petitio Principii

Biconditional sentence: A compound sentence in which the components are said to imply one another. Example: The Yankees will win if, and only if, they play the Orioles. (5,6,7,8)

Categorical sentence: A sentence composed of a quantifier (All/No/Some), a subject term (S), a copula (any form of the verb 'to be'), and a predicate term (P). Examples: All S are P; No S are P; Some S are P; Some S are not P. (2)

Categorical syllogism: An argument consisting of three categorical sentences in normal form. (3)

Checked formula/sentence: In truth trees, a sentence to which a rule has been applied. (6,8)

Closed branch: In truth trees, a closed branch is a branch on which there exists an explicit contradiction. (6,8)

Composition: An informal fallacy occurring when one argues that because something is true of the parts of some whole it is therefore also true of the whole itself. (4)

Compound sentence: A sentence consisting in two or more simple sentences. (5)

Conclusion: The sentence in an argument that is supposed to follow from a number of other sentences, called the premises. (1)

Conclusion indicator: A word or phrase, e.g., 'hence', marking the presence of the conclusion in an argument. (1)

Conditional sentence: A conditional sentence in which one sentence is said to imply or entail another sentence. (5,6,7,8)

Conjunct: A component sentence in a conjunction. Example: 'A' and 'B' are conjuncts in '(A • B)'. (5)

Conjunction: (Conjunctive Sentence) A compound sentence in which it is asserted that both components are true. Example: The Yankees lost their game and Yogi Berra hit two home runs. (5,6,7,8)

Consequent: The component in conditional sentences that is implied by the antecedent. Examples: 'it will rain' is the consequent in 'If the wind blows from the north, then it will rain'; 'B' is the consequent in '(A → B)'.

Contradictory sentences: Two sentences are contradictory if and only if they have opposite truth values under all interpretations. Contradictory sentences cannot both be true at the same time and cannot both be false at the same time. Examples: '(A • B)' and '-(A • B)' are contradictories, as are 'All musicians listen to the Beatles' and 'Some musicians do not listen to the Beatles'. (2,6,7,8)

Contradiction: A contradiction is committed either when one asserts a logically false sentence or when one asserts any sentence and its negation as both true or both false. (2,6,7,8)

Contraries: A relation holding between 'A' and 'E' sentences in Aristotelian Logic. Contraries cannot both be true at the same time but may both be false at the same time. (2)

Contraposition: A method of inference in Aristotelian Logic holding for 'A' and 'O' sentences whereby the subject term is replaced by the negation of the predicate term and the predicate term is replaced by the negation of the subject term. (2) Also, a Principle of Replacement in Natural Deduction whereby the antecedent in a conditional is replaced by the negation of the consequent and the consequent is replaced by the negation of the antecedent. (7,8)

Conversion: A method of inference in Aristotelian Logic holding for 'E' and 'I' sentences whereby the subject and predicate terms are exchanged. (2)

Copula: A form of the verb 'to be' positioned between the subject and predicate terms in normal form categorical sentences, usually 'are' or 'are not'. (2)

Counterexample: An argument designed to show the invalidity of a different argument by having the precise form of the other argument, but which has true premises and a false conclusion. (1)

Deontic fallacy: An informal fallacy occurring when one draws a conclusion which is prescriptive in nature based only on descriptive statements as premises. (4)

Disjunct: The component sentences in disjunctions. Example: 'A' and 'B' are disjuncts in '(A v B)'. (5)

Disjunction: (Disjunctive sentence) A sentence in which it is asserted that one or the other of two sentences is true. Example: 'Either the Yankees will win or the owners will be mad'. (5,6,7,8)

Division: An informal fallacy occurring when one argues that because something is true of the whole of some object it is also true of the parts of the whole. (4)

Distributed term: A term is said to be distributed in a normal form categorical sentence if the sentence refers to every member of the class designated by the term. (2)

Dot: Logical symbol used to designate conjunctions. Example: (A • B). (5,6,7,8)

Double arrow: Logical symbol used to designate biconditionals. Example: (A ↔ B). (5,6,7,8)

Equivalent sentences: Two sentences are said to be equivalent if and only if they are true under the same interpretations *and* false under the same interpretations. Example: (A → B) and (-A v B) are equivalent. (6)

Equivocation: An informal fallacy occurring when one uses a word or phrase in two or more senses (meanings) within the same sentence/paragraph/context. (4)

Existential quantifier: The logical symbol designated by words and phrases such as 'some' and 'a few'. The logician takes its literal meaning to be 'there exists at least one'. The symbolic representation for 'there exists at least one x' is '(∃x)'. (2,8)

False cause: An informal fallacy occurring when one draws a conclusion on the basis of an erroneous causal relationship. (4)

Figure: One of four forms of placement of the middle term in a normal form categorical syllogism. (3)

Hasty generalization: An informal fallacy occurring when one argues to a generalization on the basis either of atypical cases or an insufficient number of cases. (4)

Ignoratio Elenchi: An informal fallacy occurring when a different conclusion is drawn from a set of premises rather than the expected conclusion. (4)

Incompatible sentences: Sentences that have the same truth values under some interpretations and different truth values under other interpretations. Example: (A v B) and (A • B) are incompatible sentences. (6)

Individual constant: See Name Letter.

Instantiation: The process of replacing instances of variables with individual constants. Example: '(Ai v Bi)' is an instantiation of the quantified sentence "(x)(Ax v Bx)". (8)

Interpretation: Each row in a truth table, each branch in a truth tree, and each instantiation, is considered an interpretation. (6,8)

Invalid argument: An argument in which it is possible for the premises to be true and the conclusion false. (1,3,6,7,8)

Law of Excluded Middle: The 'law of thought' expressing the fact that every sentence is either true or false and that no sentence is both true and false. (5)

Limited alternative: An informal fallacy occurring when an arguer suggests/presents a lesser number of [obvious] alternatives than there actually are. (4)

Logic: The study of correct and incorrect reasoning. (1-8)

Logically false sentence: A sentence that is true under no interpretations. Example: (A • -A). (6)

Logically indeterminate sentence: A sentence that is true under some but not all interpretations. A sentence which is neither logically true nor logically false. Example: (A → B). (6)

Logically true sentence: A sentence that is true under all interpretations. Example: (A v -A). (6)

Major premise: The premise in a normal form categorical syllogism containing the major term. (3)

Major term: The predicate term in the conclusion of a normal form categorical syllogism. (3)

Middle term: The term which appears once in each premise of a normal form categorical syllogism. (3)

Minor premise: The premise in a normal form categorical syllogism containing the minor term. (3)

Minor term: The subject term in the conclusion of a normal form categorical syllogism. (3)

Mood: A designation, using **A**, **E**, **I**, and **O**, of the type of sentences comprising normal form categorical sentences and syllogisms, in the following order: major premise, minor premise, conclusion. (3)

Name letter: The logical symbol (a lower case letter from 'a' to 'o') representing an individual or constant, e.g., 'a' in 'Ra'. (8)

Necessary Condition: In a conditional sentence, the necessary condition is represented by the consequent. Example: In '(A → B)', 'B' is the consequent, hence a necessary condition for 'A'. (5)

Obversion: A method of inference in Aristotelian Logic holding for **A**, **E**, **I**, and **O** sentences whereby the quality of the sentence is changed from affirmative to negative, or vice-versa, and the predicate term is negated. (2)

Open branch: In truth trees, an open branch is a branch that does not contain a contradiction when all formulas on the branch that can be checked have been checked. (6,8)

Particular Affirmative sentence: A categorical sentence of the form 'Some S are P'. An **I** sentence in Aristotelian Logic. (2)

Particular Negative sentence: A categorical sentence of the form 'Some S are not P'. An **O** sentence in Aristotelian Logic. (2)

Petitio Principii: A fallacy occurring when one assumes the very conclusion for which one is arguing. Alternatively, also occurring when one fails to make explicit a premise that is at the heart (usually very controversial) of the issue/point about which one is arguing. (4)

Predicate: In symbolic logic, 'R' in 'Ra' is the predicate. In natural language, the predicate indicates what is said about an individual or object, e.g., "Rachel is an architect", in which 'is an architect' is the predicate. (8)

Predicate letter: In symbolic logic, the symbol (an upper case letter) which represents the predicate, e.g., 'R' in 'Ra'. (8)

Predicate term: The word or phrase directly following the copula in a normal form categorical sentence. (2)

Premise(s): The sentence(s) in an argument designed to provide support for a further sentence, called the conclusion. (1)

Premise indicator: A word or phrase, e.g., since, marking the presence of a premise in an argument. (1)

Primary connective: In a symbolized sentence the primary connective is the connective with the widest scope, i.e., ranges over all other symbols in the sentence. Example: In '[(A • B) → C]' the arrow is the primary connective. (6)

Proof: A demonstration of the validity of an argument in Natural Deduction. (7,8)

Quantifier: A word, phrase, or logical symbol in a sentence that indicates the quantity of class membership. (2,8)

Quantifier Exchange: The process of replacing one quantifier form with another, equivalent, quantifier form. Example: '-(x)Rx' can replace or be replaced by '(∃x)-Rx'. (8)

RAA: Abbreviation for *'Reductio ad Absurdum'*. (7)

RCP: Abbreviation for 'Rule of Conditional Proof'. (7)

Reductio ad Absurdum: A method of determining validity in which one assumes the conclusion to be false and attempts to derive a contradiction using the premises in conjunction with the denied conclusion. Alternatively, a rule stating that if the conclusion of a given argument is assumed to be false and a contradiction results, then the original argument is valid. (6,7,8)

Rule of Conditional Proof: In Natural Deduction, the use of a rule whereby one assumes any sentence (ϕ), derives another sentence (ψ) through a finite number of applications of the rules of inference and/or principles of replacement, then closes the scope of the assumption, after which a further sentence (χ) is derived, in the form of a conditional in which ϕ is the antecedent and ψ is the consequent. (7)

Self-contradiction: A logically false sentence. (2,6,7,8)

Simple sentence: A sentence expressing essentially one idea. (5)

Sound argument: An sound argument is one that is valid and has true premises. (1)

Subalternation: A relation existing between **A** and **I** and between **E** and **O** sentences in Aristotelian Logic, where the first of these pairs implies the second in the pair. See the Traditional Square of Opposition. (2)

Subcontraries: A relation holding between **I** and **O** sentences in Aristotelian Logic. Subcontraries can both be true at the same time but cannot both be false at the same time. (2)

Subject term: The class term or phrase directly following the quantifier in a normal form categorical sentence. (2)

Subordinate connective: Any connective in a symbolized sentence that is not the primary connective. Example: In '[(A • B) → -C]' both the dot and the bar are subordinate connectives. The arrow is the primary connective. (6)

Sufficient condition: In a conditional sentence, the sufficient is represented by the antecedent. (5)

Tautology: A logically true sentence. (1,5,6,7,8)

Traditional Square of Opposition: A diagram indicating the various relationships holding between normal form categorical sentences in Aristotelian Logic. (2)

Translation: A replacement of a sentence in natural language, e.g., English, with a sentence in symbolic notation. (5,6,7,8)

Translation dictionary: A dictionary for sentence letters used in translating sentences from natural to artificial language. (5,6,7,8)

Truth functional connective: The words or phrases, e.g., and/or/if and only if, connecting the simple sentences in conjunctions, conditionals, disjunctions, and biconditionals. In symbolic form, the truth functional connectives are represented by the arrow, dot wedge, bar and double arrow. (5,6,7,8)

Truth table: A method by which arguments are shown to be valid or invalid and by which sentences are shown to be logically true, logically false, or logically indeterminate. (6)

Truth tree: A method by which arguments are shown to be valid or invalid and by which sentences are shown to be logically true, logically false, or logically indeterminate. (6)

Truth value: In truth functional logic (sentential logic), which is a two-valued system, the values are 'truth' and 'falsehood'. In truth tables, we assign 't' for true (truth) and 'f' for false (falsehood). A sentence has the truth value 'true' if the sentence is true and has the value 'false' if it is false. (6)

Universal Affirmative sentence: A categorical sentence of the form 'All S are P'. An **A** sentence in Aristotelian Logic. (2)

Universal Negative sentence: A categorical sentence of the form 'No S are P'. An **E** sentence in Aristotelian Logic. (2)

Universal quantifier: The universal quantifier is designated by words and phrases such as 'all', 'every', 'each', 'no', 'none'. The symbolic representation is '(x)'. (2,8)

Valid argument: An argument in which it is impossible for the premises to be true while the conclusion is false. (1,3,6,7,8)

Variable: In symbolic logic, a letter (e.g., x, y, z) used as a placeholder for individual constants. Example: $(x)Ax$. (8)

Venn Diagram: For categorical sentences: Two overlapping circles, each representing a class of individuals or objects, which are marked to indicate class inclusion or class exclusion. (2) For categorical syllogisms: Three overlapping circles, each representing a class of individuals or objects, which are marked to indicate class inclusion or class exclusion. (3)

Wedge: Also known as the 'vee' or the '*vel*'. Logical symbol used to designate disjunctions. Example: '(A v B)'. (5,6,7,8)

Rules of Inference

Modus Ponens
$(p \rightarrow q)$
 $p \vdash q$

Modus Tollens
$(p \rightarrow q)$
 $-q \vdash -p$

Disjunctive Syllogism
$(p \lor q)$
$-p \vdash q$

Simplification
$(p \bullet q) \vdash p$

Hypothetical Syllogism
$(p \rightarrow q)$
$(q \rightarrow r) \vdash (p \rightarrow r)$

Addition
$p \vdash (p \lor q)$

Constructive Dilemma
$[(p \rightarrow q) \bullet (r \rightarrow s)]$
$(p \lor r) \vdash (q \lor s)$

Conjunction
p
$q \vdash (p \bullet q)$

Axioms of Replacement

DeMorgan's Theorems
$-(p \lor q) \Leftrightarrow (-p \bullet -q)$
$-(p \bullet q) \Leftrightarrow (-p \lor -q)$

Commutation
$(p \bullet q) \Leftrightarrow (q \bullet p)$
$(p \lor q) \Leftrightarrow (q \lor p)$

Material Implication
$(p \rightarrow q) \Leftrightarrow (-p \lor q)$

Contraposition
$(p \rightarrow q) \Leftrightarrow (-q \rightarrow -p)$

Material Equivalence
$(p \leftrightarrow q) \Leftrightarrow [(p \rightarrow q) \bullet (q \rightarrow p)]$
$(p \leftrightarrow q) \Leftrightarrow [(p \bullet q) \lor (-p \bullet -q)]$

Replication
$p \Leftrightarrow (p \bullet p)$
$p \Leftrightarrow (p \lor p)$

Association
$[p \bullet (q \bullet r)] \Leftrightarrow [(p \bullet q) \bullet r]$
$[p \lor (q \lor r)] \Leftrightarrow [(p \lor q) \lor r]$

Double Negation
$p \Leftrightarrow --p$

Distribution
$[p \lor (q \bullet r)] \Leftrightarrow [(p \lor q) \bullet (p \lor r)]$
$[p \bullet (q \lor r)] \Leftrightarrow [(p \bullet q) \lor (p \bullet r)]$

Exportation
$[(p \bullet q) \rightarrow r)] \Leftrightarrow [(p \rightarrow (q \rightarrow r)]$

Truth Tables

(p • q)	(p v q)	(p → q)	(p ↔ q)	-p
t t t	t t t	t t t	t t t	f t
t f f	t t f	t f f	t f f	t f
f f t	f t t	f t t	f f t	
f f f	f f f	f t f	f t f	

Truth Tree Rules

Conjunction
(p • q)

p
q

Negated Conjunction
-(p • q)

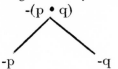

-p   -q

Disjunction
(p v q)

p   q

Negated Disjunction
-(p v q)

-p
-q

Conditional
(p → q)

-p   q

Negated Conditional
-(p → q)

p
-q

Biconditional
(p ↔ q)

p   -p
q   -q

Negated Biconditional
-(p ↔ q)

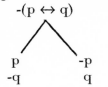

p   -p
-q   q

Double Negation
--p
p

Rule of Conditional Proof

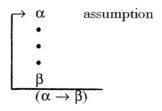

α assumption
.
.
.
β
$(\alpha \rightarrow \beta)$

Reductio ad Absurdum
(**P**redicate **L**ogic)

$-\alpha$ assumption (denial of conclusion)
.
.
.
$(\beta \bullet -\beta)$ explicit contradiction
α conclusion

Rules for Quantifier Exchange

$(x)\Im x \Leftrightarrow -(\exists x)-\Im x$ $-(x)\Im x \Leftrightarrow (\exists x)-\Im x$
$(\exists x)\Im x \Leftrightarrow -(x)-\Im x$ $-(\exists x)\Im x \Leftrightarrow (x)-\Im x$

Rules for Instantiation

Universal Instantiation: $\dfrac{(x)\Im x}{\Im a}$

Existential Instantiation*: $\dfrac{(\exists x)\Im x}{\Im a}$ *Restriction: 'a' must not have occured prior to the line of instantiation.